Screening the East

Film Europa: German Cinema in an International Context
Series Editors: **Hans-Michael Bock** (CineGraph Hamburg);
Tim Bergfelder (University of Southampton); **Sabine Hake**
(University of Texas, Austin)

German cinema is normally seen as a distinct form, but this new series
emphasizes connections, influences, and exchanges of German cinema
across national borders, as well as its links with other media and art
forms. Individual titles present traditional historical research (archival
work, industry studies) as well as new critical approaches in film and
media studies (theories of the transnational), with a special emphasis on
the continuities associated with popular traditions and local perspectives.

SCREENING THE EAST

Heimat, Memory and Nostalgia in German Film since 1989

Nick Hodgin

Berghahn Books
New York • Oxford

Published in 2011 by

Berghahn Books

www.berghahnbooks.com

Library of Congress Cataloging-in-Publication Data

Hodgin, Nick.
   Screening the East : Heimat, memory and nostalgia in German film since
   1989 / Nick Hodgin.   p. cm. – (Film Europa: German cinema in an
   international context) "Introduction – Mapping Identity – Heimat Stories:
   East Meets West – Lost Landscapes – At the Back of Beyond: Heimat East
   – Berlin: Disorientation/Reorientation – Good Bye, Ostalgie? –
   Conclusion." Includes bibliographical references and index.
   ISBN 978-0-85745-128-6 (hardback : alk. paper) – ISBN 978-0-85745-129-3
   (ebook)
   1. Motion pictures–Germany–History–20th century. 2. Motion
   pictures–Social aspects–Germany. 3. Motion pictures–Political
   aspects–Germany. 4. Germany (East)–In motion pictures. 5. Nostalgia in
   motion pictures. 6. Culture in motion pictures. 7. Stereotypes (Social
   psychology) in motion pictures. I. Title.
   PN1993.5.G3H63 2011
   791.430943'1–dc22

                                                           2011006255

British Library Cataloguing in Publication Data

A catalogue record for this book is available from the British Library
Printed in the United States on acid-free paper.

ISBN: 978-0-85745-128-6 (hardback)
E-ISBN: 978-0-85745-129-3

CONTENTS

List of Illustrations

ACKNOWLEDGEMENTS

This project would have been impossible without the help and support of a great number of people. I would like to offer my thanks to a number of scholars who were kind enough to provide me with copies of films. Tony Coulson furnished me with several films which were not available commercially and seldom screened on German television, as did Dina Iordanova. A number of filmmakers, producers and distributors sent me copies of titles that were equally difficult to come by. I am indebted to those filmmakers, producers and distributors who generously allowed me to include film stills. While in Berlin, I was happily ensconsed all day, every day, for a number of months in the new, hi-tech surroundings of the Hochschule für Film und Fernsehen Konrad Wolf in Potsdam (a far cry from its old site where I had previously viewed East German films in a converted toilet cubicle). The school granted me access to countless films, newspaper archives and their well-equipped library. I am especially grateful to the ever helpful and resourceful Frau Illing there. A number of directors were ready to meet or correspond at length with me about their work. Jan Ralske provided some useful insights into the industry and supplied me with materials and films. Andreas Dresen, too, was kind enough to take time from his busy schedule and to meet me in Potsdam. Others, such as Klaus Gietinger and Andreas Höntsch, helped me locate more obscure films. A number of people offered helpful information, clues as to the whereabouts of certain films or forwarded me copies of articles that were either hard to locate or not yet published. My thanks, then, to Sean Allan, Daniela Berghahn, Joshua Feinstein, Dave Robb and Moray McGowan.

This research began with the encouragement of the Department of Germanic Studies at the University of Sheffield, whose support and welcome atmosphere I greatly appreciated. Not the least of this support was the generous funding in the form of a three-year bursary and a travel stipend for one of my extended research trips to Berlin. My thanks go to Michael Perraudin, Peter Thompson, and Jonathan Woolley. The Conference of University Teachers of German (now AGS) was also generous in providing me with a research grant.

Tim Bergfelder was assiduous in reading through the manuscript several times and offered useful advice about the book's structure. My former colleague, Andrew Plowman, also made a number of useful comments about the sections he read. Thanks are also due to Mark Stanton for his forbearance and editorial support. I am grateful to them and to two anonymous readers for their suggestions and guidance. If any faults remain, these are my own.

Above all, I am grateful to my friends in Germany, to Dieter Aichele, Kurt Gardella and Falk Krentzlin who sent me books, newspaper cuttings and videos that were relevant to the project, and finally to my family and partner, Lucy.

INTRODUCTION

People don't want to see a German film made by a German any more, not unless it's some trash.[1]

German film is gathering speed. The age of the rom-coms is over, the auteur film has finally given up. With courage, passion, irreverence and imagination, a new generation of actors, directors and scriptwriters has given German cinema a creative boost. [2]

By the final decade of the last century, German cinema, once regarded as a serious challenger to Hollywood and later associated with exciting, oppositional filmmaking, had, as the quotation from Werner Herzog indicates, been reduced to banality. Herzog's reputation as Germany's 'visionary' director seemed justified: the 1990s saw the release of a series of trite, formulaic comedies, whose debt to Hollywood was obvious. These popular mainstream films are, according to Eric Rentschler, part of the 'cinema of consensus', which shuns the perceived obscurantism of the New German Cinema and, instead, 'cultivates familiar genres and caters to public tastes'.[3] The satisfaction derived through recognition and anticipation, familiarity breeding contentment, as it were, was one that Adorno and Horkheimer had previously described:

> Pleasure hardens into boredom because, if it is to remain pleasure, it must not demand any effort and therefore moves rigorously in the worn grooves of association. No independent thinking must be expected from the audience ... Any logical connection calling for mental effort is painstakingly avoided.[4]

This is not to say that German filmmakers have avoided making films requiring mental effort. In terms of box-office success, the 1990s may be associated with hackneyed genre filmmaking, but the decade produced some critical and inventive works, even if the public was seldom swayed by the films' success at international film festivals or by enthusiastic reviews.

Not everyone is as discouraged by contemporary German cinema culture as Herzog, as the second of the above quotations indicates. Some commentators have even spoken optimistically of a 'third golden age' (after the cinema of the Weimar period and the New German Cinema of the late 1960s and 1970s). This optimism, which led to talk of German cinema's renaissance, was largely based on the unexpected success, nationally and internationally, of two films (both produced by the Berlin film collective, X-Filme Creative Pool), Tom Tykwer's *Lola Rennt* (*Run Lola Run*, 1998) and Wolfgang Becker's *Good Bye, Lenin!* (2003). German cinema's continuing fascination with its past(s) has further sustained its critical and commercial success as seen, in varying degrees, with films such as *Der Untergang* (*Downfall*, Oliver Hirschbiegel, 2004), *Sophie Scholl - die letzten Tage* (*Sophie Scholl – The Final Days*, Marc Rothemund, 2005), *Die Fälscher* (*The Counterfeiters*, Stefan Ruzowitzky, 2007), *Das Leben der Anderen* (*The Lives of Others*, Florian Henckel von Donnersmarck, 2006) and *Der Baader Meinhof Komplex* (*The Baader Meinhof Complex*, Uli Edel, 2008).[5]

While these films may go some way to legitimizing those optimistic projections about German cinema's future, it should be noted that this is not the first time such optimism has been heard. When the German Democratic Republic (GDR) collapsed in 1989, its state-owned enterprises were sold off, including its film industry, Deutsche Film-Aktiengesellschaft (DEFA), which was bought by the French company, Compagnie Immobilière Phénix. The acclaimed West German filmmaker and 1979 Academy Award winner, Volker Schlöndorff, who was made one of the studio's co-directors, was similarly prone to making such bold statements, especially those concerning the former GDR studios, which he imagined as a super-studio of the future: 'Wim Wenders or Werner Herzog will be directing in one studio, in the one next door there'll be Louis Malle or Claude Chabrol, and English directors like Peter Greenaway will be here or Americans like Martin Scorsese. And they will all meet up in the canteen.'[6] Neither Schlöndorff's vision of transforming the mighty Babelsberg studios into a viable, if internationally constructed, challenger to Hollywood, nor his declared intention of consolidating and applying the talent at DEFA has come to fruition. A dozen years after their purchase of Babelsberg, the French conglomerate (later renamed Vivendi) finally decided to part company with the studios, which had been running at a loss for a decade, and sold Babelsberg in July 2004 to the investment company Filmbetriebe Berlin Brandenburg GmbH (FBB) headed by the west Germans, Carl Woebcken and Christoph Fisser, for the symbolic price of €1 – and a debt of €18 million.

Though an important financial success, the real value of a film such as *Good Bye, Lenin!* lay in its boost to industry morale. With domestic audiences exceeding six million, Becker's film counted as a major accomplishment for a film industry that had long accustomed itself to the dominance of Hollywood. *Good Bye, Lenin!* was not the biggest German film of recent times. That title still goes to Michael Herbig's *Der Schuh des Manitu* (*Manitou's Shoe*, 2001), a parody of the Karl May westerns (but undoubtedly the lowbrow mainstream fare to which Herzog objects), which attracted almost double the number of people. Despite Herbig's sensational returns, it was the films made by Becker and von Donnersmark and Hirschbiegel which seemed to restore German cinema's reputation abroad. This was principally due to their perceived cultural significance, which, unlike the majority of other recent (successful) German films, reflected contemporary issues relating to German history and society in ways that were accessible to international audiences.[7] The ways in which *Good Bye, Lenin!* addresses the most important event in recent German history was considered of such importance that a gala screening was even held for the Bundestag, and the Federal Agency for Civic Education (BpB) was quick to publish an accompanying booklet designed for educational purposes.[8] It hardly needs to be said that such high-level endorsement is not a common occurrence, even in a country that values the arts as highly as does Germany. What distinguishes Becker's film from German cinema's other high-earners, however, is that it is prepared to reflect and engage with contemporary issues. It reflects present concerns about the recent German past(s) and is unafraid to explore issues central to (German) identity – memory, nostalgia and the communities on either side of the former wall. Rentschler included Becker's film in his summary of contemporary German films, noting that 'contemporary German films at long last once again manifest an ability to take risks, to dare to be spontaneous and tentative'.[9]

Good Bye, Lenin! is by no means the only film to address unification; and it is certainly not the most penetrating account of that time, though its success marks a significant point in the representation of the east, as the final chapter of this book makes clear. Filmmakers began addressing the dissolution of the GDR and the effects of unification on the (predominantly eastern) population almost as soon as the wall was breached. Some have surveyed the new republic from a critical position that recalls the kind of social critical filmmaking for which (West) Germany had once been renowned, though these are, by and large, low-budget films that made little impression on audiences. Others have seen the coming together of the two populations as material for light-hearted comedies and have revived old genres in order to represent the encounters between east and west. Despite the divergent approaches to unification and its related issues, one thing is clear: German unification has provided many of the country's filmmakers with a much needed focus, resulting in an intriguing audiovisual index of recent German history and contemporary society.

Films and Identity: Reflecting the Nation

Conventional wisdom has it that identity is not a fixed, immutable concept. The contributions made to identity discourse by Benedict Anderson, Eric Hobsbawm and Anthony Smith have offered a theoretical starting point for many scholars seeking to trace the developments of national identity in film. These scholars have stressed the 'constructedness' and mutability of identity. If one accepts that identity is created, that it is the product of what

Hobsbawm refers to as 'invented tradition', one can begin to investigate the means by which culture (and that includes film) participates in its construction.[10] The cultural narratives that films offer play a vital role in the discussion, and even in the shaping of identities (whether regional/national, ethnic, or gender). Regardless of the universality of their themes – love, death, betrayal, duty, fate – the manner in which they engage with these ideas often reveals something of the society in which the films are produced. Though talking specifically about filmmaking in Afghanistan, the Iranian director Samira Makhmalbaf's comment that 'cinema acts like a mirror for society to look at its spirit and correct its faults' stresses the socially purposive role the medium can fulfil in providing an image of the nation that is invaluable to its self-understanding, but it also hints at the way in which cinema can provide a portal through which others come to view a particular society.[11] Since no society remains impervious to change but undergoes a 'continuous process of cultural reproduction', one should add that film enables us to view a particular society at a particular time.[12]

Thus, for film scholars (and the discipline extends to include, amongst others, art historians, philosophers, and social anthropologists), film is an important means of examining different nations' cultural individuality. Recent years have seen an increase in publications which address the twin subject of national cinema and national identity, resulting in some illuminating studies of countries as diverse as Spain, China and Iran.[13] Until recently, the interest in German cinema and national identity had tended to focus on Germany's pasts, whether on the Weimar period, the National Socialist (NS) past or West Germany during the 1960s and 1970s. The collapse of the East German state precipitated an identity crisis within Germany as the two populations, which had been separated for four decades, struggled to adjust to their newly defined profile. Since the collapse of Communism, many scholars have sought for evidence of an east German distinctiveness, a regional particularism that denies or at least problematizes any notion of a homogenous German identity. While literature and poetry have proved fertile grounds of enquiry, resulting in a wide number of anthologies and monographs on the period's poetry and fiction, most post-unification films have rarely been subjected to the same kind of critical examination; those international triumphs such as von Donnersmark's Oscar-winning film remain an exception to the rule. The discussion of post-unification cinema has largely been eclipsed by the discourse surrounding the role played by film in the GDR. The interest in East German film is understandable. The state film industry, DEFA, was largely unknown in the west and the sudden fascination with all things East German extended also to its cinematic output, resulting in a large number of historical accounts and individual studies.[14]

Contemporary German cinema, however, has received much less attention, despite its obvious relevance to identity discourse. At least eighty films exploring issues relating to unification have been made since 1989. Many of these remain unknown, having received limited distribution even within Germany, and are accessible only to those able to attend international film festivals (though the sheer number of festivals that are now in operation provides these films with a far bigger audience than was once the case).[15] Subsequent television broadcasts allow some films an afterlife of sorts; nevertheless, the films rarely enjoy prime time slots and tend to be shown in the small hours and often only on regional stations. This is not true of those films that did enjoy considerable success at the box-office such as *Go, Trabi Go* (Peter Timm, 1990), *Sonnenallee* (*Sun Alley*, Leander Haußmann, 1999) and *Good Bye, Lenin!* which are regularly screened on television and usually at peak time. Though some films have been individually commented on in film magazines and academic journals, the majority simply vanish from view. The publication of Leonie Naughton's *That Was the Wild East. Film Culture, Unification and the 'New' Germany* in 2002 went some way to rescuing many films from obscurity and the volume counts as the first comprehensive account of the developments in filmmakers' responses to unification.[16] Naughton's study, which is weighted towards western productions, concludes quite rightly that 'the western takeover of the studios had devastating cultural implications for the filmmaking community in the former GDR as well as for East German culture'.[17] Naughton's assertion correctly describes the situation for many of DEFA's established directors. Following the collapse of their indigenous industry, which came under the control of the *Treuhand*, the trust fund that was responsible for supervising the transferral of the GDR's state businesses into joint-stock operations – or, the 'world's busiest asset-stripper', according to one observer – many careers were lost to the new market conditions. However, Naughton does not acknowledge the new generation of filmmakers from the east who have made a significant contribution to contemporary German film culture.[18] Despite the problems experienced at Babelsberg and the decline of many DEFA directors, filmmaking in eastern Germany has not dried up. The film school in Potsdam, where many GDR filmmakers learnt their craft, is now open to students from all over Germany, and a number of the films discussed in the following chapters were made by its graduates. Where one might have expected some contribution from the once politically minded proponents of the New German Cinema, these remained strangely silent when it came to dealing with the complicated issue of unification. Wenders, Herzog, Jean-Marie Straub and Danièle Huillet, and Hans-Jürgen Syberberg have, in fact, shown little interest in the troubled dialogue of unification, preferring to make quirky documentaries, experimental films, or working in Hollywood. Of the directors associated with the German new wave, Helma Sanders-Brahms (whose 1992 film *Apfelbäume* (*Apple Trees*) is discussed in Chapter 2) and Margarethe von Trotta (whose GDR melodrama, *Das Versprechen* (*The Promise*), was released in 1994) and Ulrike Ottinger, whose documentary film *Countdown* (1991) chronicled the last ten days before unification, are among the few to have responded to unification. It has mostly fallen to young directors to chart Germany's progress since the two states were sutured, and to see how the east has recovered from this operation and what kind of scars it may have left.

The subject of German unification has spawned a vast number of books and articles across a broad range of disciplines, from economics to gender studies. From the beginning of the GDR's end, the debate surrounding German identity was one of the critical issues. The subject aroused passions as a wide range of people entered the fray, from politicians to filmmakers, footballers to intellectuals. Despite the images of jubilation and of cheerful defiance that for many came to define the autumn revolution, many articles tended towards gloomy prediction and remained unconvinced by Chancellor Helmut Kohl's confidence that the grey east would transform into 'blossoming landscapes' (a vision that he later recanted, explaining that he too had been caught up by the general optimism of the times). This tendency continued to be a feature throughout the 1990s, but the *a posteriori* consideration resulted in a more thoughtful, less emotional consideration of the situation. The tenth anniversary of unification inevitably aroused media attention but, with spirits tempered by the experiences since 1989, the celebrations were muted, and the failures and disappointments of unification received as much attention as its achievements. Two decades on, the questions surrounding Germany's post-Cold War identity continue to provoke debate and lively media coverage.

The ongoing economic problems that are most evident in the new federal states (the area comprising the former GDR) and the financial burden placed on the states that previously comprised the Federal Republic are well documented.[19] In 2004, the east Germans showed themselves capable of mass demonstrations once again, as thousands took to the streets in order to protest against the so-called 'Hartz IV', the controversial package of economic reforms that appeared to encumber still further a region already suffering from high unemployment. The disillusionment with unification has manifested itself in other ways too, a fact arguably revealed in the electoral support for the Party of Democratic Socialism (PDS, later renamed The Left Party) in the east. What is more, increasing numbers of commentators have offered evidence suggesting that, rather than overcoming the differences between east and west, which was the ardent hope of unification's architects, the opposite may in fact be the case.

Heimat, Memory and Nostalgia

Screening the East sets out to investigate how these differences have come to be represented in the films since 1989 and, in so doing, assesses their contribution to, and reflection of, the debate surrounding east German identity. For all the rhetoric of integration and the (contested) notion of cultural commonality inherent in the idea of the *Kulturnation* (an idea of

German exceptionalism that was promulgated by various sides in both German states), the populations of the east and west did not naturally co-alesce once the barrier that had divided the nation was removed and geo-graphical and political union established. The following account reveals how the east Germans' post-unification frustrations have, in some films, led to a regrouping of their local/regional community and the emergence of a post-GDR eastern identity. This reconstructed identity has not resulted in a single, unambiguous sense of belonging observable throughout the films. It is possible to single out two clearly definable east German identi-ties at play in post-unification discourse and both are ultimately regres-sive. One involves the return of a Heimat (home, homeland) identity, an identity that largely ignores the features of modern life and celebrates instead the traditions of an imagined, ostensibly apolitical, all-German past. The other also celebrates aspects of the past, specifically of the GDR. Other films offer narratives that focus not on any revitalized identity but on the decline of the east German community and its repercussions. Unable to escape their stultifying eastern environment, or hindered by the memo-ries of the GDR or by other markers of their easternness, the protagonists of these films can neither separate themselves from the east nor are they able to find an alternative home within the so-called Berlin Republic.

Certain questions arise from this investigation into the representation of east German identity: how, and to what end, is the east encoded (visu-ally represented)? What are the perceived effects of unification on the ter-ritory and its population? Do clear, discernible differences emerge in the characterization of the east and west Germans in the films and, if so, do these differences preclude the notion of a homogenized national identity or do they broaden it? A number of themes that have emerged in the films made since 1989 are germane to the construction of identity. Three con-cepts in particular have come to preoccupy filmmakers interested in screen-ing the east: Heimat, memory and nostalgia.

Heimat has always involved a dialectic of difference and identity. It may serve to distinguish *them* from *us*, though the manner in which this oppo-sition is expressed changes according to context. Heimat is, after all, a pol-ysemic notion: it can refer to the sentimental celebration of the folkloric tradition and be tied up with ideas of rurality and local culture; but it has proved a malleable concept to politicians of different hues, whether they are addressing the wider theme of nation and a sense of national belong-ing or focusing on narrower issues as part of a regional particularism. Indeed the left's recent appropriation of a concept traditionally promoted by the right has been met with some incredulity.[20] In a period in which the Germans' notion of home has (once again) been destabilized by political and historical events, Heimat surfaces as one of the key themes in post-unification film, frequently providing a context for the conflict between east and west, a clash of cultures in which the Heimat that is defended rep-resents 'something more elementary, more contingent, and thus more real than life seen in a larger scale perspective'.[21] Heimat is not just a confrontation between the global and the local, however. It can also be a site of contested space and attitude within established neighbourhoods. No longer held together by the ideological glue that appeared to bind communities in East German film, the post-GDR Heimat is for some filmmakers a location beset by prejudice and characterized by friction.

Memory, too, plays an important role as a point of orientation for the east German community. How communities see, or imagine, themselves is defined as much by the present as by the past. A fundamental component of identity, memory is likewise a protean concept, subject to change and manipulation. Memory of the GDR past has been crucial to preserving some cultural specificity. But while memory is crucial to identity, enabling communities to coalesce through shared experiences and reminiscences, which are assembled in order to construct some collective framework for identity, it can also be divisive, serving to exclude those without a legitimate claim to the collective memory bank. The East German past has been subjected to conflicting accounts, which either reify or vilify the GDR. Memories are often fiercely disputed, especially during times of upheaval when a community's unsteadiness prompts it to cling to the (imagined) security of the past. The past is then reinvoked through certain symbols and rituals, which may continue to offer a point of orientation for the community and perpetuate identity. This is not to suggest that memories of the past go unchallenged within a community, that it is only those outside its boundaries who doubt its authority; as some of the films show, there are competing memories of the past even for those whose life stories intertwine.

Nostalgia, the third recurring theme, is closely related to memory and offers a further inroad into identity. Nostalgia's focal point, however, is less precise than that of memory which often narrows in on particular points in the past. Indeed, the tendency towards nostalgia is interpreted by others who do not participate in its sentimental yearning as a provocation, for 'disparagement of the present' is, as Christopher Lasch has noted, 'the hallmark of nostalgia'.[22] The evocation of a vague past is central to its appeal and this retrospective desire is exploited by everyone, from politicians to tourist boards to television producers who contribute to what Frederic Jameson calls the 'aesthetic colonization' of favoured periods.[23] In recreating a vision of the past, films often prompt nostalgia, even – and this is where nostalgia and memory differ – among those who have no recollection of the past that is being performed before them. Nostalgia, then, may describe a regretful yearning for something one never had, for something that did not exist in the first place. Like memory, nostalgia is often at the centre of disagreement; 'a utopian diversion from the real tasks ahead', the retrospective realization of what has been lost can, and has, further exacerbated dissatisfaction with the present.[24]

This book examines these interrelated factors as represented in film in relational terms and considers them with reference to, among others things, socio-economic issues and political developments which have all influenced the post-unification experience. Chapter 1 looks at the factors that are involved in the development of the east Germans' contentious post-GDR identity and establishes the social and political context against which the films that are considered in subsequent chapters may be analysed. According to many observers, the various measures employed by the East German state in order to establish a separate national consciousness ultimately failed.[25] Moreover, the mandate given to Kohl's Christian Democratic Union (CDU) in 1990 and the support for subsequent monetary union appeared to offer conclusive proof that its population had no problem in identifying with the west and had happily abandoned any GDR distinctiveness. The east Germans' enthusiasm for the west was more likely prompted by their desire to enjoy the material benefits associated with the neighbours across the former border than proof of any profound bond. The euphoria of the early days was short-lived, and the assertion of pan-German solidarity soon disappeared. The regeneration of the east has proved far more of a challenge than was initially expected and the anxieties and disappointments associated with life in a free market society have been central to the emergence of a separate identity, which (in the early days at least) was unafraid to hoist the tattered banner of the left.

Discussion of the films is, as the book's subtitle suggests, organized thematically, though there is naturally some overlap; memory of the GDR for example runs through many of the narratives. Within the chapters, the films are discussed chronologically. I have opted to present an exegetic account of numerous films that are pertinent to the themes outlined above. A few of these have received some critical attention, many have gone unnoticed. Not all the films made since unification are easily categorized. Though many of the films that situate their narratives in the east do conform to certain generic conventions, a fact that may, in part, be explained by their reliance on funding from television stations and regional film funding boards, there are also several idiosyncratic productions, which are experimental in both narrative and form, and which resist classification. *Screening the East* considers films regardless of their generic character or the merits of their representation. The categories 'popular film' and its standard antonym the 'art film' are, as others have pointed out, problematic concepts when it comes to considering a nation's self-representation, with the critical weight often falling on those films which do not accurately reflect the national taste.[26] The popular, mainstream films may be critically derided, dismissed as flummeries because they fail either to engage with social issues or reveal anything about the society that produced them, but this is a prejudice born of the high art preferences that have long dominated film studies and working within such narrow confines risks a limited and limiting understanding of national film production.[27]

Taking as a given Gerald Mast's conclusion that 'even the most light-hearted, escapist piece of fun inevitably implies serious values', Chapter 2 addresses a number of comedies that focus on the encounters between east and west.[28] Ostensibly humorous accounts, which often make use of cabaret performers, the films – including Wolfgang Büld's and Reinhard Klooss's *Go Trabi Go II. Das war der wilde Osten* (*Go, Trabi, Go. That was the Wild East*, 1992) and Vadim Glowna's *Der Brocken* (*Rising to the Bait*, 1992) – reflect substantial divisions between the two peoples and should not be discounted as 'the social bad conscience of serious art'.[29] It has been argued that these films revive the post-war (West German) genre, the Heimatfilm. Though the most successful genre of the 1950s and 1960s and arguably the country's only indigenous genre, the traditional Heimatfilm for a long time received little academic attention, with film scholars subscribing to the long-held view that it was a reactionary genre, which replaced real-life concerns with 'idyllic images of rural simplicity'.[30] This chapter provides an overview of the Heimatfilm and includes recent reappraisals of the genre, which argue that the films did acknowledge post-war tensions, albeit in a subtle fashion. Progress and the development of a forward-looking social-ist culture were some of the guiding principles in the GDR, and the film in-dustry was expected to support these notions. The celebration of the local and the traditional that was central to the idea of Heimat did not corre-spond with the ideologues' vision, though they recognized its importance for the population, and the chapter examines the efforts made to redefine it according to a socialist perspective; inevitably, DEFA was expected to play a part in portraying this new version of Heimat. Having established the Heimatfilm's genealogy, I then consider its revival in some of the come-dies of the period. Claims that the Wende comedies simply recycle themes associated with traditional Heimatfilme can be misleading. I therefore assess the appeal of the genre and question its purpose, looking particu-larly at its use in the articulation of a collective identity mustered in defence of an east German Heimat that is firmly set in the provinces.[31]

Chapter 3 continues the enquiry into the Heimat theme though not the Heimatfilm. The provinces are still the focus of films such as Helke Misselwitz's *Herzsprung* (*Heart Leap*, 1992), *Stilles Land* (*Silent Country*, Andreas Dresen, 1992), and *Verlorene Landschaft* (*Lost Landscape*, Andreas Kleinert, 1992), but these narratives share none of the cheer found in the comedies. The chapter focuses on those communities no longer character-ized by solidarity or a group identity but portrayed as either irreversibly divided or on the verge of extinction. Memories of the GDR past figure strongly in these narratives, which repeatedly use the landscape as a way of reflecting the east Germans' sense of loss since unification, a loss that reflects the GDR's unrealized potential rather than nostalgia for the halcyon days of life behind the wall.

The discussion of Heimat is drawn to a close in Chapter 4, after looking at a number of films that have received very little attention in the literature on the subject. These meld the gloomy vision of the east that informs the narratives of the previous chapter with a comedic take on unification and on the stereotypes that have come to dominate in post-wall discourse. These black comedies (for example, *Tolle Lage* (*The Perfect Site*), Sören Voigt, 1999), *Not a Love Song* (Jan Ralske, 1997)), which are partly reminiscent of non-German filmmaking – the lo-fi cinema of Jim Jarmusch, the grotesques of Mike Leigh – highlight the continuing social and economic problems in the east but do not champion the local population in their struggle against the west.

In Chapter 5, the attention shifts from the community to the individual and from the provinces to the city; in post-unification cinema this is short-hand for one city alone: Berlin. Though the city has long been portrayed as an alienating place, an *unheimlich* location, the anxieties that are articulated in these films reflect a general unease and restlessness associated with the loss of guidance once provided by the state. The architectural makeup of the city plays an important role in these narratives, serving to alienate and estrange the inhabitants, who, in the films of the 1990s, are often seen struggling to find their way in the new capital. Like the protagonists of the films examined in Chapter 3, these urban protagonists, in films such as *Der Kontrolleur* (*The Border Guard*, Stefan Trampe, 1994) and *Wege in die Nacht* (*Paths in the Night*, Andreas Kleinert, 1999), are caught between the past and the future, between memories of life in the GDR and their present lives in the Berlin Republic. Negotiating these two temporal coordinates is, as we shall see, seldom straightforward and even perilous.

The focus of Chapter 6 is on nostalgia, specifically Ostalgie, the east Germans' nostalgia for their pre-wall past. The nostalgic turn has been a central factor in post-unification identity discourse; reconstituting an idealized, inauthentically authentic past has naturally impacted on attempts to structure a dominant cultural hegemony and this final chapter explores some of the controversies surrounding the east German community's attachment to their past and considers it implications. Having traced the evolution of Ostalgie and examined it in its social and economic context, I then turn to those films which generated the most debate in post-unification cinema, the so-called Ostalgie films, and question the appropriateness of the label and assess whether these retro narratives, among them *Sonnenalle* (*Sun Alley*, Leander Haußmann, 1999) and *Good Bye, Lenin!* (Wolfgang Becker, 2003), really do indulge east Germans' nostalgic longing.

The number of films offering insight into issues of contemporary east German identity is far larger than the few articles on post-unification film might suggest, and no single study could offer a detailed account of each film. I have therefore chosen to concentrate on feature films, rather than television or documentary films (though the funding practices in Germany which see some films part-financed by television companies and given a short release at cinemas mean that some films are both television and feature films). To include the many television films and series that have in some way or other engaged with unification issues would have burdened the study unnecessarily. This is more a logistical question than a matter of taste; there is simply not enough room within this account to offer a satisfactory survey of the large number of relevant television productions, though I occasionally refer to some television dramas and series where this enhances my discussion of a particular film or films. Equally, the many documentary films made since unification have been omitted from the research. While these films often provide invaluable accounts and insights into individual reactions to the historic changes that have taken place in east Germany, my focus is specifically on feature films. These may not be guided by the putative objectivity that generally governs the documentaries, but the films' contribution to the identity debate is not diminished by their subjectivity. As with other modes of representation, they 'creatively interpret and refract … complex worlds of significance and actively contribute to the construction of new forms of self-understanding'.[32]

Notes

1. Herzog, cited in G.S. Freyermuth, *Der Übernehmer. Volker Schlöndorff in Babelsberg*, Berlin: Ch. Links Verlag, 1993, p. 27. All translations, unless otherwise indicated, are the author's.
2. M. Töteberg, 'Vorwort', in M. Töteberg (ed.), *Szenenwechsel. Momentaufnahmen des jungen deutschen Films*, Reinbek: Rowohlt Verlag, 1999, p. 7.
3. E. Rentschler, 'From New German Cinema to the Post-Wall Cinema of Consensus', in M. Hjort and S. Mackenzie (eds), *Cinema & Nation*, London and New York: Routledge, 2002, p. 264.
4. T.W. Adorno and M. Horkheimer. 'The Culture Industry: Enlightenment as Mass Deception', in T.W. Adorno and M. Horkheimer, *Dialectic of Enlightenment*, London, New York: Verso, 1979, p. 137.
5. See N. James, 'German Cinema. All Together Now', *Sight and Sound*, December 2006: 26–31.
6. R. Schenk, 'Zerissene Seelen und gefundene Fressen', *Berliner Zeitung*, 20 May 1996. Retrieved 4 March 2002 from http://www.berlinonline.de/wissen/berlinerzeitung/archiv/1996/ 0520/kultur/0004/index.html. Note: I follow the convention whereby any reference to the pre-unification population/state/region is referred to by using upper-case spelling (East/West) and employ lower case (east/west) when referring to the period since unification.
7. Of course, Herbig's film is of cultural significance, even if it has received little, if any, scholarly attention. One possible analysis might consider the film's nostalgic value, since it engages with the popular Karl May films of the 1960s. Similar might be said of Herbig's other huge hit, *(T)Raumschiff Surprise – Periode 1* (2004), which parodies cherished sci-fi films.
8. See C.M. Kaupp, *Good Bye, Lenin! Film-Heft*, Bonn: Bundeszentrale für politische Bildung, 2003, and N. Hodgin, 'Aiming to Please: *Good Bye, Lenin!* and the Cinema of Consensus', in P. Cooke and C. Homewood (eds), *New Directions in German Cinema*, London: I.B. Tauris (forthcoming).
9. E. Rentschler, 'Post-Wall Prospects: An Introduction', *New German Critique* 87 (Special Issue on Post-Wall Cinema), 2002: 5.
10. See E. Hobsbawm and T. Ranger (eds), *The Invention of Tradition*, Cambridge: Cambridge University Press, 2003.

11. In D. Calhoun, 'Afghan Aftermath', *Sight and Sound*, February 2004: 222.
12. G. Schöpflin, *Nations, Identity, Power. The New Politics of Europe*, London: Hurst, 2000, p. 15.
13. See R. Tapper (ed.), *The New Iranian Cinema. Politics, Representation and Identity*, London: I.B. Tauris, 2002; Y. Zhang, *Chinese National Cinema*, New York and London: Routledge, 2004; and N. Triana-Toribio, *Spanish National Cinema*, London and New York: Routledge, 2003.
14. There are a growing number of titles that address DEFA. For an indispensable guide see R. Schenk (ed.), *Das Zweite Leben der Filmstadt Babelsberg DEFA-Spielfilme 1946–1992*, Berlin: Henschelverlag, 1994. Other useful histories include S. Allan and J. Sandford (eds), *DEFA. East German Cinema, 1946–1992*, New York and Oxford: Berghahn, 1999, and D. Berghahn, *Hollywood Behind the Wall. The Cinema of East Germany*, Manchester and New York: Manchester University Press, 2005.
15. Elsaesser suggests that the multitude of festivals has given rise to a new genre, the 'festival film'. See T. Elsaesser, *European Cinema: Face to Face with Hollywood*, Amsterdam: Amsterdam University Press, 2003, p. 88.
16. L. Naughton. *That Was The Wild East. Film Culture, Unification, and the 'New' Germany*, Ann Arbor: The University of Michigan Press, 2002.
17. Ibid., p. 235.
18. The situation at DEFA had allowed many directors to wither on the vine. The state's collapse came at a time when several promising directors were too old to be considered fresh talent and not nearly experienced enough to command any kind of attention; not that the older DEFA directors were necessarily in demand. Only the biggest names in the East German film industry successfully completed the transition from nationalized industry to the highly competitive privatized industry in the west, and even their presence is difficult to detect. In 1994, the respected (and former GDR) film journal, *Film und Fernsehen*, sent questionnaires to various former DEFA directors, in order to assess their experiences since unification. Few of the responses suggested that the directors had mastered the new market. The journal folded after twenty-seven years in 1999. See 'Lebenszeichen aus dem Osten. Antworten auf eine Umfrage', *Film und Fernsehen* 3, 1994: 22–27 (no author).
19. See, for example, M. Münter and R Sturm, 'Economic Consequences of German Unification', *German Politics* 11(3), 2002: 179–94.
20. See C. von Ditfurth, cited in P. Thompson, *The Crisis of the German Left. The PDS, Stalinism and the Global Economy*, New York and Oxford: Berghahn Books, 2005, p. 98.
21. A. Appadurai, cited in D. Morley, *Home Territories. Media, Mobility and Identity*, London: Routledge, 2000, p. 11.
22. C. Lasch, *The True and Only Heaven. Progress and Its Critics*, New York and London: E.E. Norton, 1991, p. 82.
23. F. Jameson, 'Postmodernism, or the Cultural Logic of Late Capitalism', *New Left Review*, July/August 1984: 67.
24. A.D. Smith, 'The "Golden Age" and National Renewal', in G. Hosking and G. Schöpflin (eds), *Myth and Nationhood*, London: Hurst & Co., 1997, p. 38.
25. According to K.H. Jarausch *et al*, assessing the success of the state's attempt to create a GDR identity is difficult, given the paucity of empirical data and relevant surveys before 1989. In K.H. Jarausch, H.C. Seeba and D.P. Conradt, 'The Presence of the Past. Culture, Opinion, and Identity in Germany', in K.H. Jarausch (ed.), *After Unity. Reconfiguring German Identities*, Oxford: Berghahn, 1997, pp. 41–2.
26. R. Dyer and G. Vincendeau, 'Introduction', in R. Dyer and G. Vincendeau (eds), *Popular European Cinema*, London and New York: Routledge, 1992, p. 1.
27. See G. Vincendeau, 'Issues in European Cinema', in J. Hill and P. Church Gibson (eds), *World Cinema. Critical Approaches*, Oxford: Oxford University Press, 2000, p. 58.
28. G. Mast, *The Comic Mind. Comedy and the Movies*, Chicago and London: University of Chicago Press, 1979, p. 17.
29. Adorno and Horkheimer, (1979), p. 135.
30. See T. Elsaesser, *New German Cinema. A History*, London: BFI Publishing, 1989, p. 141. R.P. Kolker and P. Beicken, *The Films of Wim Wenders. Cinema as Vision and Desire*, Cambridge: Cambridge University Press, 1993, p. 64.

31. The term Wende (literally 'turning point') originally referred to the transition from the GDR's planned economy to the west's market economy but has since come to mean the period of unification and the period that immediately followed.
32. M. Fulbrook and M. Swales, 'Introduction: Representation in Literature and History', in M. Fulbrook and M. Swales (eds), *Representing the German Nation. History and Identity in Twentieth Century Germany*, Manchester: Manchester University Press, 2000, p. 10.

Chapter 1

MAPPING IDENTITY

Angela Merkel's accession to Chancellor of Germany in October 2005, which counted as a double triumph since she was both the first woman and the first east German to head the German government, would appear to disprove any suspicion that the east Germans have been denied the opportunities for advancement in the new Germany or sidelined from positions of power. But what was interesting in judging Merkel's rise through the CDU is quite how much her eastern background was used as a point of reference. Although she emphatically criticized the former GDR regime, something that was necessary if she was to convince diehard CDU voters of her candidature, she was and continues to be described in terms of reductive eastern stereotypes. Evelyn Finger, writing in *Die Zeit*, noted how journalists focused on what were considered to be distinctive (and mostly negative) east German qualities: 'her malleability and her unscrupulousness, that deviousness, suspiciousness and, above all, ingratitude'.[1] Not long after Merkel's pyrrhic victory, *Der Spiegel* ran a lead article on the new chancellor and her fellow east German politician (albeit for the rival Social Democrats), Matthias Platzeck, in an issue whose cover page also invoked the GDR past by parodying an East German propaganda poster from 1952.[2] Politicians are rarely able to dodge their past; biographical details have a habit of surfacing at awkward moments in their political careers, often compromising their present commitments and undermining their reputation in the process. But in eastern Germany the past is ever present in the lives of ordinary east Germans, too, and the limiting reference points and stereotypes that accompany many discussions regarding the head of the German government are part of the complex identity discourse which began almost as soon as the two states became one. The debates have often been divisive. Failed expectations, perceived injustices, mutual suspicions and emerging prejudices have been central to the debate.

Issues of German identity have long been a subject of scrutiny for historians, social scientists, political scientists, cultural commentators, and filmmakers alike. Konrad Jarausch claims that 'Germans keep searching for a collective sense of themselves, while outside commentators continue trying to define what these perplexing people might really be like', while Mary Fulbrook describes the quest to discover national identity as a 're-markably dogged search for a remarkably elusive holy grail'.[3] There are, however, a number of useful theoretical guides to mapping identity. Anthony D. Smith's influential work on national identity signposts routes one might take in order to arrive at a satisfactory account of identity and his research might usefully be applied to the Germans' post-unification sit-uation.[4] 'Unity', he suggests, 'has a plain and a more esoteric nationalist meaning. At the simplest level, it refers to unification of the national terri-tory or the homeland, if it is divided, and the gathering together within the homeland of all nationals'.[5] Those who remain beyond these boundaries are, according to Smith's thesis, considered lost by the remaining popula-tion. This was, to some extent, evident in post-war Germany, where it was the population of the GDR who were considered absent from the 'real' Germany. Over the years, the FRG (Federal Republic of Germany) began to show signs of having accepted the division and the East Germans, stranded on the other side of the German/German border, were given up as victims lost to the exigencies of the Cold War. With little hope or belief in unifica-tion, an idea that strengthened rather than weakened, the FRG appeared to have accustomed itself to the post-war arrangement. Certainly, it seemed as if the FRG had more or less come to terms with the East German irre-denta: a survey conducted in the very month in which the East Germans took to the streets revealed the extent to which the West German popula-tion had come to accept division, with only 24 per cent of respondents ex-pressing a belief that reunification might one day be possible.[6] But unification ceased being a 'nostalgic phantasm' after 1989.[7] Finally a reality, it created something of a predicament for the west German population. To be suddenly confronted with 16 million new compatriots was almost certain to provoke some hostility and to problematize the position of ab-stract sympathy (or indifference) that had typified the West German atti-tude.[8] Previously, the sympathy directed at the East Germans had been aroused by a vague understanding of their plight. This centred mostly on the East Germans as victims of political repression, geographical restric-tions, and, above all, of the Stasi, the notorious State security (though the actual extent of the Stasi's dealings had been underestimated, and post-GDR revelations came as a shock to many). By the following spring, a survey commissioned by the public television corporation, ZDF, gave some indication of the disparate reactions to recent events. Where 41 per cent of those in the east were 'very pleased' with unification, less than half that figure were as enthusiastic in the west, leading some commentators to con-clude that 'West Germans were quite sympathetic to the East Germans as a people and quite hostile to East Germany as a state'.[9] Unification ulti-mately affected this sympathy when those previously given up as lost became the newly arrived and only briefly welcomed.

Theories of national identity tend towards individual self-perception based on a shared sense of who we are – the 'imagined communities' to employ Benedict Anderson's influential phrase. Anderson's seminal study holds that a collective identity evolves from shared historical, cultural and linguistic experience, and is disseminated via the printed word. Though Anderson's study focuses on print capitalism, his analysis has gained vital theoretical cachet among film scholars keen to stress film's role in producing and shaping a national consciousness.[10] Applied to the two German states, such a culturalist perspective would hold that the intra-German borders did not inhibit a pan-German national identity. The idea that the two states had always in a sense been one, the forty years of separation notwithstanding, was indeed one of the attitudes expressed at the time of unification. It signalled the desire by some former GDR citizens to participate in the economic success of the FRG, but it also signalled a degree of political triumphalism among commentators on the right who were keen to discredit the communist state and deny the existence of a separate socialist German identity – an argument that appeared to be vindicated by Chancellor Kohl's first resounding electoral triumph in the east. These were early days, however, and it soon became apparent that the two states' historical, cultural and linguistic experiences, those precepts that help determine national identity, had left their imprint on the two populations, and it was in these areas that one might identify factors that distinguished the two nations. Forty years of separation had seen to it, for example, that the populations of both states viewed their past through different ideological prisms, which the subsequent removal of communist heroes from street signs and the renaming of certain public holidays could not undo at a stroke. Unlike the more substantial reminders of the previous regime such as the state statuary, street names were easily changed, making them 'tempting targets for politicians eager to make a symbolic gesture'.[11] However, the new nomenclature was often understood by east Germans as a further attempt to wipe clean the GDR past.

The culture and language of each state had also been shaped by their respective political, economic and social environments, and the many differences were perhaps even more apparent after 1989. Language, a key element in collective national consciousness, had developed many distinguishing features. These were not just distinctions of dialect characterizing regional linguistic differences, but informed by cultural distinctions. The everyday socialist rhetoric and jargon that made little sense to those from the West was, according to one observer, part of a strategy of using 'language that set the GDR apart from the Federal Republic and created its identity'.[12] That the two Germanys did share a common history and past culture was a fact recognized by each and, unless supervised appropriately, had serious implications for their individually assumed identity and sovereignty. The West had preferred to think of itself in terms of the real Germany, continuing the cultural tradition that had been briefly hijacked by the National Socialists (NS), and of the GDR as the renegade state, the Sozialistische Einheitspartei Deutschlands (SED – Socialist Unity Party of Germany) as Soviet lackeys. The GDR, on the other hand, never made any claim upon the other Germany, seeing itself as the breakaway state. Yet, paradoxically, it also saw itself as the legatee of a carefully defined Germany, as the final link in a concatenation of historical revolutionary thought and action. Thus, the GDR simultaneously sought to balance these two ideas, that of a new Germany which could look eastwards, towards Moscow, for inspiration and support, and as a Germany that could continue to draw upon the (state sanctioned) traditions of the German past.

The differences between the two states were not as easily dismantled as the wall, and were still manifest after 1989. Fashion, commodities, and language came to serve as cultural signifiers distinguishing east from west. These often lent themselves to stereotyping, be it the east Germans in their snow-wash jeans and Trabant or the well-attired west Germans driving their Mercedes – symbols and props that have proved especially popular in post-unification film. References to the east Germans' post-unification unease have not been uncommon. This appears to have been confirmed by the data collected in social surveys and questionnaires, in voting behaviour and in artistic self-expression. It is reflected, too, in a number of issues associated with unification: high unemployment (a fact more acute in the east than the west), the political marginalization of the east, the related social problems and Ostalgie. This significant 1990s neologism was coined in order to describe the east Germans' post-unification nostalgia for their GDR past. Over time it also came to express an attitude that reinvigorated and celebrated a problematic east German identity whilst simultaneously rejecting or eliding many of the less appealing features associated with unification and with the west.

After Unity: Stereotypes and Dissent

The GDR was, as I have indicated, a more abstract land to West Germans than were its western neighbours, France, Britain and especially the US, which had, as one of the characters in Wim Wenders's *Im Lauf der Zeit* (*Kings of the Road*, 1976) memorably observed, colonized their consciousness. As for actual experiences of life in the GDR, only 10 per cent of West Germans could reasonably claim to have witnessed it first-hand, and then only temporarily.[13] For some commentators, the rush to unification constituted a threat to the west's post-national republic. The political triumphalism that followed the GDR's implosion risked a return to a national patriotism rather than the 'constitutional patriotism' (and its implicit commitment to European integration) that had been proposed and supported by intellectuals like Jürgen Habermas.[14] Some on the left perceived the collapse of the East German state as a critical blow to utopian ideals, something that is certainly borne out in a number of films made after 1989.

Ill-prepared for dealing with the events that had taken place, their situation has been described as one in which 'mourning utopia replaced an engagement with the new realities'.[15] Nevertheless, the *coup de théâtre* that was the success of the demonstrations in the East came initially as a happy surprise for those in the FRG, a large percentage of whom had given up expecting to see unification in their lifetime, though their interest in coming together was less enthusiastic than that of the east Germans. One commentator summed up the asymmetrical interest, wryly noting that it was only on east German cars that one saw stickers declaring 'we are one people'.[16] A further indication of the imbalance in the Germans' interest in one another was confirmed by the west Germans' singular lack of interest in visiting the eastern states, with less than 3 per cent choosing to go east even after the borders had opened.[17] Traffic continued to be a one-way affair.

As memorable as the sight of sputtering Trabis crossing into the west was the image of determined east Germans storming once-dreaded Stasi headquarters and the documents and dossiers spilling out of the windows of its centre of operations at Normannenstrasse in Berlin. A population so long kept in check by the invidious activities of the Stasi was naturally eager to have access to their files, to expose the Ministry's employees and the thousands of unofficial informants. Allegations, recriminations and revelations were commonplace, and those that involved some of the high-profile cultural figures, notably the acclaimed east German writer Christa Wolf, aroused frenzied media interest that was inevitably disproportionate to the actual facts. This (mostly west German) media focus on the apparent moral and ideological transgressions of such a key cultural figure not only served to undermine her position. It put the FRG's intellectual left into an uncomfortable position of continuing to support their old GDR colleagues amid a series of problematic accusations and highlighted the extent of the east Germans' collusion with the regime. The dissolution of the GDR had already precipitated a crisis for the left, whose intellectual credibility had been undermined by their support for East Germany, a state whose population had just overwhelmingly voted for Kohl's centre-right party. These gleeful accusations of hypocrisy have in turn been criticized. John Milful has suggested that, 'It will be a tragic irony if those writers who were once stylized in the West into dissidents … are now condemned as quislings who failed to lead their people to the barricades.'[18] Certainly, key dissidents, who before 1989 had been fêted in the west for their criticism of the regime, were, following revelations of their apparent duplicity, condemned as hypocritical collaborators, who had duped colleagues and good-natured liberals in the FRG. Daily disclosures ensured that the GDR was regarded as a 'land of Stasi agents, Stalinists, privileged elites [and] fellow travellers' leading many west Germans to view their eastern compatriots with an increasing amount of suspicion.[19]

There are mitigating factors in the emergence of this attitude, of course, not least the fact that the GDR's relative stability was largely due to its tightly structured and controlled nature. It was also a society controlled by a regime that knew how to punish and reward. Scholars often describe the socialist regime as a corrupt and corrupting force, which sought 'to govern by concluding bargains with each citizen, or potential dissenter'.[20] This 'informal, tacit "social contract" between ... state and society' was instrumental to the GDR's relative longevity.[21] The actual number of Stasi agents and informants exposed contracts of a more insidious nature, and the subsequent disclosure of Stasi files revealed just how widespread their activities were. The DEFA studios, too, had been home to a diligent network of spies. With roughly two informants for every hundred employees (as opposed to the usual ratio of one per hundred throughout the wider GDR population), the potential subversion at the Babelsberg studios was clearly a matter of some concern for the SED, and many screenwriters and directors were monitored by the Stasi, a theme that was central to what is perhaps the best-known post-unification film, *Das Leben der Anderen*.[22] Nevertheless, it was, and continues to be, a source of frustration to east Germans to be judged according to such a narrow frame of reference and could only harm plans for social integration.

The West Germans' abstract solidarity with those in the GDR, which had required very little in the way of active support, was ruptured by unification. The reasons for the ensuing change in attitude are manifold: the disclosure of Stasi activities, the assumed culpability of the GDR population (either as participants or passive onlookers); the revelations of environmental damage caused by irresponsible heavy industrial practices; the huge cost of restructuring; and, above all, the sheer lack of gratitude, even hostility expressed by the east Germans. Suddenly, the codified features offered a stick with which to beat those they previously pitied. Political repression and the violation of human rights in the GDR were recognized as a feature of the SED dictatorship but the Stasi revelations implicated the population as potential informants. A growing mistrust of the eastern population's biographies was evident early on. Their maintained innocence vis-à-vis their ideological convictions was often doubted. Suspicions such as these effectively robbed the east Germans of their revolution, which threatened to be overshadowed by allegations of collusion and of lack of personal responsibility. The focus switched from the state's repressive character and its mismanagement of the economy, to collective responsibility in perpetuating an unjust system.

After 1989, the east Germans' commitment to pluralism and to other modern democratic values was found wanting. The violent attacks on refugees and on members of the ethnic minorities, which received widespread media coverage in the early 1990s (both in national and international news reports and as a stock theme in film), confirmed the suspicion that the east Germans were as unmodern in their opinions as their industries were obsolete. The validity of some of the surveys and opinion polls investigating the difference in attitudes between east and west has been

questioned by several social and political scientists who point to methodological problems, particularly in the wording of the questionnaires.[23]
Much has been made, for example, of the east Germans' apparent shibbo-
leth, 'second-class citizen'. This is a term repeatedly heard in post-unification identity discourse, yet the description is seldom analysed and its
origins rarely considered. Rudolf Woderich states that it first gained currency in an early survey compiled by the ENMID Institute, which allowed
respondents only two choices of description (a 'citizen accorded equal
rights' being the other).[24] Repeatedly employing a new post-unification vocabulary that emphasizes stereotypes, such surveys and questionnaires
have, he argues, themselves been a contributing factor in the construction
of an east German identity.

Yet the negative reception of such terms does not diminish their accuracy. Though their use is often derogatory and their effect divisive, generalizations and stereotyping are not necessarily without foundation.
Moreover, the use of stereotypes is not always an attempt to 'lock a cate-
gory irrevocably into its place, in an apparently settled hierarchy of relations'.[25] The ownership of the caricature problematizes the use of
stereotyping. By this, I mean not just the target of the caricature, but its
agent. It is not uncommon for the same kind of images and characteristics
ascribed to the typical Ossi – the unglamorous garb, a nasal Saxonian
dialect, the comic-provincial outlook – to be used by *both* west and east
Germans.[26] What differentiates them is, of course, the purpose of the caricature. While east Germans can hardly be said to be lacking in their capacity for humour, they clearly object to such depictions, regardless of how
close these may be to their own comic self-representation. The reasons for
this are linked to the complex process of transition from socially and economically disadvantaged underlings to fully accepted and respected
members of the Federal Republic, an evolution that, arguably, has not yet
been fully realized.

The east German depiction of the west Germans as the arrogant expo-
nents of a shallow, consumerist culture abound, but such generalizations
have less of an impact upon their targets. Partly this impact is minimized
by the fact that it was precisely to this culture that many GDR citizens had
aspired, as evidenced by the frenzied accumulation of western consumer
goods during the early stages of the Wende and the blanket support for
Kohl (modes of behaviour and expression that dismayed those on the left).
The image of the provincial dim easterner even functions as a vent for self-
mockery in the east; as Wolfgang Thierse, former President of the
Bundestag, conceded: 'You have to complain about the east Germans sometimes, don't you? I'm allowed to since I am one myself.'[27] There is undoubtedly an element of truth to Thierse's comment; nevertheless, such
rational self-reflexivity is less likely when a community feels threatened
by particular categorization.

The problem in the two populations' relationship by no means post-dates unification. Tensions were in evidence at 'neutral' locations long before the Wende, with East Germans often feeling that they were treated as second-class citizens at the favoured international camping grounds in Hungary because of the attention paid to the West Germans or, more accurately, western currencies.[28] Hungarians at modern day campsites might find it more difficult to differentiate between Germans from east or west, and the Germans, too, can no longer rely on the old signals of regional identity. A Mercedes, for example, is no longer a rare sight on the streets of Dresden, and the shopping malls that have sprung up around the old east provide the latest fashions. Still, a degree of unfamiliarity, a lack of direct experience of one another persists, and the contrasts between the two are frequently amplified and sustained in the filmic representation of the east and west.

In May 2002, *Stern* magazine felt that the title, 'The Ossis. What they want, what they can do and what they hate', merited a front cover and leading article. Interestingly, the cover, depicting six eastern caricatures, among them the politicians Gregor Gysi (clutching a PDS flag) and Angelika Merkel, a skinhead clutching a swastika-labelled beer and footballer Michael Ballack, all squeezed into a Trabant. The use of these figures as archetypal *Ossis* suggested that, a dozen years on from unification, the preconceptions of the east had not diminished, and that the stereotypes had a longer shelf life than one might have initially expected. Strangely, the

Figure 1.1 *Der Spiegel* (cover)
Reproduced with kind permission
of Spiegel

Figure 1.2 Stern (cover)
Reproduced with kind permission
of Stern

Representing the east Germans with old references and new stereotypes accompanying article, by the Leipzig based journalist, Holger Witzel, countered precisely the kind of imagery used on the magazine's front cover. As he wearily noted, '[the editors] mean well; they don't just want to increase circulation but to understand – but then they go and stick a Trabi, a naked woman and Gysi on the cover page and that's your Ossi right there.'[29]

The article contains several thumb profiles of a cross section of east Germans, from sportsman (and youth icon) Stefan Kretzschmar, to politician Cornelia Pieper. The articulation of an eastern identity is consistent throughout these brief profiles. Some express this through an appeal to take pride in certain achievements in the New Federal States but avoid any direct comparison with the west; others demonstrate a critical attitude to the prevailing negative images of east Germans. Else Buschheuer, a writer and broadcaster, offers a particularly sardonic response to the west Germans' view of their eastern compatriots, when she highlights the Ossis' fondness for crappy clothes, nudism, bashing foreigners, and greasy food. Buschheuer's statement encapsulates a series of associations that have become integral to the east/west stereotypology. These images and generalizations, which appear frequently in post-unification film, connote a provincialism apparently prevalent in the east. Since the features and kind of behaviour mentioned by Buschheuer are deemed to be symptomatic of the east (again further problematized by the fact that they are in use among east Germans, too), the implication is that the west is all those things which the east is not. Right-wing extremism, previously seen as a blight on the FRG's otherwise healthy liberal democracy, suddenly became more of an east German problem. The attacks on asylum seekers in the east have been well documented, as have the underlying reasons for such antagonism.[30] The dire economic situation and the dismal social conditions that typify most of the environments where the attacks and killings have taken place are usually brought into the analysis. Invariably, the explanation of right-wing extremism in the east focuses on the unfortunate combination of poor socio-economic circumstances in a region that has not had contact with foreigners. This is not quite accurate. Foreign workers and asylum seekers were not an unknown entity in the GDR; nor, indeed, was right-wing extremism. But, the media focus on racist incidents in the new federal states provoked fundamental anxieties in the west about their eastern neighbours' commitment to a pluralist, democratic society and consequently underlined apparent differences between the two.

Buschheuer's indignation is interesting, too, since it does not seek to challenge the described modes of behaviour. Instead, it redeploys these different codes into a single homogenized composite. As a whole, and lacking any context, they are revealed as nothing more than laughably exaggerated qualities, which have little relevance or actuality for east Germans such as Buschheuer. Nevertheless, the markers of otherness continue to occupy east/west discourse. This is no great surprise; similarities are axiomatic and require little in the way of challenge or disputation; differences, meanwhile, are frequently and heatedly debated. They are also, in a sense, malleable quantities, which can be rearranged and reconfigured within competing discourses. Journalists, politicians, comedians, and academics thrive on such differences, which allow endless interpretation and analysis. The usefulness of the assumed differences for writers and filmmakers should not be underestimated, since they usher in a potential for conflict and division that does not always require further explication. Often the differences between east and west are givens, with the assumption being that the audience or the readers are aware of an underlying tension, or at least the potential for such tension. Clear, distinguishing features have developed that help announce these differences; they have evolved within the public imagination to become recognizable indicators of east and west, frequently conforming to crude partisan positions. They are so often repeated and employed that they become almost unavoidable. Obstinacy and recidivism are thus considered characteristic of those in the new federal states, while west Germans are linked to such unappealing tendencies as egotism and superciliousness. These unattractive characteristics correlate with other semiotic signifiers and confirm certain preconceptions. Cars provide such an example, with the unfortunate Trabi evidence of both the GDR's lack of choice in such an important status symbol, and of the GDR's lack of style, efficiency, and individualism. Zooming along the well-maintained motorways of the west, by contrast, is the Mercedes, emblem of the FRG's prosperous economy writ large. Efficient and desirable, the brand functions as a symbol of a long (if sometimes dubious) heritage. Where the Trabi is abandoned to the scrap heap of history (the final insult being the difficulties it posed even after death, with its cotton fibre 'Duroplast' frame making it impossible to crush effectively, let alone recycle), the Mercedes continues to command national and international respect. Representing the mechanized superiority and technical innovation of the FRG, it is able to draw upon a grand, illustrious tradition of German manufacturing whilst also demonstrating cutting-edge technology. The Trabi, then, remains the spluttering symbol of the GDR, the product of resourceful, if limited technology, and of a market that was never able to satisfy its consumer demands. The two-stroke engines could never compete with the powerful engines across the border and, as with the general attitudes to the GDR itself, east Germans display a fondness for it that does not quite extend to wishing its return other than as a novelty ride for tourists wishing to take up one of the Trabisafaris offered on the streets of Berlin and Dresden.

A Post-GDR Identity?

The discourse surrounding east German identity has not resulted in any universally accepted and conclusive answers, and, rather than waning, the debates look set to continue. Some commentators maintain that there was never any specific GDR identity despite, and possibly because of, the SED's best efforts. The simple article switch chanted by the demonstrators in 1989, substituting 'we are *the* people' for 'we are *one* people', is often invoked as evidence of some self-perceived essential German 'oneness' that, not recognizing any border, or ideological polarity, persisted over the forty years of separation. Detlef Kannapin, meanwhile, rejects the concept of identity altogether and advances instead 'the concept of consciousness, which insists on the fact that the GDR had an existence and that the citizens living in this state had, in some way, a conscious opinion about it or attitude towards it'.[31] These epistemological issues aside, questionnaires and social surveys do appear to document a shift in attitudes that bears out the existence of a post-wall identity. Steußloff even goes so far as to claim that an east German identity is now so frequently referred to that it no longer requires justification as a subject for research.[32] Others argue that, although the intended socialist identity that the ruling Party endeavoured to promote was never successfully forged, an east German identity nevertheless developed.

The emergent identity was considered by some to be a lingering symptom of indoctrination and met with suspicion in the west. Such suspicion is evident in *TAZ* reporter Anna Jonas's unrestrained invective:

> What East German identity is supposed to be saved if identity is simply a synonym for nationalism? The identity of a cringing society condemned to unquestioning obedience? The identity built up around 'people's own business' and 'agricultural production co-operatives', which deprived the country and its citizens of their rights, exploited and literally poisoned them? The identity based on a niche society? On the contrary, one can only hope that as little as possible or even nothing remains, since this would be the only chance for a shared and better society.[33]

These signposts of identity, as Jonas sees them, were undoubtedly fixed features within GDR life, yet such blanket rejection ignores the complex attitudes that existed towards them, and simultaneously reduces east German identity to nothing more than a by-product of SED policy (one can only imagine an east German's reaction to such reductionist classification).

Other, competing issues persist and further confuse the debate over an east German identity. Among these is the complex and often contentious process of *Vergangenheitsbewältigung* ('coming to terms with the past'). A bitter intellectual debate concerning the FRG's connection to the NS past had already taken place in the West during the 1980s. The Historians' Dispute, as it came to be known, saw intellectuals divided between those who believed that the (West) Germans could begin to unburden themselves of the NS past and reconstitute a positive and normalized identity, and those who did not agree that the modern West German state could separate politics from history. East German culpability was never worked through in the same way that it was (forced to) in the west. The initial discussion of the East Germans' guilt quickly faded; self-inquiry and contrition were surrendered to ideological expediency as the east concentrated on promoting its antifascist profile, a mythology of resistance that exonerated the GDR's citizens of any blame. If coming to terms with the past had been a process delayed by more than two decades in the west (when the so-called '68er' finally challenged the previous generation's reticence), it was overdue by some forty years in the east. When the GDR collapsed, so too did antifascism as an article of faith. The ensuing full-scale economic restructuring and the democratic overhaul of the political system drew comparisons between the post-war and post-wall periods. Inverting the SED's rhetoric, which had previously linked the FRG to Hitler's Germany, some commentators sought to equate the SED regime with that of the NS, a view that found some support among those who had been victims of the East German system. Milful has warned of the dangers of treating GDR history in the same condemnatory fashion with which NS history was often portrayed, because of the east Germans' visceral attachment to their past.[34] Certain calendrical coincidences indirectly link the GDR to NS history. The most obvious of these is the anniversary of unification, which falls on the anniversary of Kristallnacht, the 1938 Nazi pogrom against Jews in Germany and Austria. In recent years, the latter has even come to overshadow the former in media coverage of events. Furthermore,

> any joyful celebration of the bringing down of the Wall and any celebration of unity between east and west has been superseded by grim and divisive memories of the GDR, a struggle to find new (political) roles in a united Germany, and a continuing unease about the legacy of the Third Reich.[35]

The historian Jürgen Kocka agrees that there were certain structural similarities in both regimes, similarities that are characteristic of all modern dictatorships.[36] According to Kocka, both dictatorships confirmed Germany's so-called *Sonderweg* ('special path'), even if their ideologies were diametrically opposed. But he acknowledges that the regimes were also very different, not least in their domestic and foreign policies. Most commentators therefore avoid direct comparisons and acknowledge German unification as a historically unprecedented event, and have applied themselves to the task of examining it according to their discipline or particular field of interest.

The iniquities of the GDR and the secrecy that characterized the state's control of its population could not remain a closed subject to be filed away and forgotten. The reassessment of the GDR was a necessary if awkward and painful task, with many issues requiring examination and reconciliation. A problem for many east Germans was that the GDR past was portrayed within a narrow context. As a result, such GDR inventions as the Stasi continue to exist as reference points in much western coverage of eastern Germany. The GDR's sinister side has lent itself to dramatic interpretation, and writers and filmmakers have engaged with these aspects of East German life, producing numerous books, films and plays that chart their narratives according to these co-ordinates. Interestingly, these accounts now compete with other, less sensationalist versions of the GDR. Recent years have seen a steady publication and release of personal accounts of life in the East German state. These are not limited to attempts to address any apparently unresolved issues of the past. Bringing some balance to the more sober memoirs of life in the GDR (for example, Günter de Bruyn's 'Vierzig Jahre') are the factual and fictional comic recollections offered by numerous autobiographies and memoirs of the period, particularly by a younger generation of authors, of which Jakob Hein and Falko Henning are just two examples.[37]

These subjective accounts are significant in shoring up an east German identity, for they mark an important shift in the east Germans' view of their past, which balances the top-down, historical accounts of the GDR. The novels frequently organize their narrative around childhood experiences in the GDR and, in so doing, contribute to a group consciousness, which, according to Rolf Reißig, 'is more likely considered amusing and dismissed as a nostalgic reminiscing by the mainstream'.[38] Such reminiscences typically focus on adolescent and family life. These often irreverent biographies serve as counter-narratives of the state, and mark a departure from the paradigms established in earlier examples of the genre, which, as Fulbrook has noted, 'might best be summarized as contributing to a tale of heroes, villains, victims – and Trabi drivers'.[39]

The narrow frame of the familial environment serves to wrest the GDR past from contemporary medial analysis. Partly this involves an emphasis of the ordinary, a view from below, with recognizable figures and familiar dramas. The state is not absent from these narratives, but has assumed a cameo role that oscillates between the absurd and the sinister. The GDR's failings frequently operate as a springboard for comedy rather than as a source of frustration. The books' relatively good sales suggest that they have connected with a public that is keen to partake in the bittersweet reminiscences that they offer. These developments within contemporary east German fiction correspond with new directions in German cinema. Films such as *Sonnenallee, Helden wie Wir* (*Heroes Like Us*, Sebastian Peterson, 2000), and more recently *Good Bye, Lenin!*, have demonstrated that this kind of engagement with the GDR past is able to perform well at the box-office, too.

The developments in fiction and in film are not simply a question of experimentation or economic opportunism (though these motives cannot be wholly discounted), but mirror shifts in the east–west relationship and in post-unification discourse. That unification has not proved to be the success that its architects predicted is hardly disputed, though the prognoses for its future are less uniform. Tensions between the populations of east and west continue to exist, exacerbated by the still fragile economic situation in the east and the west's post-unification slump. The strain in relationship between east and west has given rise to stereotypes and prejudices, usually with the easterners accused of lacking sincere commitment to the project of integration and the west accused of exploitative business practices and a colonial mentality.[40]

The grounds for a separate post-GDR identity lie not, it seems, in the desire to replicate the GDR but in reaction to the east Germans' increasing ineffectuality. The west's alleged policy of colonization is a claim that is not taken seriously by many academics or politicians and is mostly limited to polemical texts, from readers' letters to online sites (older cadres preferring 'western imperialism'). Such a claim is erroneous but not irrational. The eastern population's clear support for unification, together with the inalienable freedoms enshrined in the German constitution, naturally problematizes any allegation of colonial interests and domination. But the east's considerable economic difficulties do offer some explanation for such resentment. East Germany's industries were remodelled or closed down, and many employees found themselves declared superfluous to the new demands of a free market economy. Subsequent circumstances demanded that many accustom themselves to that relatively novel (for East Germany) experience of redundancy. Angela Merkel's election success belies the fact that most of her compatriots were, in effect, excluded from the elite positions in supervising reintegration, with few east Germans figuring in any of the top positions in the new federal states in the first decade after unification.[41] With the west effectively assuming responsibility for stage-managing the changes begun on the streets of the GDR's towns and cities, the east Germans were largely obliged to accept the role of spectators, exacerbating the already widespread inferiority complex, that sense of being second class citizens. Those who held on to their jobs in any case found their work affected by the changes taking place in the nature of the work itself, which for many was suddenly subject to new regulations and conditions, and within the actual work environment. The tensions that inevitably arose between the new, usually western managers and original employees could easily be played out according to wider tensions between east and west. Statistics, such as those offered by Ahbe, provide some explanation for the kinds of grievances that have arisen amongst the east German working population.[42] That the collective east German wage levels were 60 per cent of those in the west (rising to 89.5 per cent in 1997) neither improved their self-esteem nor lessened the feeling of discrimination, though some of these figures should be considered in conjunction with other factors, such as the cost of living and taxation.[43] Though freed from the yoke of a planned economy, businesses continued to be subject to close scrutiny, not by Party members and institutions, but by western-based parent companies. According to one observer, these companies exerted greater management control in their eastern business ventures than was ordinarily the case with their other subsidiaries.[44] These practices may not have been widespread, and there is some question as to the interpretation of statistical data and the methodological principles used, but what is clear is that the workplace and the conflicts that have developed there since 1989 have, to some extent, consolidated stereotypes and perpetuated certain prejudices vis-à-vis east and west.[45]

Ostalgie – Recharging the Batteries of Identity

The past, as Maurice Halbwachs observed in his influential treatise on memory, 'is not preserved but is reconstructed on the basis of the present'.[46] Given the east Germans' (perceived and actual) discrimination, it was perhaps to be expected that, far from embracing a collective national German identity, they would cling to vestiges of their past and even begin reviewing the GDR with some affection. In recalling their former lives, many east Germans focus on the stability and comfort offered by the state's programme of socialism rather than its tyranny, its abuse of basic human rights. They indignantly defend, for example, such features as the GDR's low crime rates, free health care, crèches – benefits which explain Jarausch's description of the SED's style of governance as a 'welfare dictatorship'.[47] Just as the GDR may be remembered by its opponents according to its failures and injustices, some east Germans' private memories of the past inevitably result in an idealization of life in the GDR. This, together with the continuing problems of adjustment since unification, goes some way to explaining the rehabilitation of an east German identity. It has often been noted that the east Germans exhibited a greater attachment to the GDR state once it ceased to exist. When he mutters 'only when I saw my country dying did I realise that I loved it' in his cameo appearance in Jörg Foth's *Letztes aus der DaDaeR* (*Latest from the Da-Da-R*, 1990), the author Christoph Hein neatly encapsulates the mixed emotions that many east Germans felt as they watched their state implode. The attachment to GDR iconography is therefore not a belated indication of SED loyalty or uncritical GDR patriotism. Rather, it can be seen as a means of countering the elision of an east German identity and of being able to embrace aspects of GDR culture that are finally severed from the party.

A further reason for the emergence of a pronounced east German identity may be, as Lyn Williams has proposed, because 'the more vigorous the policy of assimilation the stronger will normally be the resistance it meets'.[48] The policy of integration has been subject to harsher analogies; other commentators have variously observed that the GDR was effectively 'raped', 'annexed' or, in Mark Blacksell's less emotive term, 'absorbed' by the FRG.[49] Each gives some measure of the negative light in which unification has been considered and reflects the neglect and exploitation that many east Germans associate with unification. The idea of colonization has proved particularly appealing, not least because of the current academic vogue for (post-)colonial theory. While reference to post-colonial theory may risk, as Terry Eagleton warns, 'a romantic idealization of the "other", with a simplistic politics which regards the reduction of the "other" to the "same" as the root of all political evil', such reductionism has been a mainstay of post-unification discourse and reflects the east Germans' perceived subjugation.[50] A number of films indulge in the 'simplistic politics' that Eagleton fears, offering plots that establish the west as the faceless threat, employing all its administrative might against seemingly defenceless east Germans, an essentializing process that may give some impression of the kind of conflict between east and west but which hardly allows for any diversity within those two communities, and which addresses the politics of unification as a simplified dialectics of colonizer and colonized.

Some commentators had, from the start, warned that unification might not be the smooth process that so many wanted to imagine. Struggling to be heard above the noisy celebration of contemporary accounts of the Wende, a few editorials and articles did urge greater sensitivity towards the process of unification. In a leader in the provincial *Badische Zeitung*, Leopold Glasner, for one, was moved to warn against triumphalism: 'We must not come across as jingoistic or arrogantly brag, nor seek to take cultural, material, spiritual and economic possession of the other Germany.'[51] Caveats like this had little impact on the swiftly implemented strategies for unification that followed.

Though difficult, the project of structural and institutional integration proved a not insurmountable challenge. Certainly, it was more easily accomplished, albeit at enormous cost, than was the project of social integration, which was not eased by the mass redundancies and the feeling amongst many east Germans that their home – their Heimat – had become a destination for west German prospectors. Recognizing numerous lucrative business opportunities, these entrepreneurs duly ventured into the eastern states, no doubt encountering many of their compatriots heading in the opposite direction for the same reasons. Seen in this context, a programme of resistance, further qualified by the profound disappointments following unification, was inevitable. How far the disillusion with unification has engendered a programme of actual, conscious resistance to the dominance of western values and codes since 1989/1990 is hard to gauge. The east Germans' developing preoccupation with all things East German, as it was routinely represented in the media, did mark a 180-degree shift in their attentions from west to east and, perhaps more significantly, from the present to the past, a fascination with their own past that was quickly branded Ostalgie. Much used in the media, Ostalgie initially described the east Germans' blithe nostalgia. Newspapers reported GDR-themed events at night-clubs where Honecker look-a-likes served east German beer paid for in Ostmarks, whilst revellers danced to old Eastern Bloc tunes.[52] This celebration of the past aroused hostility and amusement in equal measure. To its critics, Ostalgie was a sign of a risibly selective memory; those who indulged their memories of the past demonstrated a lack of interest and commitment in overcoming the present problems brought about by unification and jeopardized the future of the Berlin Republic. Other commentators initially underestimated its significance, dismissing it as nothing more than a quirk in fashion, albeit one that existed only in the new federal states. The media focus on the rise of a few GDR brands, such as *Rotkäppchen Sekt* (a sparkling wine), *Rondo* coffee, and *F6* cigarettes, only distracted from more pressing concerns – racism, unemployment, suicide, economic paralysis – that were linked to the east Germans' post-unification disenchantment. The success of these old brands was initially derided, apparently owing more to nostalgic familiarity than to any obvious differences in quality. But the goods came to assume a new level of semiotic significance that transcended the actual product. Whether *Rondo* actually tasted better than *Jacobs* was to miss the point. What these products offered the consumer was a rejection of the west and a celebration of the east that ran counter to the dominant consumer values. The specifically political images that Ostalgie frequently employed were seen simply as examples of ironic decontextualization and little more. In any case, the sudden interest and enthusiasm for a 'retro' GDR hardly extended to actually wishing the former state to be resurrected. Although some scholars doubt its impact – Maier is of the opinion that 'nostalgia is very easy to indulge in when it is deprived of consequences' – to reject Ostalgie as a mere trifle of fashion, as nothing more than superficial posturing in yesterday's clothes, also belies the trend's impact and its significance to the east Germans' evaluation of their past, and their adjustment to the present.[53] For Woderich, Ostalgie has had a significant role in rescuing the population in the east from their 'structural inferiority' and conferring on them a 'virtual superiority'.[54] His analysis points to Ostalgie's psychological influence, in terms of identity, but also its relative impotence, for although persuasive in its articulation of identity, he claims it barely registers at any political level. Jarausch, by contrast, argues that Ostalgie's influence can be traced within politics, where it briefly 'fuelled the electoral rise of the PDS'.[55] For Milful, it demands more serious consideration than it was typically given, being

> less a nostalgia than a neuralgia, an ache where something has forcibly been removed, not so much a desire to return to the past as a sense of a gap in the present, a gap which dare not speak its name.[56]

Moreover, Ostalgie threatened to exacerbate divisions between east and west, being by its very nature a club with a membership limited to those who had grown up in the east. In providing a resort of camaraderie based on certain shared experiences and memories, it constituted a trend that necessarily excluded the population of the old Federal states. Despite its resonance, one should, however, resist the urge to imagine the whole of the east German population rushing to iron their *FDJ* (*Freie Deutsche Jugend*) shirts and polish their Party lapel badges, since the more demonstrative aspects of the trend were manifest among the younger generation alone. Nevertheless, Ostalgie is not simply a matter of late night revelry and bad taste parties. Nor is it an attempt either to relive the past or to restore it; the past is certainly invoked and recalled, sometimes even yearned for, but, other than a few feckless internet users who claim otherwise, no one seriously seeks to reinstate the GDR. It was, and continues to be, an analogue of fundamental anxieties among the population of the east.

The East German administration was certain that a separate GDR identity would develop as the result of a pervasive ideology, which would inform East German society in all areas, from history text books to newspaper coverage of the cosmonaut space flight. Obsessed with proving the legitimacy of an east German identity, ideologues repeatedly sought to link the past to the present, while also looking forward to the future. To what extent the SED was successful in actively engendering a distinct GDR identity predicated on socialist principles is hard to measure accurately. Open resistance was essentially futile and, given the kind of control exerted by the Stasi and the lengths to which the Party was willing to go in order to assert its authority, not recommended. The events of June 1953, which saw the Red Army deployed in order to subdue the demonstrations and strikes taking place throughout the state, demonstrated how seriously threatened the Party felt by such actions and how ruthless they could be in quashing them. For many East Germans, the only means by which to express their dissatisfaction with the system was through 'inner exile' or actual emigration, with over four million of its citizens leaving the GDR for the west over the forty years of its existence.

That so many people took the opportunity to leave the GDR as soon as was possible indicates a profound sense of dissatisfaction with the state. Although it was rather late in the day for the GDR authorities to begin examining the causes of the exodus, a Stasi document on 'Motives for Emigration', produced in 1989, did report on the reasons given by those wishing to leave the country. These included such unsurprising observations as 'dissatisfaction with the supply of consumer goods' and 'annoyance at bureaucratic behaviour'. Significantly, it also identified what it considered to be the apparent '"illusions" about Western lifestyle, especially expectations of a life with "better" material security and "better" earnings, more "freedom" enabling one to attain a lifestyle based on selfish striving for consumption and ownership'.[57] The tone may be incredulous, yet the impact that those western images had on eastern viewers, offering them the opportunity of regularly absconding from their republic, if only mentally, is a fact that cannot be underestimated. For many east Germans, life in a newly unified Germany did not meet with their expectations. Disappointed by their experiences since unification, many have discovered an emotional attachment to their region and local culture, resulting in an identity that is linked to a coinciding rejection of certain western values and a renegotiation and reordering of past memories. Social researchers largely failed to understand the significance of this issue during the first decade following unification. Woderich argues that it was not uncommon to discredit social surveys which appeared to corroborate the emergence of an east German identity (since it went against the project of integration), though this is less usual now.[58] Ostalgie effectively fostered a culture of remembrance, which sought to counterbalance outsiders' constant scrutiny of GDR history, and the calls to do away with all vestiges of its society. However risible it may seem to outsiders, such recourse to the familiar amid such momentous changes is not unusual. In times of tremendous upheaval, it is natural that those affected should at least seek to protect their memories, their own biographies.[59] The issue of personal biography is particularly important, since a great deal of the GDR past is traduced through its association with the SED regime. This, according to Reißig, explains both the absence in official discourse of east Germans' personal experiences and the pressure that east Germans feel to modify and revise their biographies according to a west German model. [60]

Ostalgie has, then, perpetuated and further complicated the discourse surrounding post-unification identity. While a pre-existing GDR identity had, according to some, been denied by the demonstrators' choice of grammar in 1989, its desire to be 'one people' confirming the essential failure of the SED's proselytizing, the subsequent, apparently uncritical appreciation of the GDR seemed to indicate an emerging post-communist identity, which in Ostalgie found its most animated form.

Notes

1. E. Finger, 'Der Ossi als Wessi', *Die Zeit*, 25 August 2005: 35.
2. 'Aufbruch Ost', 2005, *Der Spiegel*, 45.
3. K.H. Jarausch, 'Reshaping German Identities: Reflections on the Post-Unification Debate', in Jarausch (ed.) (1997), p. 2. M. Fulbrook, 'Heroes, Victims, and Villains in the History of the GDR', in R. Alter and P. Monteath (eds), *Rewriting the German Past. History and Identity in the New Germany*, New Jersey: Humanities Press, 1997, p. 194.
4. A.D. Smith, *National Identity*, London: Penguin Books, 1991.
5. Ibid., p. 75.
6. See P.H. Merkel, 'A New German Identity', in G. Smith et al. (eds), *Developments in German Politics*, Durham: Duke University Press, 1992, p. 332.
7. The phrase is from A. Huyssen, *Twilight Memories. Marking Time in a Culture of Amnesia*, London: Routledge, 1995, p. 74.
8. See H.-G. Benz, 'Perplexed Normalcy: German Identity after Unification', in R. Alter and P. Monteath (eds), *Rewriting the German Past. History and Identity in the New Germany*, Atlantic Highlands, New Jersey: Humanities Press, 1997, p. 50.
9. Ibid., p. 48.
10. B. Anderson, *Imagined Communities. Reflections on the Origin and Spread of Nationalism*, London: Verso, 1991, p. 37. Anderson's relevance for film studies and theories of national cinema is evident in the essays collected in Hjort and Mackenzie (2002).
11. B. Ladd, *The Ghosts of Berlin. Confronting the German History in the Urban Landscape*, Chicago and London: University of Chicago Press, 1997, p. 208.
12. A.L. Nothnagle, *Building the East German Myth. Historical Mythology and Youth Propaganda in the German Democratic Republic, 1945–1989*, Michigan: University of Michigan Press, 1999, p. 26.
13. See R.Thomas and W.Weidenfeld, 'Identität', in W. Weidenfeld and K.-R. Korte (eds), *Handbuch zur deutschen Einheit 1949–1989–1999*, Frankfurt am Main: Bundeszentrale für politische Bildung, 1999, p. 436.

14. See J. Habermas, *Die nachholende Revolution*, Frankfurt am Main: Suhrkamp, 1990a, pp. 151–2.
15. J.W. Müller, *Another Country. German Intellectuals, Unification and National Identity*, New Haven and London: Yale University Press, 2000, p. 134.
16. A. Püschel, 'Grenzenloses Grenzgebiet Der "Zonenrand" außer Rand und Band', in *Facetten der Wende. Reportagen über eine deutsche Revolution Band II*, Frankfurt am Main: Institut für Medienentwicklung und Kommunikation GmbH in der Verlassungsgruppe Frankfurter Allgemeine Zeitung GmbH, 1991, p. 42.
17. A. Staab, *National Identity in Eastern Germany. Inner Unification or Continued Separation?*, Westport and London: Praeger, 1998, p. 121.
18. J. Milful, 'Who Owns GDR Culture? Against Analogy', *Debatte* 5(2), 1997: 130.
19. T. Koch, 'Deutsch-deutsche Einigung als Kulturproblem: Wird die Bundesrepublik in Deutschland aufgehen?', in R. Reißig and G. J. Glaeßner (eds), *Das Ende eines Experiments. Umbruch in der DDR und deutsche Einheit*, Berlin: Dietz Verlag, 1991, pp. 329–30.
20. C.S. Maier, *Dissolution. The Crisis of Communism and the End of East Germany*, Princeton, NJ: Princeton University Press, 1999, p. 40.
21. C. Kleßmann, 'Workers in the Workers' State: German Traditions, the Soviet Model and the Magnetic Attraction of West Germany', in C. Kleßmann (ed.), *The Divided Past. Rewriting Post-War German History*, Oxford and New York: Berg, 2001, pp. 13–14.
22. V. Baer, 'Das andere Gesicht der DEFA', in *Film Dienst* 8, 1998: 12–14.
23. See H. Steußloff, 'Zur Identität der Ostdeutschen. Merkmale und Tendenzen eines Phänomens', *Hefte zur ddr-geschichte* 66, Berlin: Forscher- und Diskussionskreis DDR Geschichte, 2000, p. 23.
24. R. Woderich, 'Ostdeutsche Identität zwischen symbolischer Konstruktion und lebensweltlichem Eigensinn', Schriftfassung des Referats auf der Konferenz 'The German Road from Socialism to Capitalism', Harvard University, Centre for European Studies, 18–20 June 1999. Retrieved 22 August 2008 from http://www.biss-Online.de/download/ostdeutsche_identitaeten.pdf, p. 12.
25. M. Pickering, *Stereotyping. The Politics of Representation*, Basingstoke and New York: Palgrave, 2001, p. 4.
26. The *Ossi* was a term that was originally applied pejoratively to east Germans. It has since been reclaimed by some in the east for whom it functions as a marker for positive attributes that distinguish them from their western counterparts. It has its antonym – the *Wessi*. Variations of these types have evolved over the years, from *Jammerossi* (whinging east Germans) and *Besserwessi* (know-it-all West Germans), to *Wossi* (west Germans living in the east who are sympathetic to the locals).
27. W. Thierse, '"Vom Westen ist hier nicht mehr viel zu lernen."' Interview with Thierse conducted by F. Gless and H. Witzel, *Stern* 18, 2002: 58.
28. See Steußloff (2000), p. 17.
29. H. Witzel, 'So sind wir, wir Ossis', *Stern* 18, 2002: 45.
30. See G. Braunthal, 'The Rise of Right-wing Extremism in the New Germany', in C. Anderson et al. (eds), *The Domestic Politics of German Unification*, London and Boulder: Lynne Rienner Publishers, 1993, pp. 97–113. See also M.Y. Mehr and R. Sylvester, 'The Stone Thrower From Eisenhuttenstadt' [sic], *Granta* (Krauts!) 42, 1992: 133–43.
31. D. Kannapin, '"GDR identity" in DEFA Feature Films', *Debatte* 13(2), 2005: 189.
32. Steußloff (2000), p. 5.
33. Cited (in English) in G. Facius, 'Integration of the East German Media into an All-German Structure', *Aussenpolitik*, 41(4), 1990: 393.
34. See Milful (1997), p. 197.
35. U.H. Meinhof, 'The New Germany on the Screen: Conflicting Discourses on German Television', in P. Stevenson and J. Theobald (eds), *Relocating Germanness. Discursive Unity in Unified Germany*, London: Macmillan, 2000, p. 32.
36. See J. Kocka, *Vereinigungskrise. Zur Geschichte der Gegenwart*, Göttingen: Vandenhoeck und Ruprecht, 1995, pp. 93–95. See also D. Schmiechen-Ackermann, *Diktaturen im Vergleich*, Darmstadt: Wissenschaftliche Buchgesellschaft, 2002, pp. 83–7.

37. G. de Bruyn, *Vierzig Jahre*, Frankfurt am Main: Fischer Verlag, 1998; J. Hein, *Mein erstes T-Shirt*, München: Piper Verlag, 2001; F. Henning, *Alles nur geklaut*, München: btb Verlag, 1999.
38. R. Reißig, 'Die Ostdeutschen – zehn Jahre nach der Wende. Einstellungen, Wertemuster, Identitätsbildungen', 1999. Retrieved 25 August 2008 from http://www.bissonline.de/download/Die_Ostdeutschen_zehn_Jahre_nach_der_Wende.PDF.
39. M. Fulbrook, 'Heroes, Victims, and Villains in the History of the GDR', in Alter and Monteath (1997), p. 180.
40. See W. Dümcke and F. Vilmar (eds), *Kolonisierung der DDR. Kritische Analyse und Alternativen des Einigungsprozesses*, Münster: Agenda, 1995.
41. The east Germans' lack of representation in elite positions is discussed by A. Segert, 'Problematic Normalisation – Eastern German Workers Eight Years After Unification', *German Politics and Society* 16(3), 1998: 105–24.
42. T. Ahbe, '"Hammer, Zirkel, Kaffeekranz." Ostalgie als Methode. Wie sich die Ostdeutschen stabilisieren und integrieren', *Berliner Zeitung* , 5 February 2000. Retrieved 8 August 2004 from http://www.kulturinitiative-89.de/Texte/Ahbe_Thomas.html
43. See C. Flockton, 'Employment, Welfare Support and Income Distribution in East Germany', in C. Flockton and E. Kolinsky (eds), *Recasting East Germany. Social Transformation after the GDR*, London: Frank Cass and Company, 1999, p. 38.
44. See W. Carlin, 'The New East German Economy: Problems of Transition, Unification and Institutional Mismatch', in S. Taberner and F. Finlay (eds), *Recasting German Identity. Culture, Politics and Literature in the Berlin Republik*, Rochester, NY, and Woodbridge, Suffolk: Camden House, 2002, p. 19.
45. Reißig and Steußloff, for example, have each disagreed with the results drawn by their contemporaries' research.
46. M. Halbwachs, *On Collective Memory*, London and Chicago: University of Chicago Press, 1992, pp. 39–40.
47. K.H. Jarausch, 'Care and Coercion: The GDR as Welfare Dictatorship', in K.H. Jarausch (ed.), *Dictatorship as Experience. Towards a Socio-Cultural History of the GDR*, New York and Oxford: Berghahn Books, 1999, pp. 47–72.
48. L. Williams, 'National Identity and the Nation State: Construction, Reconstruction and Contradiction', in K. Cameron (ed.), *National Identity*, Exeter: Intellect Books, 1999, p. 14.
49. M. Blacksell, 'State and Nation: Germany Since Reunification', *Europa* 3, 1997. Retrieved 23 August 2008 from http://www.intellectbooks.com/europa/number3/blacksel.htm
50. T. Eagleton, *Literary Theory. An Introduction*, London: Blackwell, 2002, p. 205.
51. L. Glasner, '"Eine deutsche Revolution." Leitartikel von Leopold Glasner in der Badischen Zeitung vom 11. November, 1989', in D. Golombeck and D. Ratzke (eds), *Facetten der Wende. Reportagen über eine deutsche Revolution*, Frankfurt am Main: Institut für Medienentwicklung und Kommunikation GmbH, 1991, p. 156.
52. It should be noted that the term was generally associated with an irreverent attitude towards the past and was not used to describe the east Germans' nostalgia *per se*. An article that appeared in *Der Spiegel*, for example, reported on the inhabitants of Eisenhüttenstadt who by 1992 were already voicing regret that the security and comforts they had known no longer existed. Not once does the word Ostalgie appear in the text. See J. Fleischhauer, '"Ick will meine Ruhe wieder"', *Der Spiegel* 19, 1990: 117–24.
53. Maier (1999), p. xx.
54. Woderich (1999).
55. K.H. Jarausch, 'Reshaping German Identities: Reflections on the Post-Unification Debate', in Jarausch (ed.) (1997), p. 12.
56. Milful (1997), p. 197.
57. A. Mitter and S. Wolle, cited in K.H. and V. Gransow (eds), *Uniting Germany Documents and Debates, 1944–1993*, Oxford: Berghahn Books, 1994, p. 37.
58. Woderich (1999). R. Ostow talks of a population who must be the most interviewed in the world. See R. Ostow, 'Restructuring Our Lives: National Unification and German Biographies', *The Oral History Review. Journal of the Oral History Association* 21(2), 1993: 1–8.

59. This may apply to a community as a whole, too, when, as Lowenthal has suggested, 'heritage is invoked to requite displacement'. See D. Lowenthal, *The Heritage Crusade and the Spoils of History*, Cambridge: Cambridge University Press, 1998, p. 9.
60. Reißig (1999).

Chapter 2

HEIMAT STORIES: EAST MEETS WEST

The strongest sense of community is … likely to come from those groups who find the premises of their collective existence threatened, and who construct out of this a community of identity which provides a strong sense of resistance and empowerment. Seeming unable to control the social relations in which they find themselves, people shrink the world to the size of their communities, and act politically on that basis. The result, too often, is an obsessive particularism as a way of embracing or coping with contingency.[1]

The early years after unification witnessed the release of several 'first encounter' films in which the east and west Germans come face to face for the first time. Drawing from a reserve of symbols and ideas that were to become fixed tropes in Wende discourse, these early films encapsulate many of the preconceptions about the east Germans. Stereotypes that have been variously deployed in the years since unification are central to Peter Timm's film, *Go Trabi Go*, the most successful and perennially popular film of the Wende, and appear in other banal comedies such as Manfred Stelzer's *Superstau* (*Super Traffic Jam*, 1990). The inclusion of stereotypes – typically, east Germans as straightforward, provincial figures, struggling to understand the values of the new society – bears little evidence of the resentment with which they would later be associated. The films, still regularly broadcast on television, delight in the east Germans' naivety, often emphasized in their reaction to the west's unknown and exotic features, though their innocence is portrayed as a positive attribute and an indication of the easterners' honesty – something that is lacking in the west Germans whom they encounter. Their innocence does not go unnoticed: alert to the profit to be made from the gullible *Ossis*, west Germans repeatedly exploit the visitors' lack of cultural nous, thereby exacerbating the east Germans' 'collective feeling of inferiority'.[2]

Despite its focus on east Germans shortly after the collapse of the GDR, the films make little reference to either recent events or to the past. The Wende is mostly viewed as an opportunity, a vital escape from uneasy times and limited options, an approach that, in the case of Timm's film, evidently resonated with eastern audiences, who were coming to terms with the challenges of transition. Given that *Go Trabi Go* was released so soon after unification, it seems extraordinary that the film should so actively avoid any mention of the GDR. Tropes and stereotypes frequently associated with the east Germans in post-GDR discourse are included in Timm's road movie, but remain strangely separated from their historical context. Nevertheless, the surfeit of east German details, of which the Trabant is the most conspicuous, together with the protagonists' provincial manner, emphasizes the Struutz family as the embodiment of the east German people and of the east German experience. The GDR's most famous icon, the Trabant, is in Timm's film more than just a prop for visual gags. The little car with the two-stroke engine, mocked and doted on in equal measure, had become one of the most recognizable GDR symbols since the border first opened, and is here elevated to star status. In *Go Trabi Go*, as with many of the early post-unification comedies, the car is not the contemptible emitter of dangerous fumes that it was to become, but the amusing old-fashioned contraption that was to endure as the butt of a thousand gags. Impractical and unreliable, it serves as a quaint reminder of the GDR's lofty ambitions and material shortcomings.

Not all the films to be made in the first years after the Wende viewed the encounter of the two populations in the same comical fashion. The general optimism of films like Timm's is challenged by the satires of this period. A number of filmmakers quickly sought to expose the west's exploitation of the east (and the east Germans' gullibility) in satires that deflated the Germans' chiliasm. In *Deutschfieber* (*German Fever*, 1992), a sequel of sorts to his acclaimed *Der Willi-Busch-Report* (*The Willi Busch Report*, 1977), Niklaus Schilling, one of the few directors associated with New German Cinema to respond to unification, focused on two small towns on opposite sides of the former border, charting the initial excitement of the two populations' meeting which soon gives way to rancour as the commercial interests and the political corruption of both administrations are revealed. The surrealism of Schilling's film did not win the director much praise. In Ralf Schenk's round-up of German films in that year's Berlin Film Festival, the respected film critic was of the opinion that the film was so abstruse as to be almost impossible to understand.[3] Schenk's doubts were confirmed at the box-office, where Schilling's impression of unification was considered out of step with the times.[4]

The most caustic of the satires, Christoph Schlingensief's *Das deutsche Kettensägenmassaker* (*The German Chainsaw Massacre*, 1990), also examined the first encounters between east and west, but did not, as the film's title suggests, accord with the optimism and confidence of the Kohl administration. Schlingensief's narrative promotes integration in terms of digestive rather than national union with the east Germans embraced by west German cannibals looking to butcher their eastern visitors. Schlingensief's grotesque, which references Tobe Hooper's notorious *Texas Chainsaw*

Massacre (1974), combines documentary with splatter movie aesthetics to offer a dystopian vision of the new unified Germany. Schlingensief's supporters were not to be found only within avant-garde and experimental film circles. For Helmut Schnödel, writing in *Die Zeit*, a paper not known for its support of such underground figures, the film was something of a revelation, and worthy of comparison with Fassbinder's work.[5] Others, meanwhile, noted that the director's promptness in responding to contemporary issues distinguished him from other filmmakers, who were still wondering how best to react to events.[6]

These low-budget counter-hegemonic narratives, which were often experimental in form, showed little concern for either commercial preferences or the audiences' mood. This disregard distinguishes them from mainstream filmmaking but is typical of the avant-garde's 'antagonism toward the public, toward the convictions or conventions characterizing the public, by a polemical jargon full of picturesque violence, sparing neither person nor thing, made up more of gestures and insults than of articulate discourse'.[7] With its provincial protagonists, whose spirit in the face of adversity reveals a family unit that, though inexperienced, is able to withstand the various challenges of their journey, it was Timm's film that resonated with audiences. Its stereotypes and banal dialogue notwithstanding, it was *Go Trabi Go* that came to be seen as the definitive Wende film. The director's cautious approach in representing the eastern states offers a clue about the film's appeal for east German audiences, for the narrative does not denigrate specific features of GDR life. The derogatory remarks about the Ossis are made by a number of characters who constitute a cross-section of west Germans. But the legitimacy of their attitudes is intentionally diminished through their characterization, since these exaggerated figures – overweight Bavarians, haughty garage owners, petulant shop assistants – are themselves parodied. In characterizing those unreceptive to the east Germans as somehow deficient, be it in manner or appearance, the director underlines the inadequacy of the (western) prejudice against the east Germans, without abandoning clichéd representations of the *Ossis* (their gracelessness, obduracy and material inadequacy). This latter feature did not go unnoticed, and the film received some hostile reviews. Daniel Simons, writing in the provincial east German *Volksstimme*, was peculiarly sensitive to the various depictions, and, in a strange misreading of the film, claimed that only a west German could imagine the east Germans to be as dim witted and the west Germans to be as cool as they are depicted in this film.[8] Timm's east Germans are certainly not without their flaws, but the portrayal is parodic, and not the malicious distortion that Simons suspects. Understanding the danger of such interpretation, Wolfgang Stumph, who plays the lead role, was keen to counter such charges, when he explained that 'we didn't want our fellow east Germans to be laughed at, let alone mocked ... nor did we want, as far as this was possible, Wessis playing Ossis. If anyone's going to make fun of us, let it be us'.[9]

Stumph's statement echoes Wolfgang Thierse's mentioned above. It is also an interesting response to the emerging stereotypology of the east Germans in unification discourse. Stumph initially rejects any possible derision of the east Germans before justifying his own caricaturing as a sort of pre-emptive parody. In so doing, he acknowledges the ambivalent power of the stereotype, recognizing that its effectiveness is not exclusively determined by the information it disseminates, but also by the way the information is disseminated. It is likely that a west German's portrayal of the innocent and unsophisticated Ossi would certainly have been less tolerated than Stumph's representation, not least because of Stumph's reputation in the east and his credentials as a satirist with Dresden's celebrated cabaret, the Herkuleskeule.

The Heimatfilm: Past Genres for Present Tensions

Most of the unification narratives discussed so far exploit the encounters between east and west, either viewing such meetings as an opportunity for comic misunderstanding and humorous antagonism or as a means of critiquing unification. The films make use of a diverse range of genres and traditions, from road movies to horror films, dystopian fantasies to surreal allegories. The satirical approach to unification is evidenced by the cabaret performers who were frequently engaged for these early east/west encounters, from Hans-Eckhardt Wenzel and Stefan Mensching (cult subversive clowns in the GDR) in *Letztes aus der DaDaeR* to Bavarian cabaret star Ottfried Fischer (*Superstau* and *Go Trabi Go*). The exaggerated performances that were central to these films, from the experimentalism of *Das deutsche Kettensägemassaker* to the broad farce of *Go Trabi Go* later waned, and though the films discussed below – Glowna's *Der Brocken* and *Go Trabi Go II. Das war der wilde Osten* (*Go Trabi Go. That was the Wild East*, Wolfgang Büld, Reinhard Klooss, 1992) – maintain the satire of those above, they couch it within the conservative paradigm of the Heimatfilm.

In her study of post-unification film, Naughton offers a strong case for viewing many of these early Wende films as a re-engagement with the Heimatfilm genre of the 1950s.[10] The unification films resurrect familiar Heimatfilm themes and ideas, among them the inheritance motif, utopian desires and the potential disruption caused by an outsider's arrival within an established community. Crucially, Naughton says, the unification films share with the much-derided West German genre a desire to 'present fantasies of social integration, opportunity, and prosperity rather than evidence of the suspicion, hostility, and resentment provoked by unification'.[11] Naughton tells us, moreover, that these films actually revive the same kind of characters and antagonisms typically found in the original genre. She identifies a number of generic topoi, among them the country *versus* the city, a source of hostility in the original post-war films and which, several decades on, is used to reflect variations on the conflict between tradition and progress.[12] Certainly, the post-unification comedies suggest that those from the city – always west Germans – are frequently represented as materialistic and exploitative. These urban interlopers typically constitute a threat to their country cousins, who are mostly portrayed as simple, decent folk, steeped in old-fashioned ways and innocent to the modern vices and suspect principles with which they are confronted.

Despite the narratives' apparent sympathy for the rural protagonists and their sense of tradition, the post-wall films are, according to Naughton, careful to avoid any mention of the past that might compromise the idyllic rural communities that are depicted. She argues that this approach, too, is reminiscent of their cinematic forbears: 'neither Heimatfilme nor western unification films depict the relics of the previous regime – the fascist dictatorship in the case of the Heimatfilme or the communist dictatorship in the case of the 1990s variant'.[13] This is not quite accurate in the case of the former; nor is it true of some of the comedies, whose mise-en-scène occasionally includes symbolic remnants of the SED administration. Naughton even makes reference to the portraits of departed GDR gerontocrats and the flags and banners of the old regime are on display in the musty attic room in which one of the characters in *Der Brocken* (*Rising to the Bait*, Vadim Glowna, 1992) spends his time. In *Go Trabi Go II*, meanwhile, the previous administration is evoked in at least one scene, which takes place in a building previously housing the *Bezirksleitung* (District Leadership) but later converted into a strip-club, while Detlev Buck's film *Wir können auch anders* (*No More Mr. Nice Guy*, 1993) acknowledges the past in its briefly glimpsed images of the disused observation towers dotted along the former border.

Though only fleeting in appearance, the features of the SED-state that frequently surface in post-unification discourse hint at a problematic comedic interpretation of the East German dictatorship that has not occurred in the Germans' reflection on National Socialism, an inconsistency described by Martin Amis as an 'asymmetry of indulgence'.[14] Naughton's point is that the films, like those of the 1950s, do not fully address the issues related to the narrative context; that is, although the films are situated within a specific time and place, they do not acknowledge, indeed are reluctant to engage with, the social and political implications of their milieus: 'the films invest in the construction of a national imaginary …, ignoring the disparity and discord that have characterized German-German relations in the 1990s'.[15] More tendentious, though, is her assertion that those films produced or made by filmmakers from the west 'display historical and political myopia by avoiding reference to invidious aspects of life in the ex-GDR'.[16] Directors from the east (or productions made with eastern backing), on the other hand, offer a more sombre approach that tends to focus on unification's negative consequences. Similar claims have been made of the decade's literary output, as Stuart Taberner notes in his survey of post-unification literature, with fiction from the east seen to be operating at a tragic level as opposed to the less serious fiction of the west.[17] Both Naughton's and Taberner's accounts occasionally engage in the kind of generalizing principles that have become all too common in post-unification discourse. Tempting though it is to stress distinguishing features in filmmaking from the east and west, a sufficient number of films contradict such sweeping statements. Films by western directors such as Helma Sanders-Brahms, Ula Stöckl and Christoph Schlingensief, for example, offer a clear, often provocative interpretation of unification and the narratives are not afraid to address the politics and the history of the east (though the impact that these films had on cinema audiences was, admittedly, marginal). Naughton's failure to acknowledge the west German director, Heiko Schier, whose *Alles Lüge* (*All Lies*, 1992) satirizes both the GDR past and the new Germany, reveals her own somewhat short-sighted approach in an otherwise comprehensive account of post-unification film.[18] Naughton's observation that many of the post-unification films invoke the Heimatfilme genre is, however, sound. In a sense it was inevitable that that these post-unification comedies which appear to provide a flight from reality would be compared with the post-war genre. After all, the Heimatfilme of the 1950s and 1960s have typically been discussed in terms of their escapist tendencies and of the distraction they offered from the unwelcome realties of the post-war period.[19] That both the post-war Heimatfilme and these post-wall films met with critical indifference but audience approval seemed to underline the similarities still further. How accurate the comparison is requires a closer inspection of the Heimatfilm tradition and of the attitude towards Heimat in the GDR.

Heimat as Refuge

The popularity of the original Heimatfilme has been widely attributed to the reassurance it offered the audiences of the 1950s, who, scarred by the psychological traumas of the war, could find some comfort in the rural tranquillity and uncomplicated lives that the films offered. The realities of the post-war period – the ruined cities, the arduous reconstruction of the urban centres, the daily suffering – was absent from the genre and audiences flocked in their millions to see the Heimatfilm during the post-war years. The moral certitude and the focus on individuals that the films provided offered an escape from such complex and unwelcome issues as collective guilt and moral responsibility. The films served to entertain rather than to instruct. Instead of challenging German audiences to review the recent past and to reflect on the realities of the present, a task taken on by contemporary writers like Heinrich Böll and others associated with the influential literary grouping known as Gruppe 47, these films preferred to portray an idealized Germany, which might, in Fehrenbach's phrase, 'serve as social and psychic balm'.[20] Audiences were presented with beautiful landscapes inhabited by wholesome Germans, who appeared to live in a spatial and historical limbo beyond the realities of Germany's recent experiences. The genre restored a vision of Germany that, for the most part, denied the pernicious influence and support of the NS regime. The films appeared to confirm the Germans' innate decency and moral constancy and, in so doing, offered a corrective to the temporary immorality of the NS dictatorship. Those antagonisms that did arise in the films – in addition to those between city dwellers and the people in the country, the films represented tensions between those displaced by the war and the host communities, and between the generations and between the sexes – were reconciled by the end. The films' organizing principle generally attempted to re-establish the pre-war gender order as part of its drive to 'reinforce the conservative agenda'.[21] Audiences could find some encouragement in the representations of Germans who were not confronted with the kind of moral dilemmas and material privation of the real post-war world.[22] For many commentators, the films effectively presented a 'dream world', a fantasy of harmonious rural communities, where differences could be easily resolved.[23]

Many scholars have focused on this escapist impulse, emphasizing the significance of such distraction for post-war audiences and underlining the 'high-brow lament' that has accompanied Heimatfilm discourse.[24] At the same time, what the genre excluded is as significant as what it included; according to such interpretation the films function as a corollary of certain post-war attitudes. While post-war writers and philosophers like Karl Jaspers probed and challenged the national conscience, filmmakers were generally reluctant to address morally awkward subjects. The films seldom foregrounded contemporary concerns regarding moral responsibility and material questions concerning the loss of territory and post-war hardship; this reflected the population's own disinclination to confront its past but was also symptomatic of the emerging Cold War, which necessitated immediate, ideologically certain positions, and not a lengthy process of contrition or self-inquiry.

New readings of the genre, however, offer a compelling re-interpretation that challenges the traditional view of the films as romantic fantasies. According to such readings, the films do not simply provide prelapsarian visions of a mythical landscape that deny modernity's corruption, but reflect fundamental post-war issues such as the redrawn borders and forced migration.[25] In recent accounts, scholars have argued that the genre was able to act as a kind of curative, not in terms of the distraction from everyday suffering and the contaminated past that it effected, but in facilitating an easier encounter with modernity and with the present. Persuasive though these counter-claims are, they do not deny that the films lacked the kind of socio-historical acuity that would define the New German Cinema.

The apparent complacency of the genre and of that generation, together with their unwillingness to analyse recent and contemporary events, was eventually challenged in the 1960s by a group of young directors (though this did not immediately hasten the genre's retirement). Their rejection of the 'deceitful movie kitsch' that they believed typified post-war genres like the Heimatfilm was subsequently made explicit in the confident declaration, 'Papas Kino ist tot' ('Papa's cinema is dead'), a slogan that advertised a screening of radical new films at Oberhausen in 1962.[26] These directors compensated for the reticence and conservatism of the previous generation by embarking on a course of boldly confrontational and experimental filmmaking, which delighted some critics as much as it horrified domestic audiences. A number of films made in the 1960s and 1970s demonstrated the willingness of the manifesto's signatories to confront the older generation of filmmakers on their own territory – the provinces. The Heimatfilms' gentle melodramas and the saccharine representations of country life were caustically undermined; village life in these new films was no longer synonymous with neighbourliness and cosy tradition. For Germany's new wave filmmakers, Heimat was not simply 'the nicest name for backwardness', as the writer Martin Walser had suggested, but was profiled as a repository of intolerance and malice.[27] In films such as *Jagdszenen aus Niederbayern* (*Hunting Scenes from Bavaria*, Peter Fleischmann, 1969), *Jaider, der einsame Jäger* (*Jaider, the Lonely Hunter*, Volker Vogeler and Ulf Miehe, 1970/71), and *Der Plötzliche Reichtum Der Armen Leute Von Kombach* (*The Sudden Wealth of the Poor People of Kombach*, Volker Schlöndorff, 1971), the standard cinematic representations of Heimat were recalibrated, prompting some critics to talk of a new anti-Heimatfilm genre. Although some later scholars have questioned the appropriateness of referring to anti-Heimatfilme, arguing that the films were individual pieces and did not comprise an aesthetic agenda that collectively sought to challenge the 1950s dramas, the films might be more accurately categorized as examples of a new, critical Heimatfilm genre.[28]

The claim that certain films renegotiated the Heimatfilm genre led to further critical differences a decade later when, in the 1980s, a decade that witnessed the revival of Heimat discourse, critics sought to classify some contemporary films as 'neo-Heimatfilme'. Films like *Erst die Arbeit und dann?* (*First Work and Then?!*, Detlev Buck, 1985), *Novemberkatzen* (*November Cats*, Sigrun Koeppe, 1985), *Der Flieger* (*The Flyer*, Erwin Keusch, 1986) and *Daheim sterben die Leut'* (*Folks are Dying Back Home*, Klaus Gietinger, 1985) and, above all, Edgar Reitz's mammoth television series, the internationally successful *Heimat* trilogy (1984–2004), marked a return to the provinces. However, unlike the deeply sceptical narratives of the New German Cinema, this new generation did not seek to expose the countryside as home to prejudice and brute intolerance (an absence that was considered especially problematic in Reitz's portrayal of village life during the National Socialist years); nor did they aim to re-present those rural spaces as the idylls of the original genre. Opting for a pseudo-documentary style that was emphasized through the use of lay actors, they offered realistic studies of country living that were both critical and sympathetic. The significance of these films and their disputed generic relevance is considered in the following chapter, which proposes that a considerable number of Wendefilme similarly came to articulate and engage with a critical Heimat discourse.

Locating Heimat in the GDR

Heimat initially posed an awkward problem for GDR ideologues. Although they recognized that Heimat might be mobilized to support state ideology, the traditional idea of Heimat represented a particularly provincial, inward-looking way of thinking and identifying that clashed with the scheme of a progressive, all-inclusive trans-regional socialism. Marxist theoreticians naturally sought to debunk the West's hold on traditional Heimat values.[29] Günther Lange, for example, attempted to explicate the incompatibility of the true sense of Heimat in the context of capitalism, arguing that Heimat served only to construct an 'illusory community' in the FRG that ultimately validated the interests of those in power.[30] According to Lange, it was in the GDR that one could find a pure understanding of the Heimat values. Perhaps mindful of Marx's phrase regarding the 'idiocy of rural life', communities in the GDR were not to be predicated on local tradition and values, but according to an understanding and appreciation of their place in a wider socialist community that would admit other peoples and recognize a common struggle against the west.[31]

An identity that transcended the local and aspired to the international was not easily achieved. For all the rhetoric of socialist communality, hostilities and prejudices towards their eastern neighbours continued to exist and it proved difficult to inculcate an immediate aversion towards the Germans in the west, though such antagonism becomes a given in post-unification films. It was therefore imperative that the concept be reassessed and redefined within a socialist context; not to do so would have been tantamount to acknowledging the supremacy of a *German* national identity over a *socialist* identity. Realizing this to be the case, GDR ideologues reincorporated the idea of Heimat into East German culture, redefining and recasting it within a politically reliable framework. It could no longer be allowed to perpetuate the celebration of localized tradition over the state; nor could it be seen as a return to a quaint, pre-industrialized Germany that denied the modern East German state with its emphasis on progress and development. Lange envisioned a socialist Heimat in terms of man's control of the landscape. Only in the bourgeois west would they seek to ignore man's labour and productivity when looking at the landscape.

Lange's uncompromising ideas were not wholly representative. Heimat in East German terms involved a difficult balancing act. It could sanction an essentially German identity that celebrated the local and traditional, so long as this did not actually contradict the wider socialist project. This turn-around was partly due to extenuating circumstances. The authorities soon realized that membership of a coalition of socialist states could not provide an adequate substitute for an East German identity. Moreover, the growing lure of the west posed a serious threat to the GDR's future. It was impera- tive not only to convince the population of its future prospects but also to make life in a contemporary GDR sufficiently appealing. The concept re- quired new political and cultural cachet that would separate it from its tra- ditional regressive tendencies.[32] The word therefore came to be directly associated with the state, appearing on official banners and flags, in songs and anthems. In 1956, Johannes R. Becher, the state's leading poet and future Minister for Culture, a pivotal figure in GDR culture, published a collection of his poems titled 'Schöne Deutsche Heimat' ('Beautiful German Homeland'). Though ostensibly a collection of innocent, bucolic verse, which celebrated the familiar Heimat topoi of mountains and meadows, the poet's introduction contextualized his poems, reminding the reader of the potential, if undefined threat to their Heimat, the GDR, and urging them to defend it against 'ruin and destruction'.[33]

Becher's caveat does not specify the origin of such a threat but, given the increasingly hostile east/west climate, the implication was clear. The pro- tectionist aspect that had always been implicit within Heimat discourse was imperative in the GDR's understanding of the concept. Love of Heimat, as Judith Kretzschmar has pointed out, meant also the defence of Heimat and was often used in rhetoric that referred to the National People's Army (NVA).[34] The implied antagonism was simply a politicized positioning of the self against the other, a dynamic that had always been at the heart of Heimat. The difficult relationship with the west inevitably re- quired that the East German Heimat came to be articulated through its de- clared distinction from the FRG. The authorities therefore envisaged the GDR as an antifascist Heimat, which existed in contradistinction to the post-fascist Heimat of the FRG.

Screening Heimat in the GDR

Although Heimat came to be redefined in a way that would make it com- patible with the state's Marxist-Leninist profile, the Heimatfilm was not a genre that could be adapted to serve either the GDR's historical interpre- tation or its socialist vision. This was hardly surprising, given the genre's conservative character. The values celebrated in the West German melo- dramas contrasted sharply with the enlightened political understanding that the East's gritty socialist realist films aimed to provide. The compla- cency and backwards-looking nature of the Heimatfilme was the antithe- sis of the GDR's thrust to forge a progressive national identity which could be imbricated within that of the wider socialist community. Yet this did not signify an absolute rejection of East German Heimat discourse per se. As Harry Blunk has noted, 'the task of winning the hearts and minds of the populace for Heimat and Vaterland was seen primarily as that of the artistic media'.[35] Where the West German audiences could find some escape from the past and avoid the suffering of the present in the scores of Heimatfilme made after the war, audiences in the East were routinely reminded of the NS dictatorship in DEFA's most prevalent and enduring genre, the antifascist film.

The 1970s saw the regime directing its energies into promoting a more pronounced GDR identity, which required a re-emphasis of an East German Heimat. With this in mind, a series of documentary films were made by one of the state's most infamous figures and propagandists, Karl-Eduard von Schnitzler. His short films were intended to play an important role in shoring up GDR identity and promoting a specific GDR 'Heimatliebe' (love of Heimat). Such paeans to the socialist Heimat did not meet with the same kind of enthusiasm with which the eloquently acerbic von Schnitzler made them and were mostly ignored by domestic audiences, who preferred to tune into West German television.[36]

More credible documents of the GDR Heimat could be found, but these were few and far between. For Sabine Spindler, it was documentary films such as *Erinnerung an eine Landschaft – Für Manuela* (*Memories of a Landscape – To Manuela*, Kurt Tetzlaff, 1983) that explored issues pertinent to Heimat discourse.[37] Tetzlaff's film focuses on a few of the families from rural communities in Saxony-Anhalt who were relocated to the new 'progressive' housing estates on the edge of Leipzig following force-purchase plans to make way for a new open-cast mining project. The documentary, made over a period of four years, offers an insight into issues such as the relationship to family and community, the identification with landscape and the role of memory and history in the individuals' self-definition. According to Spindler, films such as this indirectly commented on Heimat topoi and presented an alternative to the preferred Heimat imagery and rhetoric espoused by the Party. By examining the Heimat of a small, long-standing rural community, Teztlaff's film departs from the state's idea of a GDR Heimat which frequently celebrated the state's modern, invariably urban profile. *Erinnerung an eine Landschaft* reveals the alienation that displaced individuals feel in their replacement Heimat, the large conurbation of pre-fabricated tower blocks that are here unmistakably linked with the state's urban planning policies. While most of the villagers accept the justification for their relocation (though they are clearly parroting the official rhetoric when they discuss these reasons), it is clear that the psychological and geographical adjustment is profoundly difficult. When the individuals comment on their new surroundings, there is a discernible hesitancy in their appraisal that is not present when they recall their old homes, the memory of which is preserved through attachment to a handful of mementoes, the village street signs and a few photographs of village get-togethers. *Erinnerung an eine Landschaft* reminds the modern-day viewer that the regime's efforts to foster an attachment to a GDR-Heimat were as unsuccessful as were its attempts to deny the population their inveterate Germanness. Ironically, maintaining some connection to the East German Heimat through an assortment of GDR keepsakes would later be common practice once the wall had fallen and the regime had disappeared.

Contesting Heimat

The Heimat concept was, as I have indicated, problematic in the GDR. The Party never succeeded in disabusing the population of its old-fashioned interpretation of Heimat as the site of local tradition and familial connection. Their connection to Heimat continued to be disputed even after the SED had ceased to exist. It was no longer the ideological and ontological meaning that was challenged, however. The increasing number of disputes regarding property in the east was understood as a material threat against Heimat since the fear of eviction meant that it was less the east Germans' idea of Heimat that was at risk than their actual physical connection to it. The eastern regions therefore became a contested site, one characterized by controversial property claims, business takeovers and by the arrival of western managers.

The property claims, which are routinely alluded to in unification films, became one of the most emotive issues of the Wende, provoking fierce debate and mutual recrimination. People filing claims naturally insisted on their right, as recognized by law, to reclaim property previously theirs. Those whose homes were thus suddenly thrown into jeopardy by these legal notices demanding restitution of property, numbering more than two million by mid 1993, perceived these claims not only as an attack on their right of residence but also, by implication, on their Heimat.[38] The journalist Daniela Dahn was one of many to become involved in the debate, detailing the reasons for her opposition in 'Wir bleiben hier, oder wem gehört der Osten' ('We're Staying Here, or Who Owns the East'), a polemic which questioned the legitimacy of such claims. Dahn focuses on the inconsistency of the claims and the adjudications, arguing that similar settlements have not been reached in property claims dating back to either the NS or the post-war period; nor were those east Germans who were dispossessed of their property by the GDR authorities accorded similar compensation.[39] In the course of her investigation, she considers the widespread suspicion that the state would favour its old members over the new, and wonders about the wider implications that such disputes will have on the two populations' relationship. The decision of the German Federation of Housing Association not to appeal to the constitutional court, despite the breach of constitutional rights that the property claims involved, because it was pessimistic about the outcome, would, she argues, do little to inspire the east Germans' confidence in the laws of the new state.

Strangely, the controversy surrounding property claims, which would seem to offer ample east/west drama, is seldom foregrounded in post-unification films (only Peter Kahane's comedy *Cosimas Lexikon* (*Cosima's Lexicon*, 1991), in which the residents of a block of flats try to save their homes from western developers, really looks at the issue). In general, the films focus not on the threat to homes but to Heimat. This allows directors to address the east Germans' post-unification anxieties, including the perceived loss of sovereignty, the threat to communities and the subsequent defence of local identity that is embedded in the idea of Heimat.

An Island Mentality: *Der Brocken*

At first sight, *Der Brocken*, actor and director Vadim Glowna's 1993 comedy, presents one of the most obvious re-engagements with the Heimatfilm of the post-war years. The film's central character, Ada Fenske, a good-natured widow living alone in her island cottage, bears a resemblance to the matriarchal figures found in those films. The widow displays a wholesomeness and integrity typical of the humble 'Oma' characters whose traditional values and lifestyle are threatened by the arrival of strangers, who challenge or cannot understand the principles of the local community. Contemporary critics, however, were less inclined to see Glowna's film as a Heimatfilm. Impressed by the lead performance of the respected East Berlin stage actress, Else Grube-Deister, reviewers made quite different connections, with Grube-Deister's character referred to as a 'Mother Courage' of the Wende.[40] The character does not only show continuity with the theatre. Strong female protagonists, and Ada is the first of many self-assured east German women in post-unification film, were a tradition in DEFA films, examples of which can be found throughout the state's production history, from Kurt Maetzig's *Die Buntkarierten* (*Girls in Gingham*, 1949) to *Solo Sunny* (Konrad Wolf, 1980). Ada's circumstances may differ from those of her cinematic predecessors, but her resistance recalls the modus operandi of those earlier women, involving a kind of principled opposition that counters the ideologically suspect or politically expedient strategies employed by her opponents. Despite this thematic continuity with GDR filmmaking, the film does invoke the Heimatfilm tradition. Like those old Heimatfilme, Glowna's film flaunts the beauty of its island location and its traditions. But despite the film's flattering visual representation of Rügen, one of the east's most popular resorts, *Der Brocken*'s narrative does not represent a holiday from history. Glowna's comedy of intrigue and underdog defiance against financially superior but politically and morally corrupt forces reflects key issues and attitudes associated with unification, even if the event is never explicitly mentioned. The film builds on only the simplest of plots – the machinations of a western undercover military agent (Zwirner, played by erstwhile Fassbinder associate Rolf Zacher) to gain control of an old family property on an east German island, and the homeowner's attempts to thwart these plans. In its isolated coastal setting, *Der Brocken* is reminiscent of other comedies in which individuals and small communities triumph over larger mainland corporations, like *Local Hero* (1982), Bill Forsyth's Scottish comedy. The narrative is played out within the confines of the small east German island, bar Zwirner's brief excursion to Berlin, and the islanders living there comprise a hermetic society, which, after years of seclusion, is suddenly exposed to western interests and intrigue, a metaphor, of course, for the east German experience of unification.

The west is mostly represented through an assortment of men – with the exception of one brief scene, there are no women from the west at all – each there to reconnoitre various business possibilities. Zwirner represents the quintessential western technocrat. A devious figure, he is determined to accomplish his mission (his purchase is connected with German military interests) regardless of the cost to others' livelihoods, an insensitive approach that had come to be seen as typical of the west's aggressive 'elbow society'. His entrance, as with many other post-unification films, is heralded by a sleek, black Mercedes, which symbol of modernity and token of material success clashes with the rusticity and provincialism of Ada's quaint house, the property in question. Although not nearly as sinister or ruthless as Zwirner, the other characters from the west are equally motive-driven and ready to exploit the provincial islanders as far as is possible, though the approaches and level of exploitation vary. Whilst Zwirner manipulates and schemes on behalf of the military, others investigate the potential for private enterprise. One Wessi, Raschke, views Ada's house for potential interior design treasures that he might use in his real estate business. Certain of his bargaining power, he offers to buy a painting by a local artist, which he sees hanging in the widow's house. Ada, surprised by its desirability but increasingly alert to such business opportunities, proves not to be the ingénue the businessman was expecting and the latter is taken aback by her confident bargaining skills:

Ada: You wouldn't find it that cheap in the west.
Raschke: I'm not here to give handouts. Especially not with today's taxes –
          I don't have to tell you who those are going to.
Ada: But you've had it better for the past forty years.
Raschke: I'm not to blame for the way things were here.
Ada: Oh, so it was my fault?
Raschke: Look, I don't want to argue with you.
Ada: But I do. Do you think you'd have behaved differently to us if
          you'd lived here?

This exchange does not simply demonstrate Ada's assertiveness; it also gives voice to two of the major issues in post-Wende Germany, the west's resentment of a taxation policy initiated to prop up the east's insecure economy, and the east Germans' refusal to accept any responsibility for the GDR's failings.[41] It heightens, too, the antagonism between east and west already detectable in previous scenes. In keeping with the conventions of the film's comedy genre, such confrontational exchanges are, however, kept to a minimum, though this does not lessen their impact when they do arise. This is not untypical of Glowna's bathetic film, which frequently punctuates the comedy-intrigue with more serious moments. Mostly the comic tempo is maintained via an assortment of exaggerated characters, ranging from effusive ex-Party functionaries hoping to exploit their connections with western interests, to simple islanders who demonstrate only a primitive understanding of events taking place around them.

The west Germans are little better served by Glowna's film, and are mostly portrayed as shrewd venture capitalists whose interests in the east are based only on its economic potential. But unlike other Wende comedies, *Der Brocken* does not rely exclusively on such overstated characterizations and Glowna brings some balance to the east/west stereotypes. The west German, Herr Naujock, for example, identifies a potential business opportunity at Ada's home and proposes that she and her friends provide him with hand-knitted pullovers, confident of their value in the west. Like the other west Germans in the film, Naujock recognizes the commercial value of the east's rustic authenticity but, in contrast to his fellow entrepreneurs, he is presented as someone prepared to combine his experience of the free market and the islanders' marketable skills in order to establish a joint venture, initiating the kind of economic co-operation that was much desired after unification. Despite the apparent fairness of such business strategies, *Der Brocken* does not focus on this kind of partnership or urge collaboration between east and west. This is partly explained by the film's indictment of western business practices in general. When Ada wonders that such labour-intensive products can make any profit, Naujock assures her that the mass-produced items, which he himself manufactures, are in fact poor quality and that hand-made goods are at a premium. This is not the only comment in the film to offer such critical truisms about the west's market economy and hints at Glowna's thesis of local, domestic products and small cottage industry being a better alternative to the mass-production of capitalist practices in the west.

If the west is represented by an assortment of carpetbaggers keen to import their business methods while they export the profits, the east is mostly represented as a naive community, inexperienced in the ways of market-capitalism. Glowna's film does, however, identify fissures within the east German community. Although the greatest threat to the island Heimat is posed by the west in the form of anonymous corporations whose decisions pose potentially disastrous consequences for the local industries, and the forceful entrepreneurs keen to exploit the islanders' naivety, the island itself is home to several disagreeable characters. Chief among these is the former local Party secretary, demoted to archival clerk in the town hall, where he presides over dusty documents amidst redundant GDR placards and the ephemera of a finished regime. Devious and rather unpleasant though he may be, Bräseke lacks the capacity for terror with which such characters are usually endowed in other films – as in Helma Sanders-Brahms' *Apfelbäume* (*Apple Trees*, 1992) or Michael Gwisdek's *Abschied von Agnes* (*Farewell to Agnes*, 1994), or *Das Leben der Anderen*. Instead, he counts as a rather pitiful figure who hopes that things will be as they once were: 'Don't get too excited', he warns his stepdaughter, 'there'll be other times'. Other undesirables include the mayor, who is vaguely linked to the Stasi and who reluctantly colludes in Zwirner's scheme for gaining possession of Ada's home. The local bank's surveyor, too, is open to a little bribery, agreeing to undervalue the house, thus weakening Ada's bargaining position.

This shifty trio, all men in their fifties and sixties, are the exception to the otherwise decent islanders, who mostly show themselves willing to help one another and make the best of difficult times: the young man who taxis Ada around in his Lada, the fisherman, who contravenes new rules and sells Ada fish fresh from the boat, and others who help steal sheep destined for slaughter. Only one family, redundant since unification and surviving on state benefits, remains impassive to Ada's 'pro-active' enterprise, and apparently inured to their marginalized and impotent role in the new Germany. When Ada challenges their apathetic outlook, ironically suggesting that 'so things were better before?', the husband responds, 'I'm not saying that. But in a way, they were.' Glowna's film (scripted by Knut Boeser) frequently ends dialogues with these rueful remarks but resists any further resolution. It is again heard in an exchange between Ada and Zwirner:

> Zwirner: D'you really think you can save the GDR with homemade jam and fruit juice, and by knitting jumpers?
> Ada: The GDR doesn't exist any more, Mr Zwirner.
> Zwirner: It still exists in many people's minds.

This device is used once more in the final scene amidst the carnival atmosphere of the celebration party in a drunken discussion between two of the west Germans. Here, Glowna's film offers an exchange that is interesting for its rare articulation of opposing western attitudes towards unification – one hesitant, the other confident – though a final line rescues it from becoming too didactic:

> Naujock: [referring to the islanders] They've woken from hibernation.
> Raschke: But not all of them. I'm scared to death about what all this is going to cost – it'll bankrupt us.
> Naujock: But not you, Mr Raschke, You're still earning.
> Drunken east German bystander: We're Germans … just like you!
> Naujock: Some hefty financial support and then it'll all work itself out. An economic miracle, that's what's needed.
> Raschke: But in a way, they are somehow different to us.

Such dialogue provides insight into Glowna's attitude to the new, united Germany. The director does not hesitate in presenting the west's interest in the eastern states as one driven by financial self-aggrandizement with little thought to the consequences for the local community. Mostly they are introduced as prospectors, who arrive in a motorcade of Mercedes speeding across the plain towards Ada's house. Even Naujock, though a more sympathetic Wessi than Zwirner and Raschke, is ultimately interested only in the profit margin of the potential business. Glowna attempts to offer greater balance in his depiction of the eastern locals, but in so doing resorts to familiar tropes, with the officious and corruptible SED/Stasi characters set up against the non-partisan, good and honest locals, who in their simple and inoffensive ways confirm the apparent *Gemütlichkeit* (cosiness) of the GDR. The solution that Glowna provides in response to the west's simultaneous exploitation and neglect of the east is a curious mix of old GDR-style socialist principles, as in the call for collective responsibility – the collective, as it were, winning the battle against diverse individual interests – policy advice (more investment, as advocated by both Ada and Naujock), and a belief in the more western concept of individual responsibility, which belies the difficulties facing such communities.

What the east Germans lack in experience, they make up for in solidarity and in a sense of communal enterprise. By the end, the successes appear to involve most of the island, even including the corrupt town officials who are permitted to share in Ada's triumph. Though those from the west essentially facilitate the island's reversal in fortunes, providing as they do the market, the impetus and the business practices so lacking among the easterners, they are mostly presented as superficial and lacking real values. Seeing the modern sculptures that Ada's nephew produces, the Wessis are only able to appreciate them in terms of functionality and material desirability, rather than simply as art in and for itself. Similarly, the importance of kinship and community – 'here come those horrible kids', one Wessi mutters on seeing his children arrive – has to them become subordinate to the primacy of business and of profit. The east Germans, meanwhile, rapidly acquaint themselves with a new way of life and with the different demands of post-unification society whilst at the same time managing to retain their fundamentally decent, east German, values. Ada confirms as much when she decides that she will forgo her dream of one day visiting Mont Blanc and, recognizing the busy times ahead, settles instead for a more modest outing, with all her colleagues, to the Harz mountains. This willingness to sacrifice her dreams and her reiterated dedication to her community echoes the kind of rhetoric heard in the GDR in previous decades, while the planned trip recalls the GDR tradition of group outings for workers that was an annual event in many companies. The celebration party at the end of the film – a standard ending in the original Heimatfilme – offers something of a didactic coda to the issues raised.[42] Asked to make a speech, the unassuming Ada takes to the stage, from which she entreats her fellow islanders to invest their money. Her final phrase, 'No future without investment … it's up to us', sounds not unlike a political slogan, and reminds those gathered (including some westerners) that the responsibility for future success lies with them all.[43]

The island's cosy community, whose members are willing to help one another in troubled times, continues the GDR's oft-mentioned *Nischengesellschaft* (niche society), which seeks to improve lives though a private system of exchange and mutual co-operation and with as little state interference as possible.[44] Whilst there is little indication of the islanders' affiliation to the previous regime – Ada's few comments hint at a self-perceived victim status – their attitude to the recent social and political changes is often ambivalent. Sufficient evidence is presented to allow a degree of (self) pity, be it in the policies affecting the fishermen, who must send their harvest to Hamburg, leaving the locals with nothing, or the shepherd, who is instructed to send his uneconomical flock to slaughter. The disagreement between the islanders and the western mainlanders ultimately confirms the widely held assessment of the conflict between east and west as one between wealthy, professional organizations and the folksier people's initiatives, which rely on communal interdependence and sheer spirit.

Der Brocken does not attempt to argue the case for the similarities between east and west; if anything, it confirms the territorial differences

Figure 2.1 *Der Brocken*
Zwirner (Rolf Zacher), the western interloper in *Der Brocken* (Vadim Glowna, 1992) © NDR/Winkler

in character and identity. Raschke's suspicion that they are 'somehow different' – the inscrutability of this difference hints at the complexity of the issue – is not the only comment to suggest this. When it transpires that Ada's nephew, Funke, is the mayor's son, the aunt exclaims, with some relief, 'then you're not a Wessi at all – not even half a one!' – even progeny and identity have managed to triumph over adversity, for the blossoming relationship between the nephew and the young woman staying with Ada is not a relationship between east and west, as previously thought, but now a pure east German affair. The film may, then, offer the case for further financial investment and advance collective responsibility as a course of action for the future, but, contrary to Glowna's appeal, it stops short of prompting east and west towards cohabitation or procreative integration, settling instead for nothing more than mutual tolerance.

Heimat Found? *Go Trabi Go II. Das war der wilde Osten*

The success of Timm's earlier *Trabi* film predictably gave rise to a sequel, which was released two years later in 1992. Though intended to capitalize on the format of its predecessor, with the *Trabi* even earning an opening credit, the follow-up, *Go Trabi Go II. Das war der wilde Osten*, showed more interest in acknowledging issues relevant to the east than had its predecessor. Where the original film had largely avoided specific references to contemporary developments, the sequel focuses on the consequences of unification for the region and examines in particular the mounting tensions between east and west Germans, a conflict that was only fleetingly acknowledged in the original.

The attention to more important contemporary issues is, one suspects, a way of compensating for the perceived deficiencies of the earlier film. Some reviewers had criticized *Go Trabi Go*'s sentimentality and its failure to address any of the significant unification issues (a fact that has not deterred television broadcasters from frequently screening it on the anniversary of unification). The mass redundancies that followed unification – 40 per cent of the labour force had lost their jobs by the end of 1992 – presumably dissuaded producers from attempting to repeat the frivolous road movie of the original.[45] Nevertheless, the replacement directors do not sacrifice the comedy of the first for an earnest representation of contemporary issues; indeed, the slapstick evident in *Go Trabi Go* is even more in evidence in the sequel, once again featuring the hapless Struutzes. The sequel's rather untidy narrative – an 'assault of preposterous and barely integrated events' according to Naughton – is the result of the directors' attempts to shoehorn a wide range of post-unification concerns including unemployment, right-wing extremism, the Treuhand, commercial takeovers, property claims and east/west hostilities into the narrative.[46]

Returning to find Bitterfeld a ghost town, a victim of new economic policies, the Struutzes, unlike their fellow (unseen) Bitterfelder, are offered a way out of this dire environment in the form of an inheritance near Dresden. The bequest is rather less auspicious than the family imagined, being a factory that produces that ridiculed symbol of German *Gemütlichkeit*, the garden gnome.[47] Nor is the business as promising as they hope, since the gnome factory too is in decline and its future enterprise seems doubtful. Unperturbed, the Struutzes decide to revive the factory's fortunes, which brings them into conflict with the local west German mayor whose grand designs for the area anticipate a rather different strategy for economic regeneration, and with western bankers, who are similarly unconvinced of their plans.[48] The Struutzes' resistance to western interests mirrors contemporary events, specifically the Treuhand's controversial widespread closure of former GDR businesses and the equally controversial arrival of west German politicians to help steward the newly democratic federal states.

Critical though it is of the western establishment, *Das war der wilde Osten* does not offer a one-sided account of the Wende's economic impact on the region. The closure of the Bitterfeld industry may be disastrous for the local population, which remains notable by its absence, but it is clearly beneficial in terms of health – the returning family can at least breathe clean air again. This is the single benefit of the new economic policy and, while the air may be cleaner, the optimistic post-unification atmosphere has been tainted by the western institutions' uncompromising policies. The administrators in charge of the transition are presented as ungracious and unsympathetic to ordinary people; the politicians are dilettantish and lack genuine commitment to, or understanding of, their constituents. The mayor is presented as a vain, conceited figure, exasperated by his slow-witted (east German) assistants and the locals' lack of initiative and vision. His scheme to rejuvenate fictional Lachwitz by introducing a motorway link, cineplexes and shopping centres corresponds with actual plans for resuscitating the eastern states. An imported project which denies the specificity of this region (the filming makes use of the picturesque sandstone mountains to the east of Dresden, and the town is possibly a reference to the nearby hamlet of Landwitz), the proposal demonstrates the west Germans' supreme arrogance and lack of understanding. The inappropriateness of such a development in Lachwitz refers to the kind of projects that were put forward in the wake of unification. In the rush to modernize the east, local opinion did often fall victim to larger commercial concerns. As corporations moved in to capitalize on the opportunities that the east offered, local people were routinely told to accept these features of progress (rhetoric that must have seemed strangely familiar). In *Das war der wilde Osten* similar proposals are rejected by Rita Struutz, who attempts to convince the Mayor that Lachwitz can prosper with its old ways. In the choice of enterprise, the product being the garden gnome, the filmmakers confirm the old-fashioned and provincial nature of the region. Corresponding with the methods for financial autonomy in *Der Brocken*, the moral implicit in

Das war der wilde Osten is that local economic recovery can be achieved by adhering to the east Germans' old and apparently preferred ways. There is even the notion that they may offer some balance to the ugly corporatism of the west, and that rather than being discarded and declared obsolete the old values can, indeed should, have a place in the new Germany. Provincial, homemade and old-fashioned, the east German ways are therefore mediated as more authentic than the established practices of the west.

The post-unification grievances of the east are, then, far more acute in *Das war der wilde Osten* than they were in the original, though the comedy consciously inhibits any inquiry into these social issues from becoming too serious. This newfound commitment to relevant issues divided critics in the east. While some approved of the characterizations and claimed that the film offered west Germans the opportunity to understand their eastern compatriots, others were unimpressed by the film's sentimentality and lack of satirical bite.[49] Günther Sobe, writing in the *Berliner Zeitung*, suggested that not even DEFA would have produced so bad a film.[50] Nevertheless, the filmmakers' volte-face in wishing to acknowledge certain problems that were considered to be consequences of unification and of the west's influence were presumably less appreciated by audiences, despite the comedic portrayal, and may have been a deciding factor in the film's disappointing

Figure 2.2 *Go Trabi Go II*
Boots maketh the man? Udo (Wolfgang Stumpf), Rita (Marie Gruber) and Jacqueline Struutz (Claudia Schmutzler) in *Go Trabi Go II. Das war der wilde Osten* (Wolfgang Büld, Reinhard Klooss, 1992) © Bavaria Film/Rolf von der Heydt

box-office returns. The film's failure to match the success of its predecessor may also have been due to the less exotic, though by no means unattractive, east German location.

The conflicts between east and west Germans that were briefly, and comically, sketched out in *Go Trabi Go* are far more vociferous in the sequel, though it is the agents of the state who are the targets of criticism: bankers, petty bureaucrats, and political representatives typically comprise the hegemonic opposition to east German interests. These supervisors of the east German states are disinclined either to compromise or empathize with the locals and are apparently motivated only by rules and regulations. Unlike *Der Brocken*, in which the community comes together in order to defy the individual challenges from the west, the Struutzes' battle with the various authorities represents east German individualism against the west German hegemony. As with most Wende comedies, their success depends not on any ideological victory, but on wildly contingent factors: providence, assistance from atypically sympathetic west Germans, and, finally, an uncanny ability to beat the west at its own game – Udo is able to secure backing from an American millionaire whose corporation is buying up the east, and thus save his factory and his employees and his rediscovered Heimat. Looking at these films, one is forced to conclude that the east Germans' chances of financial independence and future stability require nothing more than a few traditional recipes, some old-fashioned cottage industries and continued reference to their own past. 'Forward, but forgetting nothing!', the opening line to Eisler's and Brecht's 'Solidarity Song' and later a rallying cry of the GDR, might now be re-conceptualized as a mission statement for regional success.

Conclusion: Triumph of the Underdog

The Heimatfilm's aesthetic has not faded from narratives located in the east. The genre has long been a favourite on German television, which frequently screens the films of the 1950s and 1960s. In 2001, Wolfgang Panzer's short television series, *Liebesau – die andere Heimat* (*Liebesau – A Different Sort of Home*), compensated for the lack of real Heimatfilme in the index of DEFA films, by offering one that charted life in an east German village from 1953 to 1989. Three years later, Edgar Reitz returned to television screens with the third instalment of his series, *Heimat 3* (2004), which spans the period 1989–2000 and which was co-scripted by Thomas Brussig, author and scriptwriter of *Sonnenallee* and *Helden wie Wir*, two of the most significant post-unification texts. Reitz's final series may have revisited the Hunsrück region in which it had first begun, but the director remained committed to charting wider changes in Germany, including east Germans' experience of the west, the departure of the US army and the arrival of *Spätaussiedler* (ethnic Germans) from eastern Europe and beyond. The genre continues to find favour among producers and directors. Aspects of the idealized eastern Heimat surface, for example, in Gordian Maugg's *Zutaten für Träume* (*Ingredients for Dreams*, 2001), in which two former lovers and celebrated chefs face one another in a series of cooking competitions, a contest that is ultimately less about cooking than about wider tensions between east and west (characterized as a conflict between a quaint and honest community-orientated region and an individualistic and superficial society). The Heimatfilm is parodied in Klaus Gietinger's *Heinrich der Säger* (*Henry the Sawyer*, 2001). Gietinger, whose acclaimed *Daheim sterben die Leut'* was considered to have revitalized the flagging Heimatfilm, returned to the provinces, this time to Thüringen in the east, whose picturesque forests and hills were well-suited to the genre. Gietinger's comedy-drama revisits the earlier Wende comedies in which determined locals defend their Heimat against the financial interests of the west. Not the threat to property is the issue in *Heinrich der Säger*, but the threat to the local train route, which is timetabled for closure by its western owners. Using numerous tools, from hi-tech gadgets to voices from the spirit world, a trio of resourceful locals sets about sabotaging the lines and disrupting the police's investigation into the mysterious Säger's activities. Though the film's plot echoes those of *Der Brocken* and *Go Trabi Go II*, the conclusion aligns it with later films in which embattled east Germans seek an ersatz community far beyond their eastern Heimat.

Despite the comic approach the films discussed in this chapter take and the fanciful solutions they propose, they do reflect the difficult consequences of unification. One of the most important of these is the threat to Heimat and to community identity (a metaphor for the wider east German identity) posed by western interests and, to a lesser extent, eastern recidivists – the diehard communists or dim-witted fascists who periodically come into view. In engaging with these themes, the Wendefilme evoke the cinematic Heimat tradition with plot devices familiar to the post-war genre revived and redeployed in a modern context, as Naughton's study clearly illustrates. The subjects and motifs in these modern films may be recycled but their relevance is not diminished by their generic provenance, since these modern narratives, despite being comedies, politicize the Heimatfilm aesthetic.[51] The directors look to Heimatfilm topoi as a means of commenting on contemporary concerns. The conflict between community and outsiders, for example, assumes greater social relevance in these films than it was traditionally seen to in the original genre.[52] This is partly attributable to the actual circumstances of unification. The process of integrating the east with the Federal Republic, which resulted in much criticism of the specific policies, naturally had more of a direct influence on the eastern states than in the west (though west Germans have also felt the impact through increased taxation to help fund the economic re-generation of the east). These films present the east as a region explored, exploited, and colonized by the west, an interpretation that arouses sympathy for the colonized subjects.

Often the Heimatfilm heritage is perceptible in the visual look of the films. One scene in *Go Trabi Go II*, in which Rita Struutz's picnic with the mayor and their stroll through the forest – a rendezvous that initially hints at a possible union between the two Germanys – echoes the kitsch rural scenes of some Heimatfilme. However, the idyllic scene, which for Rita is the embodiment of Heimat but for the ambitious mayor a site for future development and modernization, finally leads to discord and not to any romantic alliance. The cinematographic aesthetic, a kind of Heimatfilm veneer, did not completely disappear from German filmmaking and continues to be evident in television productions and series (one thinks of popular television Heimat-soaps such as *Schwarzwaldklinik*). The genre's aesthetic influence on these films is clearly visible, and this recourse to an established cinematic tradition appears to have been a convenient means of representing the east, of making the unfamiliar familiar. Whilst these Wende comedies draw on Heimatfilm motifs, they depart from the paradigm of the original genre in a number of ways. One of the most obvious differences is the new eastern setting (Rügen and the Sächsische Schweiz); the action is historically determined by certain calendrical details (the Treuhand's period of operation; the currency union). All the same, one should recognize that these films are not concerned with accuracy or authenticity, nor are they intended as social critical narratives.[53]

The films offer an appealing mix of tradition, solidarity, individual strength, family responsibility and simple morality against the exploitation and unsympathetic policies of anonymous western corporatism. However, their appeal lies in a sympathetic representation of the underdog that is not necessarily determined by a specific regional loyalty or identity. So insensitive are the vulgar commercial plans of the west that western audiences might conceivably identify with the Struutzes' struggles against their adversaries, or Ada Fenske's resistance to the various underhand methods employed by her antagonists. In their exaggerated characterizations, these Wessis function as negative representatives of the FRG, whose conduct would be similarly inexcusable in their local context. Equally, the films' east German heroes may appeal to western audiences on the strength of their personality, rather than a specifically eastern pedigree. For western viewers, Udo's Sächsisch may announce his regional origins but the accent is more likely to amuse than to alienate. At the same time, the films include a sufficient number of specifically east German details to ensure their resonance with audiences in the east; so, whilst viewers in Schleswig Holstein might sympathize with the provincials' resistance to metropolitan intrusions, viewers in Brandenburg might identify with the protagonists in the particular social and economic context of the Wende.

The sympathy that is extended to protagonists like Udo Struutz and Ada Fenske is not unconditional; nor is it motivated simply by their dire circumstances. The characters are not sympathetic by virtue of their East German origins. Since their east German status is not by itself a signal for empathy or understanding, the filmmakers must imbue their protagonists with ostensibly ahistorical, apolitical qualities. To that end, the protagonists' east German specificity is in no way linked to the character of the SED-state. To emphasize this, the films' heroes are distinguishable from the SED goons who occasionally appear. Udo's adversary in the second of the Trabi films may be west German, but his subordinates are clearly former SED cadres – their allegiance hinted at by the red socks they still each wear. And though Ada Fenske resists those western entrepreneurs who would intrude on her community, this is not an indication of any posthumous loyalty to the defunct state, a fact that is emphasized by her opposition to the old guard, the island's insidious ex-officials and bureaucrats.

With the protagonists therefore set apart from the erstwhile SED flag-wavers, their actions in combating the various west Germans is not attributable to a specifically East German – SED – ideology. The solidarity on which the protagonists rely may be indicative of an ethos that was inscribed within East German culture but it is not the defining strategy in the communities' opposition to the west. The prime movers of this economic and social resistance are ultimately triumphant because they succeed in beating the west at its own game. Following a moment of revelation in which they realize that they must employ the same tactics that threaten them, the characters become adept at harnessing the standard practices of the west for their own protection. Udo, for example, exhibits determination – a quality that jars with his hangdog look and downtrodden attitude – in pursuing an American millionaire in order to acquire the financial backing necessary to save his business (and the livelihoods of the small rural community). Ada, on the other hand, motivates her island neighbours to produce a variety of goods whose sale to west Germans she successfully and assertively negotiates. The characters' transformation into self-assured venture capitalists overnight is not permanent, however. Despite their commercial and moral success, the characters retain an east German identity, which is confirmed when they return to type at the end of the films.

Although the films effect a rescue of an eastern identity, the traditions and customs that are under threat are not given as examples of a socialist Heimat but of a true originary German Heimat that invites all Germans to reminisce and empathize. The films reach back through history to invoke a Heimat that attempts to transcend the political and to fix itself within an idealized, apolitical cultural context. Indeed, the narratives confirm one of the prevailing opinions of the former east, namely that the region is somehow more German than the west, that, despite four decades of communist rule, the east has managed to hang on to core German values that have been eroded in the west.

The films may not celebrate a postnational identity or support modern notions of integration. They do, however, correspond with what Morley and Robins have referred to as the '"small is beautiful" ideal of ... Europe', and 'a romantic utopianism in this celebration of small nationalism and re-gionalism, *a utopianism of the underdog*' [my emphasis].[54] The appeal, then, is to an identity that seeks to connect German audiences from east to west, even if the films do not ultimately redress the east/west differences in order to make the case for true integration. The Heimat envisioned in these films finally allows the easterners the utopia they never had.

Notes

1. J. Weeks, 'Rediscovering Values', in J. Squires (ed.), *Principled Positions. Postmodernism and the Rediscovery of Value*, London: Lawrence and Wishart, 2000, p. 182.
2. H.-J. Hahn,'Ossis, Wessis and the Germans: An Inner-German Perception of National Characteristics', *Journal of Area Studies* (Perspectives on German Unification) 2, 1993: 119.
3. R. Schenk, 'Schattenboxer und Kinderspiele. Über einige neue deutsche Spielfilme während und im Umfeld der Berlinale', *Film und Fernsehen* 2, 1993: 27.
4. From author's correspondence with the film's co-producer, Elke Haltaufderheide (12 March 2004).
5. H. Schnödel, 'Würstel aus Krauts', *Die Zeit*, 14 December 1990.
6. See C. Seidel, 'Von Metzgern und Menschen', *Der Spiegel* 49, 1990.
7. R. Poggioli, *The Theory of the Avant-Garde*, Cambridge, MA: Belknap Press/Harvard University Press, 1968, pp. 36–7.
8. D. Simons, 'Ein flacher Film über den doofen Ex-DDR-Bürger', *Volksstimme* (Magdeburg), 30 January 1991.
9. H.-D. Tok, 'Wir sind doch ganz schön naiv. Auskünfte des Hauptdarstellers Wolfgang Stumph zu "Go Trabi Go"', *Thüringer Allgemeine*, 20 March 1991.
10. Naughton (2002), pp. 125–206. Reif had earlier drawn attention to a possible *Heimatfilm* revival in her review of Detlev Buck's 1993 comedy. In C. Reif, 'Die Provinz schlägt zurück. Über die Tugenden des Ländlers und Detlev Bucks neuen Heimatfilm "Wir können auch anders"', *Film und Fernsehen* 2, 1993: 28–9. See also M. Conboy, 'The Discourse of Location. Realigning the Popular in German Cinema', *European Journal of Communication* 14(3), 1999: 366.
11. Naughton (2002), p. 126.
12. Ibid., pp. 129–30.
13. Ibid., p. 128.
14. See M. Amis's polemic on Stalin in M. Amis, *Koba the Dread. Laughter and the Twenty Million*, London: Vintage, 2003.
15. Naughton (2002), p. 126.
16. Ibid., p. 127.
17. Taberner refers to *Die Zeit*'s critic, Iris Radisch. In S. Taberner, *German Literature of the 1990s and Beyond. Normalization and the Berlin Republic*, London: Camden House, 2005, p. 33.
18. Similarly, to claim *Go Trabi Go* as a west German film is not as straightforward as Naughton would like. Although she acknowledges the director's eastern origins, this fact might have benefited from some explanation before including the director in the west German camp. See 'Interview mit Peter Timm', *Dirk-Jasper Filmlexikon*. Retrieved 12 January 2007 from http://www.djfl.de/entertainment/stars/p/peter_timm_i_01.html
19. This traditional understanding of the genre continues. See I. Aitken, *European Film Theory and Cinema. A Critical Introduction*, Bloomington: Indiana University Press, 2002, p. 138; Wulf Kansteiner, 'Sold Globally – Remembered Locally: Holocaust Cinema and the Construction of Collective Identities in Europe and the US', in S. Berger, L. Eriksonas and A. Mycock (eds), *Narrating the Nation. Representations in History, Media, and the Arts*, Oxford and New York: Berghahn, 2008: 153–81, p. 161.
20. H. Fehrenbach, *Cinema in Democratizing Germany. Reconstructing National Identity after Hitler*. Chapel Hill and London: The University of North Carolina Press, 1995, p. 151.
21. H. Fehrenbach,'The Fight for the "Christian West": German Film Control, and the Reconstruction of Civil Society in the Early Bonn Republic', in R.G. Moeller (ed.), *War*

Stories. The Search for a Usable Past in the Federal Republic of Germany, London and Berkeley: University of California Press, 2001, p. 321.

22. See T. Bergfelder, *International Adventures. German Popular Cinema and European Co-Productions in the 1960s*, New York and Oxford: Berghahn, 2005, p. 29.

23. See A. Kaes, *From Hitler to Heimat. The Return of History as Film*, Cambridge, MA, and London: Harvard University Press, 1992, p. 14.

24. Conboy (1999), p. 357.

25. See, for example, S. Hake, *German National Cinema*, 2nd ed., London and New York: Routledge, 2002, p. 119. See also J. Von Moltke, *No Place Like Home. Locations of Heimat in German Cinema*, Berkeley: University of Cailfornia, 2005.

26. See Kaes (1992), p. 15.

27. M. Walser, *Heimatkunde. Aufsätze und Reden*, Frankfurt am Main: Suhrkamp, 1968, p. 40.

28. This point is discussed in T. Hoffmann and I. Steiner, 'Die Sechziger. Zwischen Jagdszenen und Jägerporno', in W. Kaschuba (ed.), *Der deutsche Heimatfilm*, Tübingen: Tübingen Vereinigung für Volkskunde e.V., 1989, pp. 101–2.

29. J. Palmowski, *Inventing a Socialist Nation: Heimat and the Politics of Everyday Life in the GDR, 1945–1990*, Cambridge: Cambridge University Press, 2009, p. 419.

30. See G. Lange, *Heimat. Realität und Aufgabe. Zur Marxistischen Auffassung des Heimatgefühls*, Berlin: Akademie Verlag, 1973, p. 44.

31. Although often translated as 'idiocy', some scholars contend that by 'Idiotismus' Marx meant isolation. Either suits my purpose here, since the point I am making is that the GDR wished to abandon the narrow provincial outlook associated with rural life. In H. Magdoff and J.B. Foster, 'Notes from the Editor', *Monthly Review*, October 2003. Retrieved 5 May 2008 from http://www.monthlyreview.org/nfte1003.htm.

32. See E. Boa and R. Palfreyman, *Heimat. A German Dream. Regional Loyalties and National Identity in German Culture 1890–1990*, Oxford: Oxford University Press, 2000, p. 134.

33. J.R. Becher, *Schöne Deutsche Heimat*, Berlin: Aufbau-Verlag, 1956, p. 5.

34. See J. Kretzschmar, 'Sein Vaterland im Film – die DDR Reportagen', in T. Prase and J. Kretzschmar, *Propagandist und Heimatfilmer. Die Dokumentarfilme des Karl-Eduard von Schnitzler*, Leipzig: Leipzig Universitäts Verlag, 2003, p. 8.

35. H. Blunk, 'The Concept of "*Heimat*-GDR" in DEFA Feature Films', in Allan and Sandford (eds) (1999), p. 205.

36. See Kretzschmar, 'Sein Vaterland im Film', in Prase and Kretzschmar (2003), p. 151.

37. See S. Spindler, '"Erinnerung an eine Landschaft. Für Manuela" – ein Dokumentarfilm', in W. Teusch (ed.), *Heimat in der DDR-Medien. Arbeitsheft zum Medienpaket 8*, Bonn: Bundeszentrale für politische Bildung, 1998, 81–101, p. 82.

38. See D. Schoenbaum and E. Pound, *The German Question and Other German Questions*. New York: St. Martin's Press, 1996, p. 155.

39. D. Dahn, *Wir bleiben hier, oder wem gehört der Osten.Vom Kampf um Häuser und Wohnungen in den neuen Bundesländern*, Hamburg: Rowohlt Taschenbuch Verlag, 1994, p. 20. Stefan Heym also dealt with the subject and, in so doing, exposed the problems of such claims, which led to even older claims from disappropriated Jews. See the eponymous story in his collection, S. Heym, *Auf Sand Gebaut. Sieben Geschichten aus der unmittelbaren Vergangenheit*, Munich: Bertelsmann, 1990, pp. 34–48. Similar claims are addressed in Ula Stöckl's film *Das Alte Lied* (*The Old Song*, 1991).

40. See for instance, D. Kühn's review in *epd film* 5, 1992: 40.

41. See, *inter alia*, H.A. Welsh, A. Pickel and D. Rosenberg, 'East and West German Identities. United and Divided?', in Jarausch (ed.) (1997), p. 121.

42. See Naughton (2002), p. 145.

43. This entreaty corresponds with Glowna's own opinion. The director told one interviewer that it was necessary to combat the 'crazy nostalgia for the GDR' and to focus on the present and the future. In R. Römer, 'Dein Lebens-Budget voll ausschöpfen', *Junge Welt*, 21 February 1992.

44. The local population is a literal manifestation of Bauman's 'vision of community [which is] that of an island of homely and cosy tranquillity in a sea of turbulence and inhospitality'. In Z. Bauman, *Liquid Modernity*, Cambridge: Polity Press, 2000, p. 182.
45. See Schoenbaum and Pound (1996), pp. 152–3.
46. See Naughton (2002), p. 173.
47. The gnome's appeal to a particular kind of provincial German cosiness is a more plausible explanation of its role here, I think, than Naughton's mythical reading according to which it somehow functions as a 'guardian of the homeland', 194. For more on its historical appeal see H. Bausinger, *Typisch Deutsch. Wie deutsch sind die Deutschen?* 3rd ed., Munich: Verlag C.H. Beck, 2002, pp. 60–3.
48. Inheritance may be a recognizable Heimatfilm motif, but the east German's attempt to manage a factory has other antecedents. In Tom Toelle's West German comedy, *Grüß Gott, ich komm' von drüben* (*Good Day, I'm From Over There*, 1978), an East German attempts to introduce socialist management principles in an inherited factory in the FRG, while one man's altruistic commitment to socialist working practices and increased production in a failing factory forms the basis of Horst Seemann's sober DEFA film, *Zeit zu leben* (*Time to Live*, 1969). On this last film, see Hake (2002), p. 133.
49. See T. Klug, '"Go, Trabi, Go 2." Stumpi jetzt im wilden Osten', *Volksstimme* (Magdeburg), 13 August 1992. Ralph Umard was among those hostile to the film: R. Umard, 'Im Kleinen Ganz Gross', *TIP* 17, 1992: 26–8.
50. G. Sobe, 'Heimkehr und Aufbruch des Udos', *Berliner Zeitung*, 21 August 1992.
51. See P. Blickle, who argues that 'in Heimat, politics is aestheticized and aesthetics is politicised'. P. Blickle, *Heimat. A Critical Theory of the German Idea of Homeland*, Rochester and Woodbridge: Camden House, 2002, p. 138.
52. Antagonism between *Ossis* and *Wessis* in the old Federal States doubtless also exists – the sheer number of east German economic refugees relocating to the west makes this more than likely – yet it is the conflicts that occur in the east that have tended to dominate in post-unification discourse. Manfred Stelzer's TV comedy, *Grüß Gott, Genosse!* (*Good Day, Comrade!*, 1993) is one of the few films to portray an east German's attempt to find footing in the west. The experience of an east German in west Germany is raised in Matthias Glasner's *Die Mediocren* (*The Meds*, 1995), a twenty-something comedy about a group of young friends whose friendship is threatened when they discover that one of them is an Ossi.
53. That *Das war der wilde Osten*'s most direct criticism of life in the New Germany should be articulated in the lyrics of the closing musical sequence (accompanying the credits and the audience's departure from the cinema) is hardly evidence of any committed social critique. See Naughton (2002), p. 204.
54. D. Morley and K. Robins, 'No Place Like *Heimat*: Images of Home(land) in European Culture', in E. Carter, J. Donald and J. Squires (eds), *Space and Place. Theories of Identity and Location*, Lawrence & Wishart: London, 1993, p. 7.

Chapter 3

LOST LANDSCAPES

By drawing on the Heimatfilm heritage, the unification comedies discussed in the previous chapter are able to present a sanitized version of the transition in which genial east Germans overcome various challenges and disappointments. The films typically centre on small communities in the east, which, despite limited means, manage to withstand the vulgar pressures of western commercial interests. Combining aptitude with a sense of collective purpose, the fictional communities stand firm against the corrupt power of anonymous corporations. Though the heroes of the films are east German everyman figures, their east German identity is not inscribed with either the politics or the ideology of the SED regime. Their values, however, often bear more than a passing resemblance to the principles enshrined in socialist rhetoric and the solidarity on display is frequently reminiscent of the communitarian values that had apparently underpinned GDR society.

Such collective resistance was, in reality, little more than a dream and the films' happy endings hardly offer an accurate portrayal of the period's economic fallout. Many east German businesses were ill equipped and not able to survive the take-overs and the aggressive competition that followed the Treuhand's administration.[1] Since the films are comedies born of the Wende and all its attendant frictions, the films cannot but acknowledge a few of the conflicts of the time. Yet, the issues do not distract from the films' primary purpose. They are, first and foremost, films which seek to entertain, and the hostilities and traumas that followed unification are therefore happily resolved, with plucky individuals mustering support against the unsympathetic agents of the state and the representatives of western business.

But does the films' tacit acknowledgement of social and political issues invalidate attempts to categorize them as a continuation of the Heimatfilm genre, a genre widely considered to have provided a German never-never world, far removed from the less than fairytale-like environments of the post-war period? Naughton has suggested that recourse to the 'Heimat heritage provides opportunity for sentimental and often reassuring reflection on national identity …, an activity that may otherwise have been the cause for bewilderment and dismay'.[2] It is true that the films do establish certain behavioural patterns and responses that may be understood as qualities constitutive of an east German identity. The solidarity and the communal resistance are here presented as natural responses to the urgency of the situation and the coercive (metropolitan, global) forces that threaten the rural and the local.

The unification comedies present a view of the east that largely contradicts the usual perception of the east as an environmental disaster zone, a landscape polluted and scarred by industries that had been able to operate, unchecked, for decades. Unable to modernize its outdated heavy industry, the GDR's industrial production had resulted in an egregious environmental record. This had an appreciable effect on the local population but pollution also caused anxiety among west Germans whose support for environmental issues had long been a feature of mainstream politics. Some commentators even warned that standards imposed by the west might be understood as a kind of 'green imperialism' by those in the eastern regions and exacerbate the resentment between the east and west.[3] The unification Heimatfilme barely acknowledge rising issues or problems such as racism and unemployment and they completely sidestep the environmental question. The Struutz family might come from the most polluted town in the GDR, but Bitterfeld only features briefly in both films, and then only as a point of departure to more distant and scenic areas (northern Italy in the first film and the forests and hills of eastern Saxony in the sequel), and it is Rügen, a long-established island resort for (east) Germans, that provides the location for *Der Brocken*.

The old Party apparatchiks would have doubtless baulked at these visual representations of the east which completely by-passed the achievements of the SED's forty-year project – the socialist Heimat was in an ongoing process of construction – but it would not be unreasonable to surmise that the films' pleasant imagery would have earned their approval. After all, 'officially, the forests in the GDR were not dying, there was no air pollution, no atomic waste. According to the picture postcard world of really existing socialism, the meadows were green, the skies blue and the babbling brooks sparkled like those in the Heimatfilms of the 1950s'.[4] The post-GDR Heimat comedies present a picture of the east as uncontaminated by the hazardous emissions and effluences of the GDR's chemical plants and heavy industry; instead, they offer meadows, rolling hills and the glittering waters of the rivers and sea. Not that this had any great effect on the western audiences. Perhaps more immune to the allure of advertising than audiences in the east, they were not suddenly induced to visiting this region of apparent natural beauty and for a long time the eastern states were not considered a viable holiday destination for anyone other than for a few intrepid tourists. Holiday traffic continued to be a one-way affair with the west and not the east the ultimate destination. Nevertheless, some of those west Germans who did venture into the east returned to report a region that was somehow more German that the west. West German journalist Irmela Hannover was, for instance, struck by the quaint backward-

ness of the rural regions of the east. Once past the obvious signs of state bureaucracy and petty officialdom that was in evidence at the border, time
and the way of life in the remote communities of Mecklenburg-
Vorpommern appeared to have stood still.[5] Perhaps, believing the SED's
rhetoric, these travellers had expected the rural east to consist of a landscape that was testimony to the highly mechanized agricultural policies of
a centrally-planned economy. The antiquated farm machinery and the simplicity of the rural homesteads that were reported contradicted such preconceptions, though they perhaps confirmed the state's self-proclaimed
farmers' state status. For some, the east offered an authenticity that had
been lost in the Federal Republic's sanitized rural districts. The GDR's arrested economic development corresponded with Walser's view of Heimat;
its perceived backwardness was not without its appeal and lent itself to a
view of the east as the quainter, more natural Germany.

But these areas were not just forgotten landscapes to be discovered by
west German journalists keen to journey east and into the past. The rural
east came also to function as a critical space of enquiry from which to
examine the idea of memory, the effects of the past, and the consequences
of unification for the people living there. If the films previously discussed
constituted a post-unification equivalent of the Heimatfilm, in which a
vision of Heimat, however anachronistic, was re-addressed, then these constituted its antithesis, presenting the east as a kind of lost Heimat, whose
communities were on the brink of collapse. Already the titles of some of the
films under discussion in this chapter indicate an alternative vision of the
east. The idea of landscape, and of home and of Heimat, is hinted at in titles
such as *Stilles Land* (*Silent Country*), *Landschaft mit Dornen* (*Landscape with
Thorns*) and *Verlorene Landschaft* (*Lost Landscape*), and certainly these films
share a fascination with the secluded provinces of the east. The east is presented not as the *Länder* of opportunity but as a hopelessly dreary province,
from which the protagonists yearn to escape. The films therefore reject the
escapist entertainment of the original Heimatfilme and of the Wende comedies. Escape is, nevertheless, a recurrent theme in the films, and the road-
movie genre is referenced, though the eastern highways are seldom routes
to a better place; in general, the roads travelled do not lead to any new beginning or way of life but back to the place of origin.

Provincial Fears and Loathing

While the directors of the Wende comedies gravitate towards narratives
that centre on east/west encounters, in many other Wendefilme the focus
turns eastwards and inwards. Filmmakers' attentions generally turn to
small eastern communities on the brink, or in the wake, of unification.
These films are less concerned with the individual impact of a few west
Germans, like the oleaginous mayor in the Trabi sequel, or the

Machiavellian undercover agent of *Der Brocken*. Instead, the west functions as a more abstract reference. Often, the free market's presence in the new federal states is perceptible only in the form of advertising and commodities, which are incongruously arranged: advertising hoardings at the sites of abandoned businesses and deserted industries promise a better future, golf courses, a new and improved lifestyle. These western signifiers emphasize the distance, economically and culturally, between the west and the east. The western goods that are a symbol of capitalism's sudden ingress into once forbidden territory appear unattainable and out of place in the impoverished east. Equally evident is the west's institutional command of the east, though the shift in power and authority is studied not in terms of its governance but in its effect. Far from the power base of the new administration, the provinces are home to communities who remain passive onlookers to the economic and social transition. Many of the films offer a portrait of communities whose Heimat is threatened by the need to adjust to new values and changed circumstances. The communities are prone to dislocation rather than coalescence; unification is seen to rupture the east's real existing communities.

The damaging effect of unification is especially noticeable in two films of the period, Helke Misselwitz's *Herzsprung* (*Heart Leap*, 1992) and Helma Sanders-Brahms's *Apfelbäume*. One of the GDR's few celebrated women filmmakers, Misselwitz had been lauded for her documentaries, particularly *Winter adé* (*Adieu, Winter*, 1985), but had never been given the opportunity to make feature films at DEFA, a decision that was the cause of some frustration for the prize-winning filmmaker. In *Herzsprung*, Misselwitz turns her attention to rural Brandenburg during the early days of unification. Misselwitz's background in documentaries explains the documentary aesthetic that informs her debut feature (prolonged, static shots of the barren winter landscape), although this is by no means consistent throughout. There are theatrical sequences, too, and moments of artifice (the actor Ben Becker plays two roles for no obvious reason), and a curious combination of styles that Nora M. Alter has described as a '"magical realist" fusion of DEFA social realism and Hollywood, UFA, or ZDF illusionism'.[6] Red functions as a colour motif, compromising the realist tone, while the film's music, a heady mix that mingles the melancholic with the exotic and upbeat, rejects the sombre soundtracks that typically accompany such gloomy material.

The Heimatfilm is also referenced by Misselwitz. The genre is clearly alluded to in the opening scene, where Heimat as a harmoniously imagined rural past is briefly invoked by a group of women sitting in a circle, plucking geese and singing an old-fashioned folk song entitled 'Süße Heimat' ('Sweet Heimat'). But *Herzsprung* is no paean to the Heimat ideal. What quaint rural past there may have been has long since disappeared. A pitiful village, its streets muddy, its buildings disintegrating, Herzsprung is far removed from the aestheticized locales of Heimatfilme. The East

Prignitz Heimat of contemporary Brandenburg is no rural idyll, providing a home for contented communities, but an area that suffered decades of neglect during the GDR and which has fared little better since. As with other rural districts in the east, it continues to be economically disadvantaged and struggles to survive. Misselwitz's film captures the pessimism, revealing a region in which business are closing or downsizing, unemployment is high and little investment is made to entice business there or to retain its dwindling population. The only profitable company is the local chocolate factory, which is supervised by a west German – a crudely conceived figure whose arrogance and manipulative behaviour corresponds with the perceived colonialist impulses of western enterprise in the east. The job he offers Johanna (Claudia Geisler), the film's central character, is conditional on her submitting to his advances: the perceived (economic) rape of the east is thus invoked in physical terms, though Johanna is able to reject him.[7] In *Herzsprung*, such violation is considered in terms of a threat to Heimat, a warning note that has already been sounded in the film's opening song.

Johanna's forceful rejection of the sleazy manager is not part of a general opposition to the west, nor does it instigate a collective sense of outrage and a desire to protect the community. The east's economic situation is not an incentive for any pro-active response or communal co-operation of the kind seen in the Wende comedies. Nor does Misselwitz's film offer any grand schemes for economic rejuvenation. The town's entrepreneurial vision amounts to nothing more remarkable than a lay-by snack-bar and a corner sex-shop, the latter an indication of the west's corrupt values, which have come to figure more frequently in later unification films. The economic circumstances of the new era threaten to sour the 'sweet Heimat'. Johanna loses her job at the same time that her husband is made redundant from the slaughterhouse where he works. In Misselwitz's film, such events are not a springboard for spirited resistance but augur tragedy: Johanna's husband kills all the cattle for which he is responsible, before turning the weapon on himself, an incident that does not appear to surprise the community.

Despite this early trauma, *Herzsprung* is not a study of bereavement. Johanna appears to adjust quickly to her redundancy and to her widow status, a fact that might be explained by her freedom from an abusive relationship. Nonetheless, a sense of loss and decline underscores the film. Implicit in *Herzsprung*'s study of a community in transition – and, like the other films, the village can be regarded as a microcosm of the wider east German community – is the community's need to adjust to a new way of life, the difficulty in adapting that led one journalist to describe the film as a 'DDR adé'.[8] Departure is accentuated, too, by the Soviet troops seen leaving early in the film. Their exit is not portrayed as a triumphant expulsion but as sad withdrawal (accompanied by melancholic melodies). Indeed, the carefully selected musical score, together with the frequently expressed regrets and lamentations, correspond with the generally mournful mood of the film.[9] Jakob, Johanna's father, muses on the places he would have liked to have visited. Others dream of a life more exotic, with Johanna's friend one of the few characters in these films able to realize her dream and escape to the Mediterranean. For Johanna, an exotic distraction to the drab reality of her life comes in the form of the proverbial tall, dark stranger, a mysterious figure, whose provenance remains unexplained, and whose name remains unspoken. He figures as an exotic composite, part dandy, part musician and traveller, a polysemic, overcoded figure according to Alter, who advances multiple readings of him, from 'racially displaced wandering Jew' and 'latter-day Pied Piper' to 'runaway slave'. The latter acknowledges the rather problematical stereotypology of the character. His sexual appetite, which clearly marks him apart from the provincial, sexually frustrated locals, confirms old racial stereotypes.[10] The stranger stands apart from the local men; where one gang member is routinely rejected by Johanna, and her father is given to voyeurism, women are magnetically drawn to him.

Whatever the specificity of his heritage, it is his otherness that eventually threatens to upset the social, not to mention racial, balance of the village. Provincial east German intolerance is provoked by Johanna's relationship with the Stranger. Disapproval is voiced by all sectors, including local officials, church members and finally the village gang, whose transformation from village thugs to paramilitary neo-Nazis appears to coincide with the stranger's arrival. The gang's increasingly provocative behaviour, from vandalizing a memorial plaque remembering those who

Figure 3.1 *Herzsprung*
Herzsprung's fateful love: Johanna (Claudia Geisler) and the Fremder (Nino Sandow) (Helke Misselwitz, 1992) © Medien Bildungsgesellschaft Babelsberg GmbH

were dispatched to the concentration camp at Sachsenhausen, to threatening and finally abusing the Stranger, counters both the GDR's self-avowed antifascist and internationalist character and marks the east's post-unification shift towards violent racism. The reference to the perceived threat posed by immigrants in the context of a new geo-political situation outlines and contemporizes east Germans' apparent hostility to others. In so doing, it confirms many west Germans' fears about their neighbours' threat to the principles of liberal democracy. At the same time, the prejudice is historicized through reference to the concentration camps. Again, this is articulated in terms of loss: the loss of certain communal values, the ebbing away of the state's antifascist ideology (even if this had never been as firmly ingrained as the GDR's leaders would have hoped). Having helped shave the gang members' heads, Johanna comments of those who will eventually, albeit inadvertently, kill her, 'I don't get it. We were at school together'. The comment reflects not only the ideological and behavioural variance between former classmates, it also implies that the gang's new direction is contrary to their political education, and their socialist heritage, values which are still recognizable in the figure of Johanna's father, a former camp prisoner and 'Altkommunist', a paternal socialist in the DEFA tradition. The film may indirectly allude to east Germany's antifascist past, but Misselwitz is not ready to identify right-wing extremism as a post-unification phenomenon and did, in fact, draw attention to its presence in the GDR in interviews.[11] Released not long after the infamous attack and murder of asylum seekers by neo-Nazis in Rostock in August 1992, *Herzsprung* gained additional and sudden relevance within the discursive context of east German xenophobia, though the director was keen to point out that this incident was not what had inspired her film – a fact that is confirmed by the chronology of the film's production.[12]

The racism in *Herzsprung* is revealed as endemic, even constituent of the east German provincial mentality. Not even Jakob (Günter Lamprecht), the solid antifascist character, is above such discrimination, even if his comments are less a question of prejudice than they are of political correctness. Though dismissive of the neologisms, Afro-American and Afro-German, he assures his daughter that he has nothing against 'Neger'. Despite these narrative developments, Misselwitz does not investigate the root of racism in her film, a failure that leads Nora M. Alter to question the director's own attitude to the issue.[13] If Misselwitz avoids any deep analysis of the youth's racism, she does at least focus on its faulty logic. The graffiti that reads 'Foreigners Out. Send them to the Camps' is a slogan that has little context in a village seemingly devoid of any other ethnic or foreign national groups. Later, one of the newly-shorn men denies his involvement, but identifies Russians, Poles and even 'Neger' as threats to the local economy, recommending their deportation to concentration camps.

The rise in right-wing extremism in the east since unification has proved a peculiarly difficult issue for (feature) filmmakers. The presence of the radical right is often acknowledged through obvious signifiers – typically skinheads in bomber jackets and jackboots – but the appeal of right-wing politics for east Germany's disenfranchised youth is rarely investigated in any detail. Instead, the turn towards such radicalism is seen as a natural and inevitable reaction to social, political and economic developments. The fact that there are very few ethnic minorities in the eastern states does not preclude such prejudice. Indeed, 'antiforeigner sentiment virtually without foreigners' is, as Patrick R. Ireland has noted, 'a puzzling phenomenon' in the east.[14] In *Vergiss Amerika* (*Forget America*, Vanessa Jopp, 2000), a film which follows the relationship between three friends, each trying to realize their dreams in a provincial eastern town, the protagonist's brother undergoes a similar transformation from sullen teenager to shaven headed 'Fascho', a development that receives little commentary, as if such a conversion were a natural reaction to small town anomie.[15] A similar explanation is proposed by Mirko Borscht in his film, *Kombat Sechzehn* (*Combat Sixteen*, 2005), in which the attraction of the extreme right is an inevitable consequence of living in the east's grimmer districts (Frankfurt an der Oder), with even its young, urbane west German (from Frankfurt am Main) succumbing to the camaraderie offered by his new right-wing peers.[16]

In many ways, *Herzsprung* resembles Bernd Böhlich's TV drama, *Landschaft mit Dornen*, also made in 1992. *Herzsprung* even offers actor Ben Becker the opportunity to reprise his earlier role of provincial gang leader. The delinquents' shift to the right is in both films strikingly similar. In Böhlich's film, racism is a symptom of post-unification malaise, though there is no identifiable catalyst. The only evidence of outsiders' presence in the town is a newly opened bank, an arrival that is perceived by some as a threat to the community, and a portent of the unwelcome changes to come. The arrival of strangers in the small community fuels the local yobs' hostility, who employ the vocabulary of the far right: 'We're not going to let ourselves be broken. Not us and not our country – Germany. We're going to take a stand against the immigrants. We're going to take a stand for Germany'.

Escaping Heimat

If, as Morley and Robins suggest, 'Heimat is rooted in that intolerance of difference, that fear of the "other"', then these films may be regarded as genuinely concerned with notions of Heimat, if not the notional aestheticized Heimat that is central to the Heimatfilm.[17] Intolerance of outsiders is frequently in evidence. It is only the chief protagonists who are willing to accept others, a sentiment that distinguishes them from their own community and disconnects them from their Heimat. Often, the rejection of local values eventuates a search for some replacement Heimat. Tangible evidence of otherness, of lives beyond the east German provinces, can therefore be seen as an attempt to connect with some distant authentic culture, one whose distinctiveness, unlike that of the post-communist east, remains assured. The distance between the east German provinces and the exoticized, far off locations reduces the probability of the protagonists ever realizing their dreams. The fantasized lands remain idealized sites onto which the protagonists, who invariably fail to escape even their immediate environment, continue to project their hopes and dreams. Gabriele Kreutzner has argued that the (west) German left felt the need to identify with remote cultures by way of compensating for a German culture, whose authenticity has been undermined by American society.[18] Similarly, one might argue that the interest these east Germans express for *extracultural* articles and people (trinkets, talismans, etc.) reflects a desire to connect with cultures far removed from western influence. No longer following a course mapped by the state, the east Germans in the films look for guidance elsewhere. Scientific Marxism is replaced by superstition and magic; exotic artefacts replace what one might call the 'objets d'état', the signifiers of 'banal nationalism' that were everywhere on display in the GDR, on murals and office walls, on desks and above classroom blackboards.[19] Ironically, it also marks the abrupt end of the east Germans' fascination for, and festishization of, western consumer products, which were especially prized in the GDR. The exotic can only retain its status if its idealized character remains unchallenged; it is only when such unverified assumptions are contested that the perceptions of the other begin to crumble. This is the case in the east Germans' view of the west. Several of the films under discussion here reflect the east Germans' declining interest in the west. The state that previously represented the ideal other, the superior counter-image of the east, is exposed as a false or corrupt ideal. Its cities prove hostile, its authorities unsympathetic. The once sought-after markers of western-ness are no longer signifiers of a more successful and appealing culture but reduced to being mere commodities. Financially beyond reach, they only confirm the east's material deficiency and emphasize their second-class status.

The east Germans' waning interest in western goods, which would eventually lead to Ostalgie's revival of GDR merchandise, is already in evidence in these films. The commodities of advanced capitalist production are rejected and interest shifts towards the products of other cultures, to items representative of more authentic or alternative ways of life. Thus, amulets and lucky charms appear repeatedly, suggesting a substituted enthralment with the exotic and mysterious, and providing characters with material evidence of an imagined magical life beyond the drab reality of their immediate borders and compensating for their delusion with the west.[20]

In Rainer Simon's first post-DEFA film, *Fernes Land Pa-isch* (*Far Away Country Pa-Isch*), made in 1993 but not released until 2000, a foreign object, this time an African artefact, similarly becomes a symbol of otherness and a mascot of escape for Umberto (non-professional actor, Jens Schumann), the teenage east German protagonist.²¹ Simon's film is one of several films to view post-unification society through the experiences of young adolescents on the run. The tendency to use lay actors in the main roles of these films was intended to lend greater authenticity to these interpretations of life in the east in which the young protagonists' course across the region offers an insight into the east Germans' material and psychological condition. In Helmut Dziuba's *Jana und Jan* (*Jana and Jan*, 1992), the seasoned DEFA director follows the route of two teenage runaways, who abscond from a juvenile detention centre just as the state is coming apart, as they make their way across the forlorn territories of the east towards the west, a journey that comes to a symbolic halt at the former border. Their final resting point is a redundant watchtower on the German–German border. Their hideout situates them not just spatially but temporally – between the GDR and the FRG, between an unforgiving past and an uncertain future. The film offers no salvation for its young couple. The hurried ending quashes any hope that the viewer may have invested in the pair's future: the scene suddenly switches from the deserted watchtower, where Jana lies pregnant and in pain, to an anonymous hospital room, where her distraught face and anguished cry provide the final sound and image. Dziuba's abrupt and unexpected conclusion refuses to mark the birth on the border as Germany's new beginning. It remains unclear whether the final yell is a consequence of Jana's labour or of a more tragic outcome.

Life is hardly more positive for the young protagonist of *Fernes Land Paisch*. Umberto lives in a small town in Sachsen, beyond the centres of political change in Berlin, Dresden and Leipzig. Like many of the characters in these films, Umberto dreams of escaping this particularly depressed and depressing milieu – a world that revolves around his alcoholic mother, violent, asocial friends with few prospects (the kind who are transformed into right-wing bullies in Misselwitz's and Böhlich's films) – and visiting Africa, the home of his one-time friend and father to Bianca, his half-sister. Simon's film is rare in allowing its protagonist to escape his environment – brother and sister relocate to Hamburg with their mother, who dreams of a better life in the west – though the destination does not symbolize any new beginning. The city's sex shops and arcades may present a colourful, neon-lit alternative to the dull greys and browns of Sachsen but the film counters the east's popular image of the west as one defined by material comfort and social freedom, and focuses instead on the extant social and economic problems. The tower block in which Umberto and his family live is, at first sight, hardly more comfortable than their home in the east, and the local environment has its own social underclass and behavioural problems in the form of prostitutes, teenage gang culture, and domestic abuse – issues that GDR propaganda always identified as a western problem. While the change in residence provides no change in his mother's circumstances, a vicious circle revolving around her alcoholism, financial problems and casual prostitution, Umberto's independence is at least facilitated by his job as a mechanic and the disposable income that this generates. Despite this, Simon's protagonist shows no interest in conforming to the society around him; nor are there any mechanisms in place to facilitate such integration. A recurring visual motif of a tightrope walker functions as a metaphor for the balancing act that Umberto must master if he is not to fall through the social net. Hamburg proves an alienating environment and the east German is drawn to other marginal groups (prostitutes, ethnic minorities). Africa continues to loom large in Umberto's imagination and the deteriorating domestic situation, his mother's prostitution, social security inspections and finally his mother's hospitalization prompt him to renew his journey to Africa, and he heads south with Bianca on a stolen motorbike. Despite the generic impulse of this narrative development, Simon's film resists becoming a road movie and any escape that might entail.[22] Umberto and his sister finally return to the east, a journey facilitated by east German solidarity – a chance meeting with a fellow compatriot, the real-life footballer, Ulf Kirsten, results in a trip back east in the Bayer Leverkusen team bus. The eastern identity and support exist only outside of the east. Such camaraderie does not manifest itself in the eastern capital, and Berlin proves as alienating as Hamburg and Simon's protagonists retreat again to society's boundaries, a strange nether world of counter cultural figures, addicts and thieves. And it is here, among the outcast and the marginalized, that the pair for the first time appear to have found some footing. But this is no cosy home for the republic's dropouts. Umberto's shelter comes at a price and, in a Dickensian touch, he is expected to steal for his supper, a course of action that he reluctantly adopts.

Of all the post-unification films, Simon's is perhaps the most despairing. In *Fernes Land Pa-isch*, the director scrutinizes German society from below and offers a narrative that stretches beyond the bleak post-GDR provinces to Hamburg's equally grim concrete estates and finally to the nation's new capital, revealing the west as a society already burdened with its own problems. There is no hope in Simon's film and certainly no blossoming landscapes; community has disintegrated and in its stead is a new society characterized by exploitation and corruption. For all their travels, the two children are unable to find a replacement Heimat. Life in Hamburg presents them with the potential for material improvement but the housing estate offers no sense of community. *Fernes Land Pa-isch* does not discover the support network of family or community that is on display in the comedies. Where those films exhibit a unity of purpose, a regional identity that buttresses the eastern communities in times of adversity, the eastern community in Simon's film is both fractious and fractured. Nor does the German welfare state, here represented by officious social workers more interested in punishment than assistance, fare well. The pair's introduction to the group of outcasts living on the periphery of society is the closest they come to experiencing some communal unity; but they are unable to transcend their second class status even within this group. The siblings' futile efforts to find a replacement home and community makes their return to the provinces, to the only Heimat they have known, inevitable. The return is no happy home-coming and the final scene, set in a desolate spot in the east, ends with his sister crying as she watches Umberto dancing wildly around a hut in flames, to the imagined rhythm of African drums. The beat becomes more feverish, as their shelter and dreams of a different, better future go up in smoke.

Compared with these endings, Johannes Hebendanz's *Asphaltflimmern* (*Flickering Roads*, 1994), is practically upbeat. The young west German di-rector's film also follows teenagers on the run, though unusually the prin-cipal characters are not east German. Hebendanz pairs a west German joy rider and a diminutive Romanian immigrant who, despite their ostensible differences, form an unlikely friendship as they travel through the east, where they are later joined by Philippa, an east German waitress and petty thief, who effectively becomes a surrogate mother to the two boys. The re-lationship that develops between the three travellers can be interpreted as a positive solution to antagonisms between east and west which even allows for the inclusion of the otherwise excluded (both Germans are ready to help the young Romanian find his brother, though the quest is unsuc-cessful). However, the characters' mutual understanding and friendship do not grow and blossom against east German landscapes. Hebendanz avoids any edifying conclusion that might outline the possibility for a har-monious and integrated society in Germany. Having established a bond that transcends age, culture and gender, the characters leave the eastern states, which are characterized as an unwelcoming environment, with Italy their spontaneously chosen destination.

Failed Utopia?

Where Misselwitz's film reports on post-Wende life in the rural east through a narrative that is confined to the geographical limits of East Prignitz, and Simon's film traces life among Germany's underclass, Sanders-Brahms's Wendefilm provides a far more ambitious study of the east. A long cele-brated filmmaker, who was actively involved in trying to save the east German film industry after unification, Sanders-Brahms was one of the few high-profile west German directors to focus on the collapse of the GDR.[23] *Apfelbäume* focuses on provincial life set within the broad sweep of Honecker's era, beginning some time in the 1970s and followed into the 1980s and up to 1990. Sanders-Brahms's film addresses a series of related Wende issues, including failed utopias, the corrupting nature of office and the GDR's economic demise, which are interlaced in an intense relationship drama that revolves around two young idealists and a corrupt Party official.
  The GDR represented in *Apfelbäume* is, despite the bucolic title, inex-orably bleak and though the periodic shots of the eponymous trees during

the different seasons represent the cycle of life, the dreariness serves as a metaphor for the state's emotional austerity. As with many of the films under discussion, the opening shot establishes the grim awfulness of the east German landscape. A voiceover, employing standard GDR phrases of progress and improvement contrasts sharply with the images on view. There is little evidence of the state's forward thinking, or of its commitment to the people in such an environment. The material deterioration of the roads and buildings hints at a related breakdown in social relations.

Sanders-Brahms's film differs from the others already mentioned in this chapter in one important aspect. The eastern provinces are portrayed as ideologically and environmentally contaminated and left to ruin by the state's political custodians long before unification had been proposed as the origin of the region's problems. Yet *Apfelbäume* is not simply an extended criticism of the GDR. The opening scene may be consistent with the director's early social critical filmmaking, but the film's formal character fluctuates between social realism and, in terms of German cinema, its generic antonym, the Heimatfilm. Having introduced the GDR of popular (western) imagination in the opening sequence, the location and tone alters. A peaceful and harmonious setting replaces the hostile environment of the former scene. At her idyllic country home, the narrator's grandmother (DEFA's grand dame, Steffi Spira) sits, sage-like in dappled light, among the trees and tall grasses adjacent to her property, offering words of wisdom to Lena (Johanna Schall), her granddaughter. Representing a traditional Germany, her old-fashioned ideas and superstitions contrast with Lena's modern paroles and parroted slogans. This pastoral life is given as dignified and pure, enveloped in an idealized conception of Heimat. The rest of the GDR is presented as the antithesis of such sentimental idealism, and the state's politics and ideology are, in practice, a matter of drab routine; the land appears as worn-out as the language of progress.

Despite this portrayal of East Germany as a dreary, ideologically complacent state, Sanders-Brahms's film does not deny the idealism of the GDR. Socialist utopianism is revealed as a project that has been undermined by the state's fraudulent officeholders, a collection of careerists and corrupt ideologues. The discrepancy between the grandmother's existence, a way of life that is traditional, natural and outside of German history, and the GDR *Alltag* (everyday life) is repeatedly emphasized. The old way of life has been lost to political reality. Lena's idealism and her grandmother's traditional values are at odds with the society around them, a society manipulated by the state. It is the state's mismanagement of the GDR that is the target of Sanders-Brahms's film and not the GDR per se. Initially, Lena and her husband, Heinz (Thomas Büchel), positively embody the idealism of the GDR. Their subsequent disillusionment is a response to the state's lack of effective progress and the administration's representatives. Their scepticism at the authorities' hollow rhetoric and the Party apparatchiks does not preclude their commitment to socialist idealism, a position that was by no means untypical in the GDR.

Criticism of the state is apparent in the characterization of the local officials, represented here by Sienke (Udo Kroschwald), who repeatedly abuses his power: influencing others for personal gain, molesting Lena and finally abandoning the state whose name and ideology he has so staunchly defended. In the end, he betrays his own community and the collective when he returns to the east after unification in order to sell the apple orchards that will be cleared to make way for a theme park. Ideologically disingenuous, exploitative and self-aggrandizing, Sienke (and other members of the local elite) confirm stereotypes of the GDR administration, an aspect of the film that was criticized by eastern reviewers but hardly noticed by those in the west.[24] Only once Sienke becomes involved in the pair's relationship does their commitment to the GDR and to one another deteriorate. His malign interest in the couple amounts to a kind of moral and ideological contamination, and the pair's relationship succumbs to paranoia and deceit. Their principles are compromised by the state as Lena conducts an affair with one of the *Bonzen* (fat cats), while Heinz betrays his ideals and his wife by becoming a Stasi informant.

The state's intrusion into individual relationships is a theme which has been explored in other post-unification narratives, notably Heiner Carow's *Verfehlung* (*The Mistake*, 1991). Carow's film, which is set in the late stages of the GDR, portrays the relationship between an east German widow, living alone in the provinces, and a west German man. The relationship is put under pressure by the woman's family who fear reprisals, and by the authorities – as the result of a jealous Mayor, who objects to the affair for personal rather than political reasons though his censure is voiced according to the latter. Like Sanders-Brahms's persecutor, Carow's villain, though portrayed as a somewhat tragic figure, embodies the chauvinism and manipulation of the GDR authorities. However, *Verfehlung* offers no redemption, no escape to pastures new. After being raped by the mayor, Carow's protagonist shoots her assailant, which results in her freedom from persecution but also in her incarceration. The east Germans' freedom from SED repression is not extended to her and in the final scene, set during the *Wende* when the east Germans have finally been released from their confinement, she must face a new period of internment.

Paradise Lost?

The films discussed in this chapter convey the feeling of loss that is linked to the difficulties of transition and the disorientation following unification. In *Apfelbäume*, such loss is more directly concerned with life before unification. Above all, it is the GDR's failings that are criticized. The GDR's forty-year existence is outlined as a wasted opportunity, a period in which idealism was sacrificed to ideological expediency. Attempts to develop a society according to a principled, honest socialism could not but fail in a state that perceived any criticism as treachery and in which lip-service and self-advancement replaced genuine ideological commitment. It is not the ideology that is the target of the director's criticism but the regime's failure to realize a truly socialist society. The end of the state is therefore understood in terms of loss – a loss of the GDR's latent potential to which the left always clung. For one sceptical reviewer, the film's narrative had more to do with the unrealized aspirations of the 1968 generation than any direct engagement with unification.[25] The criticism of the GDR's failed potential is unequivocally articulated by Heinz when he berates the drunken *Bonzen* at a harvest festival: 'A dream, it was a dream of humanity. Of freedom. And equality. And brotherliness. Not brownnosing and scams and lies.' This same line is repeated towards the end of the film, as Sienke (in a Mercedes, the western status symbol that has replaced his former GDR vehicle of status, the Wolga) cruises past the orchards made barren by the diggers. Updated, the sentiment corresponds with new disappointments and grievances, specifically the hasty dissolution of the GDR. Inflexible capitalist ethics have replaced the east's intransigent ideology as the threat to the eastern community. The hurried union with the FRG has overtaken any hope for reform and ruled out any alternatives.

Like others of her generation, the director was eager to emphasize that her criticism targeted the SED's supervision and not the state's original direction: 'it's the socialist paradise that's shown in this film, which doesn't work at all, of course. In a way *it's a sort of paradise*, until the apple trees are destroyed' [my emphasis].[26] The orchards function as a rather awkward metaphor and the director's own admission that they represent a socialist Eden and their subsequent deracination amounts to the 'degradation of the GDR' reflects the left's difficulty in letting go of the GDR, which they regard as sound in theory but flawed in practice.[27] West German intellectuals' post-GDR melancholy, where 'mourning utopia replaced an engagement with new realities', is in evidence in *Apfelbäume*, and the film's conclusion offers just such a flight from reality.[28] Though their idealism is in tatters and their state has come under the *Treuhand*'s knife, Sanders-Brahms's protagonists are given a lifeline. In an ending that is as fanciful as those of the early comedies, the reconciled couple retreats even further from their limited locality to the smallholding left by Lena's grandmother in order to tend her small orchard, a plan that denies the progressive rhetoric of the GDR and resists the development initiatives of the new capitalist order.

These films ultimately deny the integrative possibilities and the fictional opportunities put forward by the comedies. The few integrative impulses that do exist in the films are not countenanced. Discussing social communication theory and its relevance to film, Philip Schlesinger has noted that whilst nationality 'becomes an objective function of communicative competence and belonging', not all nations are able to integrate new members – foreigners or other marginalized groups – and 'may throw the process into reverse by expulsion or even extermination' of these outsiders.[29] It is not only the non-Germans in the films who become the victims of local prejudice. Those members of the community whose way of thinking departs from the hegemonic order are expelled and even in some cases murdered. Johanna's relationship with the Stranger leads ultimately to her death. Umberto's relationship with Tschibo (also a mixed race relationship) fails before it has even had time to begin. Significantly, the films also mark the passing of any localized co-operation: there is no evidence of any community identity supporting the marginalized communities against the challenges of transition; individuals are unable to find any comfort or retreat within the niche of their families. Instead, the characters are left as individuated and isolated figures, alone in a landscape of ruins. *Heimat* GDR has ceased to exist and they are left in a kind of vacuum from which they are rarely permitted to escape. Whilst the physical boundary that separated them from freedom may have disappeared, other circumstances continue to restrict their movement and their futures. Economically limited but socially adrift, these east Germans are prisoners not of ideology but of the provinces.

Post-unification Landscapes: Charting Memory

The ruined features of the GDR that are glimpsed in the films discussed above play a more prominent role in other films of the period, with the remnants of the past emphasizing the east as a site of inactivity and squandered hopes. But the foregrounding of the GDR's material conditions in these films is not intended simply to confirm the east's economic hardships; nor is it an attempt to muster sympathy for a land clearly in need of financial investment. The mining operations that have fallen into disrepair or the disused manufacturing premises serve as important reflexive prompts. They function as 'memory beacons', potent reminders of the passing of the workers' and peasants' state, highlighting the neglected condition of the east and exposing as false the official rhetoric of the GDR as a state committed to progress and achievement.[30] The films therefore counter the former state's 'monopoly on social memory' and the GDR myth of continued development and economic self-reliance.[31] At the same time, and no less important, the sites render the promised 'blossoming landscapes' as a similarly utopian vision.

The representation of the eastern territory in these films approximates to Smith's idea of 'ethnoscape', in which the territory mirrors the ethnic community and is historicized by the communal events and processes whose relics and monuments dot its landscape, so that the land comes to belong to a people in the same way as the people belong to a particular land.[32]

The east Germans may not be members of a separate *ethnie* in the sense that Smith means (though at least one scholar has suggested that the eastern population *is* ethnically distinguishable from their western com-patriots), but his analysis does have some relevance to our discussion.[33] Land and property laws did, as the previous chapter outlined, problema-tize ownership of east German land, and the countless disputes after 1989 exacerbated east/west relations. But people's connection with their sur-roundings is as much a question of historical and geographical identifica-tion as it is an issue of legal possession. The landscape is inextricably linked to the people's history – to the GDR. The ruins on display may not resem-ble the architectural remnants of a past age so beloved by the Romantics but their significance is the same, for they come to represent a lost time and serve as mnemonic landmarks that fix the local population historically and geographically. Lowenthal stresses the importance of such markers for col-lective memory:

> Tangible survivals provide a vivid immediacy that helps to assure us that there really was a past. Physical remains have their limitations as informants, to be sure: they are themselves mute, requiring interpretation; their continual but differential erosion and demolition skews the record; and their substantial survival conjures up a past more static than could have been the case. But however depleted by time and use, relics remain essential bridges between then and now. They confirm or deny what we think of it, symbolize or memorialize communal links over time, and provide archaeological metaphors that illumine the processes of history and memory.[34]

But the eastern landscape has become a kind of palimpsest, where the signs of the previous administration are under threat of erasure by new building projects, and by agricultural and economic policies.[35] Certain features (the regime's ubiquitous symbols for instance, the emblems and flags, the State statuary) have already disappeared and others will do so.[36] Some of these films therefore count as the last visual records of particular GDR markers which have all but vanished (the watchtowers are an obvious example).

Landscape features prominently in many of the films with the sites repre-senting the faded symbols and hopes of the former state. In *Die Vergebung* (*Forgiveness*, Andreas Höntsch, 1994), the representation undergoes a number of permutations. Scenes set during the GDR establish the east as a contaminated region, exposing the coal and chemical industries' detri-mental effects on the landscape (a land laid bare by open cast-mining; noxious gases that pollute the atmosphere) and on the people (skin con-tamination, respiratory complaints). In Andreas Kleinert's *Neben der Zeit* (*Outside Time*, 1995), the debris of the past is on display throughout: a derelict swimming pool, deserted army barracks, a scrap heap of old East German cars. However, the material disintegration does not simply serve as an indictment of the state's disastrous economic and environmental poli-cies. The sites featured are places of local significance and relevance, since, for good or bad, they constituted a nexus for the individual and the collective, the community and the state. So while they symbolize the state in terms of production (obsolete and fragile though many of them were), they were equally important to the people as the lifeblood of local communities, offering a source of income and as a basis for identification and professional self-esteem. Building socialism and, *ipso facto*, a socialist identity, had been the primary purpose of these industries even if the technology and manufacturing procedures had in reality made this target increasingly unlikely. The state's economic neglect and complete disregard for environmental issues not only resulted in physical health problems, it also undermined any confidence in the state's apparent commitment to the welfare of its citizens. Charges of environmental neglect typically met with official denial and counter-accusations which labelled the detractors 'enemies of the state'. This was not simply a matter of curbing any criticism of the state. It was necessary for the SED to promote the land as lovingly maintained for the socialist cause. The eastern territory was understood as inviolable, as a land in which population and state were investing in the future in order to build the east German Heimat.[37] Industry was to be instrumental in achieving that ideal; paradoxically, it was their noxious emissions and other pollutants that undermined and corrupted Heimat. Their obsolescence became proof of the state's failure to devote itself to realising its own ideals. The images of crumbling industrial sites are, then, more than just a comment on the GDR's economic mismanagement or an attempt to mirror political realities but reflect the population's precarious identity.

Though the regime is implicated as the administration ultimately responsible for the region's parlous state, the films do not represent a totalizing critique of life in the GDR. They show that the GDR is irreducible and cannot be portrayed simply in terms of moral and material decay. It is also revealed as a state in which there was room for utopian hopes and individual idealism, though these individual utopian impulses are by no means analogous to the state's progressive values, a dichotomy between citizen and state that is repeatedly emphasized. The films are less concerned with establishing a case against the SED administration than they are with tracing the east Germans' life during the transition. The focus on the east's material conditions enables them to reflect the disintegration of the means of identification, which has repercussions for both the individual and the community, as they try to come to terms with the present often whilst occupied with thoughts and memories of the past.

Andreas Kleinert's two films, *Verlorene Landschaft* and *Neben der Zeit*, Andreas Höntsch's *Die Vergebung* and, to a lesser extent, Andreas Dresen's *Stilles Land* represent a conscious recording of the passing of time, of the shift from the GDR past to the FRG present. Though many of the films reference broader issues, they centre on individual stories and on personal histories without abandoning political and social realities. These films chronicle the east's transition; the documentary-like fragments that inflect and interrupt the narratives represent a conscious decision to record the actual, to imbue the films with moments of authenticity. These moments – long takes of locals drinking beer; close-ups of worn faces; the recurring shot of an empty landscape, empty roads – offer a still life of the east. The inclusion of these genuine details clearly attempts to lend the narratives a visual authority, a degree of truth that was absent in the *Wende* comedies and which had been supplanted by popular stereotypes and histories of the east Germans. The directors' reasons for concentrating on the east's simple stories may not be driven merely by an uncritical desire for preservation, but there is an appreciable determination to make a record of that which is quickly disappearing. And generally it is to the rural locations that these filmmakers venture. In contrast to metropolitan locations, which have traditionally provided the setting for politicking and consequently for change, the provinces, and especially the rural provinces, are often the last to undergo any transformation.

Stories from the Margins

The filmmakers' tendency to restrict themselves to such enclaves, rather than embarking on ambitious narratives about the actual collapse of the SED-state, may also have been a question of practicality. Depicting revolutions is a difficult and costly affair and throughout the history of cinema there have been relatively few successful examples. In addition, the east German revolution's lack of action and, crucially, lack of leader – there were pivotal figures but no defining revolutionary hero – might explain some directors' hesitancy in representing the population's bid for freedom, though the uprising was not quite as peaceful as is often thought. To date, only Frank Beyer's two-part television drama, *Nikolaikirche* (*St. Nicholas Church*, 1993), has ventured to provide a comprehensive account of the unrest that would eventually result in the GDR's downfall. Confirming Habermas's theory that the east Germans later surrendered the revolutionary character of the uprising, the films are disinclined to acknowledge the events of 1989 directly.[38] For the most part, the films set within this timeframe acknowledge the demonstrations only in passing; the revolution's fault line is distant and its tremors are only barely perceptible.

Though the political developments are sidelined, events left to develop off-camera, the films do engage with political and social realities. Of primary concern is the social and economic collapse in the eastern territories – the torn fabric of east German society that covers communities, families, and regional identities. Avoiding a historical overview of the period, the films do not simply aim to provide an impression of the period and the place but seek to highlight individual details and to articulate the concerns of its subjects. Pierre Nora's comment that 'memory attaches itself to sites, whereas history attaches itself to events' might be seen as a description of these films' approach.[39] Indeed, it is memory, as opposed to history, that plays the more significant role in most post-unification films. The films naturally have some historical value for film scholars, but their concern is not with representing historical accounts of the GDR and the Wende, but with stimulating memories of the GDR – whether good or bad is not the issue. The significance lies in the supposed authenticity of memory over history; the local population's experiences – or 'mass individual memory' – acquire a legitimacy that was frequently occluded by the GDR's official history and which, in the new Germany, is in danger of being subverted by new historical accounts. Nora says as much when he writes: 'At the heart of history is a critical discourse that is antithetical to spontaneous memory. History is perpetually suspicious of memory, and its true mission is to suppress and destroy it.'[40] The post-GDR accounts of life in the east provide a space in which memory competes with history and which, as the final chapter will discuss, validated the popularity of Ostalgie.

Still Life: Representing the East

The young east German director Andreas Dresen's debut feature film, *Stilles Land*, avoids the familiar locations of protest and the demonstration and dramas that were on view in the GDR's urban centres in Berlin, Dresden and Leipzig. Eschewing the action, though not the significance, of the escape route to the West that was suddenly and unexpectedly made possible by Hungary's relaxed border control, and the mass demonstrations in East German cities, Dresen focuses instead on the almost inert provinces of the east (though not mentioned, the location is Anklam in Mecklenburg). The film's title works both as a description of the town's geographical distance from the tumultuous events and as a reference to a kind of mental detachment that is discernible among the small-town population. The film's characters, all members of a provincial theatre ensemble, lack the pro-active communal spirit and solidarity on display in *Wende* comedies and are generally aloof or confrontational. Dresen's film charts the attempts of young theatre director Kai Fincke (Thorsten Merten) to stage a production of Beckett's 'Waiting for Godot'. Recently arrived from Berlin, Fincke's idealism, passion and choice of material for his debut production are, initially, the source of some conflict between director and a cast that is both unfamiliar with anything but standards and unaccustomed to such idealism.[41] Their objection to the play is not based on Beckett's incompatibility with GDR ideology and dramaturgy (in fact, the play had first been staged by Wolfgang Engel in 1987) but because it strikes the provincial actors as abstruse and irrelevant. The cast members are more concerned with getting information about the events taking place at the western borders (their location being so remote that they are beyond even the west German broadcasting ranges) than they are with staging Beckett's

Figure 3.2 *Stilles Land*
Still lives: Kai Fincke (Thorsten Merten) and Claudia (Jeanette Arndt) in *Stilles Land* (Andreas Dresen, 1992)
Stills reproduced with kind permission of Andreas Dresen and Wolfgang Pfeiffer

absurdist drama. Kai's vision and commitment to the play, his explanation that it has great relevance 'for our times', initially meets with little understanding. For the actor playing the role of Beckett's Estragon, however, its relevance indeed proves too much. In one rehearsal, he reveals such profound hopelessness at the prospect of waiting for Godot that Kai raves over the power and emotional intensity just witnessed: 'it was really good; truly depressing'. But the passion the actor brings to these lines is drawn not from the play; it articulates a frustration, frequently heard in the GDR, at forever having to wait, whether for material goods, or for bureaucratic decisions or for political reform.[42]

Despite the play's bearing on the contemporary situation, *Stilles Land* is not a metafiction that presents Beckett's play as an allegory of the GDR. Its relevance is Kai's fixation, of course, and not Dresen's.[43] Kai is so preoccupied with his project and its significance for East German society that he largely fails to register the events taking place beyond the theatre, weighing up these developments only when they threaten to overtake, disturb or trivialize his interpretation of Beckett. With each new account of events taking place at the border, the director quickly redrafts his 'concept' of the play. While Dresen's film satirizes the obsessive artist and the small-town cast (one suspects a degree of self-parody, given that Dresen, like his father, had some experience as a director of provincial theatres), the film resists any explicit criticism of his characters, an approach that has come to define his films. The relative generosity of Dresen's and Laila Stieler's script even extends to the theatre manager and the Party official appointed to the theatre, neither of whom conforms to the prevailing one-dimensional characterizations of GDR bureaucrats and officials. Made at a time when the GDR past was being discussed and filed according to narrow discursive parameters which largely ignored subjective accounts (where these did not confirm the west's view of the GDR as a dictatorship), Dresen's film came under some criticism for being apolitical, and the director found himself defending the film's lack of political punch.

As with his east German contemporaries, Dresen's focus is not on the extraordinary (the escapes, the demonstrations, the arrests) but on the ordinary, an approach that has characterized his oeuvre from his film school debut, *So schnell geht es nach Istanbul* (*Short Cut to Istanbul*, 1991) to his Silver Bear winner at the Berlin Film Festival, *Halbe Treppe* (*Grill Point*, 2002) and *Sommer vorm Balkon* (*Summer in Berlin*, 2005). The film strives for an authentic representation of the daily conditions in the GDR, with the mise-en-scène revealing the daily features of the east German state – drunken men in the *Volkshaus* bar, badly maintained housing, shabby interiors. At other times, the camera's gaze is fixed on the environment, employing a visual style that tends towards documentary realism, a mode preferred by Dresen's role models and one with which he has continued to experiment.[44] The long, static shots of the bleak winter landscape emphasize both the inertia of the remote rural location and provide physical anchorage for the characters' emotional atrophy. The symbiosis of the physical and the emotional, of external and internal, is emphasized in the cutting, with scenes suddenly switching from dialogical exchanges and interior scenes, to silent, exterior shots.

The film acknowledges political and social circumstances – the east's material shortcomings, the frustrations that derive from such lack, the quietist mentality that pervaded East German society.[45] But a political reckoning is not the incentive for the film. *Stilles Land* calls no one to account. The film nevertheless provides an insight into the everyday attitudes that underpinned the regime. Typical of the niche society, the members of the theatre avoid the directly political; all frustrations are introverted, all protestations are impotent. A (drunken) decision to write to Honecker demanding openness is the sole act of political brio and comes too late, not least because the theatre manager, played by celebrated DEFA actor Kurt Böwe, does not post the appeal until after Egon Krenz has been instated as the new Secretary General and the danger of repercussions has diminished. Other circumstances inhibit any opportunities for possible heroism. The play's political edge is dulled by real-life events. The decision to witness events in Berlin is literally stalled by the aging company bus; the characters are once again stranded in the provinces.

Significantly, the troupe's most idealistic character refuses to hitchhike to the capital and participate in or witness the true *coup de théâtre*. That Kai's passion and commitment to change is ultimately limited to his production satirizes the role of the dissidents and counter-cultural figures in the GDR. Preoccupied by his work and idealistic only in terms of abstract notions of utopia, his intellectual pursuits obscure his vision of events taking place around him and finally wreck his romance with his assistant who is more tempted by the real drama happening in Berlin than by Kai and his enthusiasm for Bloch and Fromm. Desperate though he is to keep his play relevant, he is incapable of recognizing the revolution's potential and, *contra* Bloch, largely fails to grasp the new possibilities available to him.[46]

On release, Dresen's film failed to stimulate the kind of interest and acclaim it had won at film festivals, though the director's later successes (notably *Halbe Treppe* but also *Willenbrock* (2005), an adaptation of Christoph Hein's novel of the same name) and *Sommer vorm Balkon* (*Summer in Berlin*, 2005) have resulted in a belated appreciation of his earlier work, and the film is frequently screened on the anniversary of the GDR's collapse. Since there is no actual evidence to explain its lack of resonance with audiences, one can only speculate as to the reasons. Dresen himself provides a clue when he explains that his motivation for making the film was 'also to show what everyday life was like in this kind of state'.[47] *Stilles Land* engages with the realities of life in the east (an aspect of the film that was warmly greeted by eastern reviewers but questioned by those writing in western papers and journals), and in so doing, it underplays the revolution as a moment of heroic collective participation and nationwide civil disobedience, again confirming Habermas's point. The mini rally that takes place in Anklam towards the end of the film, in which a few people holding protest signs walk in circles, is looked on by a couple of bemused policemen, who are more concerned with the forthcoming football match between Berlin and their rivals Dresden. The only moment of non-compliance occurs off-screen when one of the cast is caught up in a wave of arrests by the Berlin police. What is first recounted in a factual manner to admiring colleagues assumes more heroic and mythic qualities with each retelling. The memory of the event is finally divorced from the actual experiences, the supplementary details of brave opposition compensating for its banality.[48] *Stilles Land*'s inclusion of such details is not an attempt to humorize the GDR or the historic events but simply to moderate post-wall accounts of the GDR and its collapse. The director is certainly aware of the emerging stereotypes and clichés that are essential to characterization in many of the period's narratives, and subtly subverts them: the German who arrives at the theatre from the west therefore arrives not in the standard Mercedes, but in a modest Saab. Other characterizations similarly destabilize familiar Wende figures – the unresponsive policemen, the self-styled activist.

Made within two years of the wall being dismantled, Dresen's film can be seen as an early example of archiving the GDR in a manner that resists the prevailing historical account of the period in favour of something more nuanced and ambiguous, in which subjective memory balances the objective version.

Memory and Loss

It is fitting to include Andreas Kleinert's *Verlorene Landschaft* in a discussion of films that wrestle with the idea of a lost or spoiled Heimat, even if Kleinert's film differs visually from the other films of this period. The director's use of symbolic imagery and the film's formal experimentation make for an early, abstract meditation on a re-involvement with the lost landscape of the east that distinguishes it from the social realism to which the majority of the other films mostly adhere. There are, nevertheless, commonalities here, not least the film's thematic pre-occupation. Kleinert's (debut) feature contemplates the meaning of Heimat and, in tracing the protagonist's return to his childhood home, offers a poetic treatment on the subject, which considers memory and loss, the balance of the subjective and the objective, and acknowledges the discrepancy between individual experience and depersonalized history. Memories of the past collide with new and actual confrontations of the present, offering insight into the GDR's isolation from the West and the problems faced in reconciling differences that have evolved between the two states.

But in *Verlorene Landschaft* memory is not merely adumbrated, sketched out in metaphorical images, it is the conceptual glue binding the narrative, which relies heavily on chronological disjuncture (analepsis and prolepsis are a mainstay of the film). A phone call to a west German politician informing him of his parents' recent death is the prompt for the protagonist's (Elias, played by Roland Schäfer) decision to revisit his east German Heimat, a journey into the lost landscapes of the title, which assumes both a literal and a figurative significance. Elias's trip eastwards is a journey to provinces from which he has become estranged over time and which appear not just geographically and emotionally remote, but isolated, too, from reality. As with other films under discussion in this chapter, the image of the east here does not match the touristic vision found in the unification comedies. Elias' chauffeur-driven BMW glides along empty roads into the crumbling, dilapidated geography of rural east Germany, between unkempt fields and through neglected streets before finally stopping at a secluded provincial town, where the urbane politician is a conspicuously incongruous figure.

Verlorene Landschaft is neither a study of east/west relations, nor a critical examination of the post-unification topography, despite its early narrative implications. Kleinert abandons the kind of documentary realism evident in his contemporaries' work and engages instead in formal and thematic experimentation: strange imagery, awkward gestures, mise-en-scène, and symbolism combine to give the film a tense atmosphere. The scenes are often surreal and inhabited by bizarre characters (an organ grinder playing in an empty street; a small boy dancing in tattered angel's wings; an ancient hotel porter in an old-fashioned uniform). The organ's hypnotic tune becomes something of a leitmotif, a melancholic refrain, punctuating a complex and elliptical narrative that substitutes temporal disjuncture for any linear development. The narrative flits between times, from the post-war past to the post-wall present. The initially indeterminate structure begins to acquire a more coherent pattern as the film progresses. Elias' memory is prompted by the long unseen environment of his formative years, and the scenes that cut from one period to another establish parallel chronologies, of the GDR past and the post-GDR present. Elias' visit to his family home prompts a series of remembered scenes; in each of the rooms that he enters, a moment from his childhood is played out before him. Past and present are intermingled and the scenes have a phantasmagoric, oneiric quality, where the boundaries between what is real and what is illiusion are blurred. The hallucinatory quality is sustained by formal randomness: the film switches from colour to monochrome; expressionistic moments reflect the protagonist's delirium and his disconnectedness from his erstwhile home. This aesthetic style has led to the oft-repeated description of Kleinert as a film-poet, one whose imaginative approach to filmmaking would have been impossible in the GDR.[49] Kleinert's fondness of the abstract had been noted early on by a senior staff member of the film school, who wrote disapprovingly of the student's tendencies.[50] Freed from DEFA's aesthetic straitjacket, Kleinert's debut is able to offer a formally diverse drama. But as with his film school contemporaries, Kleinert does not follow a western, that is, Hollywood paradigm. The film may not exhibit the (DEFA) documentary realism that finds some continuity in Dresen's or in Misselwitz's films, but an east European aesthetic is nonetheless discernible. In particular, the director's reluctance to supply meaning to the incomprehensible imagery betrays the influence of Tarkovsky (on whom Kleinert had written his dissertation).[51]

The protagonist's return to his family home prompts forgotten memories of his childhood and of the East German past. Elias' return to the disappeared world of his childhood is, unsurprisingly, tinged with sadness. This melancholy refers not just to the loss of innocence that typically accompanies such recollection but also, specifically, to the unrealized and unrealizable hopes of his parents (and of the GDR) to establish and maintain utopia. Certain key historical events are outlined so that the narrative presents an account of Elias' formative years and indexes developments within the East German state: Stalinism; the repression of liberals; the subsequent rejection of the Stalinist course; the steady emigration of GDR citizens. Though Elias' past is synonymous with the GDR, the memories of those times are disinvested of the historian's grip, for Kleinert refuses to represent the past as historically or factually fixed; the past is, instead, filtered through the subjective memories ôf its protagonist. The flashbacks present personal snapshots of the past that do not strive to be accepted as an objective account. Kleinert qualified this individual approach, arguing that, 'the whole film is a fantasy, a memory and sometimes a dream. This narrative perspective enables me to handle the historical material more freely than I could have done if I'd chosen a quasi-authentic formal approach.'[52]

Elias' increasing closeness to the dreamed and remembered past is emphasized by his estrangement from the present. His return to the family home, to his Heimat and its subsequent effect on him, corresponds closely to a hypothesis outlined by Nora:

> In the same way that we owe our historical overview to a panoramic distance, and our artificial hyper-realization of the past to a definitive estrangement, a changing mode of perception returns to the historian, almost against his will, to the traditional objects from which he had turned away, the common knowledge of our national memory. Returning across the threshold of one's natal home, one finds oneself in the old abode, now uninhabited and practically unrecognizable – with the same family heirlooms, but under another light; before the same *atelier*, but for another task; in the same rooms, but with another role.[53]

The protagonist's former home is the equivalent of the 'lieux de mémoire', the sites of memory that Nora discusses; the physical space offers a portal to an intangible past. Elias' memories of his childhood conform both to the traditional image of a Heimat idyll: a house in the forest, a life that strives to maintain its autonomy and resists change and external interference. It also resembles an imaginary place and time, a fairytale past that Elias once inhabited with his parents, whose construction and defence of their world (a life purposely lived within the confines of their property) blurred the boundaries between reality and make-believe, as they tried to keep their son cosseted from the world beyond. Elias' childhood and his relationship with his parents (played by Slyvester Groth and Frederike Kammer) are offered as an allegory of the East German state in the post-war years. Although his parents' clearly reject the state, their attempts to avoid becoming involved in the mechanics of day-to-day living in the GDR, to avoid involvement with life beyond their fence altogether, do not constitute clear ideological opposition. Their resistance to the state is a rejection of all outside influences, a desire to stay isolated from the world itself. While the family's rejection of the political and social world beyond their perimeter fence represents the niche society taken to its insular extreme, a sign of a quietist mentality that Marxists would criticize as secessionist, their attempts to determine their own existence echoes the GDR's utopian aspirations and desire for autonomy. [54]

The idiosyncratic childhood is of course an allegory of the east German experience itself. The parents' attempts to shelter their son from outside influences, however naive and impractical, are motivated by love and by parental protection rather than by any pedagogical or ideological convictions. At the same time, their desire to enclose themselves within the world they have created reflects the utopian ideals of the GDR. But for Elias, as for millions of east Germans, the measures undertaken create an environment that stifles as it secures; the carefully guarded borders of the family property are as restrictive as those of the state. Kleinert's film may be critical about the effects that such control has on its subjects but it is not directly critical of the GDR. The parents' instinct to protect themselves, and especially Elias, from the external ironically mirrors the SED's own concerned 'protective' policies, and just as the GDR citizens fled the state, so Elias finally escapes from the only environment he has known.[55] In forsaking the microcosmic world ordered around a familial centre, the adolescent Elias abandons his Heimat and his family's niche utopia.

Returning to his erstwhile Heimat, Elias is forced to re-examine his childhood. Heimat in Kleinert's film is the imagined landscape lost since childhood, and accords with Bloch's oft-quoted description of Heimat:'there arises in the world something which shines into the childhood of all and in which no one has yet been: homeland'.[56] His remembered past offers a kind of refuge, for Elias is alienated by the present (the strange surroundings of the eastern town) and by his western lifestyle (a life that appears materially comfortable but spiritually and emotionally empty). Yet the past is not merely a sanctuary, offering shelter from the present's real and actual challenges, but enables Kleinert's protagonist to comprehend the present. The process of return echoes what Douglas Kellner and Harry O'Hara have referred to as Bloch's dialectical analysis of the past which illuminates the present and can direct us to a better future. The past – what has been – contains both the sufferings, tragedies and failures of humanity – what to avoid and redeem – and its unrealized hopes and potentials, namely what could have been. Crucial is Bloch's claim that what could have been still can be: for Bloch history is a repository of possibilities that are living options for future action.[57]

For Kleinert's protagonist, the past is significant for the present and therefore the future. Elias's confrontation with the past represents a process of individuation and, in making sense of the past, he appears to make sense of the present. But it is not through dreams that Elias's childhood is re-activated. The strange visions of the remembered past are not the incoherent, unfathomable visualizations available to the unconscious dreamer, but conjured up through a series of conscious daydreams, which finally lead to self-realization. The politician is offered renewed insight into his past, even if the fractured hopes of the past do not positively outline future development in the sense that Bloch means when he talks of daydreams. When, at the end of the film, Elias, back in his smart apartment, reviews a recorded televised speech he previously made, he laughs derisively at the smiling on-screen politician earnestly reminding the electorate that not just the geographical borders need to be overcome during these momentous times, but the internal, private borders too. Elias' personal confrontation with the east has revealed that this may prove more complicated than such entreaties imply.

Neben der Zeit: Memories in Ruins, Ruined Memories

Memory continues to play a significant role in later films such as Höntsch's *Die Vergebung*, and Kleinert's *Neben der Zeit*. But, unlike *Verlorene Landschaft*, memory provides no redemptive possibilities; the protagonists are denied any self-understanding through memory and are, instead, torn between the process of remembering and the inability to forget. In Kleinert's second feature film, it is the consequences of repressed memory that dominates the narrative. *Neben der Zeit* demonstrates a formal restraint that distinguishes it from his debut. The controlled narrative is appropriate, given its focus on a family of inhibited individuals, who are forced to confront difficult issues and memories long stifled. Kleinert's film is set in a by now familiar east German province, far removed from the hub of political events. The village remains, as the title suggests, beyond time and beyond modernity. Only the departure of the Soviet troops and the introduction of shadowy Russians acknowledge new political developments and power shifts in the new states. The Wende appears to have had little positive effect on the villagers. The village's inconsequential status is suggested by the trains that mostly pass through without stopping, their speed and movement contrasting with the inertia of the village. The near redundant train station serves chiefly as the location for the regular drinking sessions in the grimy station bar, a recognizably provincial routine that confirms the east Germans' reputation for passivity and alcoholism.

Despite these details, Kleinert denied that the film was specifically about the GDR, an assertion repeatedly made by younger east German directors who fear being categorized as such. Yet *Neben der Zeit* clearly engages with the problems of remembering that had come to inflect unification discourse. Kleinert subsequently conceded that the film did reflect the east German tendency to stifle truth and questioned the consequences that this might have:

> There were lots of things we didn't work through; we never managed to sort certain thing out, to discuss them, to remain fair, to free ourselves of prejudices – these things will have consequences, or rather, we're having to pay the price now. There'll be repercussions for the things we never worked through. [58]

Kleinert's film acknowledges the broader issue of *Vergangenheitsbewältigung*, which had assumed a new relevance in the context of the GDR past, but *Neben der Zeit* concentrates not on the wider social and political issues; instead, it narrows its sights on a single family, suggesting that coming to terms with the past is a process that must first start at home. Again, a feeling of loss filters through the narrative. The loss of economic potency and of political authority is implied throughout. While the locals need alcohol in order to maintain some semblance of community, the family at the centre of the narrative is dependent on keeping up fixed primary roles and repressing natural feelings in order to maintain its fragile survival. Loss is evident in the material details: the abandoned barracks and ruined properties represent the state's loss of power and its subsequent dissolution; and details within the family's home similarly acknowledge loss (furniture shrouded under blankets; the dead father's clothes hanging in the wardrobe).

Following the paradigmatic Heimatfilm plot, it is the arrival of a stranger within a small, self-contained community that upsets the order and harmony that may have previously existed. Despite this generic pattern, *Neben der Zeit* is clearly not a traditional Heimatfilm, even if the east German Heimat is the backdrop to the film's narrative. Again, it is not the cosy community that is in evidence here. The locals' livelihoods are under threat as a result of economic developments, and solidarity is only manifest in collective drunkenness. The environment, meanwhile, is further evidence of a region in decline and reflects the bleak mood of the populace. The arrival of a fugitive Russian soldier threatens not the local community, but a family, whose hermetic relationship comes undone when

Figure 3.3 *Neben der Zeit*
Forbidden love, forlorn Heimat: Sophie (Julia Jäger) and Sergey (Michael Poretschenkow) in *Neben der Zeit* (Andreas Kleinert, 1995) © Kitty Logan/ öFilm

the daughter, Sophie (Julia Jäger), introduces them to the exotic Sergei (Michael Poretschenkow). Kleinert was keen to acknowledge his positive relationship with the Soviet Union and Sergei is, as with several films of this period, portrayed in a way that counters the general post-unification representation of Russians as members of the German underworld.[59] The Russian troops' withdrawal from the GDR, which was a decision that was widely supported in the east, is a departure that in post-unification films is frequently thematized in terms of loss – the loss of the GDR's connection with the Soviet superpower (and that superpower's own gradual loss of authority).[60] The relationship between the East German population and the Soviet people was never as close as the 'Society for German-Soviet Friendship' implied, yet the troops' exit is often a prompt for nostalgic reminiscences, for sudden efforts between guest and host to communicate at the point where such communication is no longer necessary.[61] In what looks like an attempt to preserve some connection with an eastern culture and tradition before the golf courses and burgers arrive, the Russians are associated with a genuine folk culture, drinking vodka, singing folk songs – signals of an authentic tradition that could, as other films show, provide an ersatz Heimat. In Kleinert's film, however, the Russian's arrival threatens to disrupt the self-enclosed family, which is as resistant to outsiders as was the family in his earlier film. Like *Verlorene Landschaft*, the close relationship between family members is intended to protect them from outsiders. Their withdrawal, which according to one reviewer confirms a typically east German retreat into a private sphere, is not as complete as that of the earlier film but is detrimental nonetheless.[62]

Maaz has noted that East German parents often failed to understand the needs of their children and were unable to provide the necessary emotional support. As with other films of the period (*Die Vergebung* for example), *Neben der Zeit* portrays relationships that correspond with Maaz's theory of emotional deficiency, despite the family's physical closeness. There is no direct suggestion of incest in Kleinert's film, but certain scenes imply an irregular intimacy between mother, daughter and son and later between the mother and her daughter's lover. The close interdependence of the family members hampers any possible development and the children, obedient and emotionally immature, remain fixed in their undeveloped filial roles. Sergei's arrival ruptures the emotionally confined domestic situation and forces brother, sister and mother to confront their emotions, a process that eventually results in tragedy – in a homoerotic scene, Sergei is asphyxiated by Georg (Sylvester Groth), the jealous brother, an assault motivated by his fears of losing his mother and sister to the stranger and his uncomfortable attraction to the Russian.

While Kleinert's film could hardly be described as positive, the tragedy does not herald the film's conclusion, as it does in other films of the period. *Neben der Zeit* does not attach a bathetic, upbeat ending, but it does offer a glimmer of optimism: the events ultimately compel the daughter to break free of her environment and in the final reel she is seen boarding a train and escaping an emotionally and physically ruined Heimat. For the protagonists of Kleinert's film, the answer finally lies in escape

Landscape and Meaning

The bleak narratives of the films discussed in this chapter present the east German Heimat as a territory enervated by post-GDR circumstances. No longer the embodiment of atomized resistance, the dispirited east German communities are seen to be on the verge of disintegration. Landscape, which so often plays a crucial narrative role in film, becomes a critical space in the post-unification films. It serves a significant, never incidental, function in the films' representation of the east, reinforcing the territory as a barren, hostile place. The material deprivation of the environment is given partly as a consequence of the GDR's agricultural and industrial policies but it also implies post-unification neglect. The landscape often appears to have been abandoned; the figures crossing empty fields and passing bare and twisted trees seem all the more solitary in such a visual context. One gains only an impression of what may have been, rather than of what is. Representing the region in such a way may signify the end of a way of life, without specifying which life has disappeared – the recent GDR communities or some older, more bucolic life, one that is central to the mythologized concept of Heimat. The visual composition of many of these films emphasizes estrangement from the local. The barren and desolate environment captures the mood of the local population. The pastures and fields assume a wild look, one that seems to anticipate a post-GDR wilderness.[63] The eastern states' synonymy with the wild west of popular imagination has already been referred to in the previous chapter. In the Wende comedies, the western motifs allowed for a comic take on the east as a wild frontier and provided a generic reference to the communities' resistance to outsiders. In a nod to the ghost towns of the western, tumbleweeds roll past the Struutzes in Bitterfeld. Other films hint at the lawless nature of the east, a territory not yet subject to the sophisticated laws and governance of the west.

The films under discussion in this chapter also acknowledge the region's wildness but they avoid the comic implications and pastiche that 'the wild east' presents in the comedies. According to John Rennie Short, 'the fear of the wilderness involved and reflected a fear of those living in the "wilderness". By definition they were not part of the formal social order. The wilderness was the residence of the marginalized elements in society'.[64] The quote is apposite since the desolate landscape perfectly reflects the sense of neglect felt by its inhabitants, who have been divested of their past and remain marginalized in the present. While the state was clearly undergoing massive structural changes, the transformations are barely per-

ceptible in the German provinces. The transition is marked only by its negative attributes: the collapse of the local industries, the rise in unemployment and the impact that this has on the local population. Infertile and
disregarded, the landscape acts as a metaphor for the psychological state
of its inhabitants. The scenery does not prompt the kind of pastoral reverie
witnessed in a film like *Das war der wilde Osten*, where the (contained and
maintained) wilderness of the nearby sandstone mountains represents a
longing for some prelapsarian Heimat, a fairytale forest retreat in which
its inhabitants will not be disturbed by any outside metropolitan interests.
If the earlier films link the countryside to fecundity, less in terms of human
reproduction, though the romance in some of the films implies sexual activity, but through the increasing yield of local goods, the rise in productivity, and a general evolution of a group identity, the barren nature of the
land depicted in these later films connotes not just a wasting of the local
economy but an allied fall in east German fertility and a threat to identity.
Studies show that in the first year after unification, fertility rates in east
Germany had indeed fallen by almost 40 per cent while those in the west
remained relatively stable.[65] Though the authors urge some caution in
reading the results as a direct response to the social and political transformation taking place, they concede that 'economic uncertainty defined in
terms of one's personal interests appears to inhibit fertility'.[66]

While the sizeable transmigration that occurred after 1989 suggests the
east as a territory abandoned to fate, the films' representation of the rural
east is not of a region abandoned to nature, transformed into a wilderness.
The east resembles not a wilderness but a wasteland – a land which has
wasted its chance for reform and which remains materially deficient and
physically exhausted. The ruined landscape is a sign, then, of the GDR's economic retardation and the regime's intransigent ideology – by the end of the
1980s, the land seemed to be withering away as rapidly as its geriatric rulers.
But the ruins frequently sighted within the landscape are not deployed as a
matter of ideological triumphalism – proof that the communist system was
bound to crumble – for loss and not victory is the subtext of the films.

Such films would have doubtless been shelved by the DEFA management, even though their formal style is evidence of an aesthetic lineage that
loosely connects them to the social(ist) realism tradition. As well as presenting a bleak picture of contemporary Germany, one should recognize,
too, that these 'lost landscapes' are a belated reckoning of issues that were
seldom aired in the GDR. Some critical DEFA films had been made during
the final decade of the GDR. Their focus on the material condition of the
GDR's cities and the villages revealed the east as a Heimat struggling to
survive. Harry Blunk has identified a small number of DEFA films – among
them, *Bis daß der Tod euch scheidet* (*Until Death Does Us Part*, Heiner Carow,
1977–78), *Bürgschaft für ein Jahr* (*On Probation*, Hermann Zschosche, 1982),
Solo Sunny and *Vorspiel* – which provide rather downbeat accounts of life
in the East German state, and which were each criticized for their pes-

simism in official reviews. These filmmakers chose their milieus in order that 'the GDR's provincialism and backwardness be understood symbolically'.[67] The films discussed in this chapter similarly convey the retarded nature of the east German provinces. Provincialism and backwardness are clearly not understood as quaintness, or as the ideal condition for some primary German identity, as the Heimatfilme propose. These films therefore problematize notions of an east German identity. While they frequently acknowledge the population's shared experience, they do not focus on the common experience as potentially unifying or as a foundation for identity. Rather, the films debunk the myth of social harmony and counter the state's self-declared tolerance. Focusing on the provinces, they explore the rural communities' 'dormant and newly-composed social conflicts' and reveal the disintegration of the east German Heimat.[68] A strong relationship between community and landscape may exist but the individuals feel stifled and constrained by their environment. Their impulse finally is not to defend or preserve their material world but to escape it.

Notes

1. For further information and details of the *Treuhand*'s management of former GDR businesses, see P.H. Merkel, 'An Impossible Dream? Privatizing Collective Property in Eastern Germany', in M.D. Hancock and H.A. Welsh (eds), *German Unification. Process and Outcomes*, Oxford: Westview Press, 1994, pp. 199–221.
2. Naughton (2002), p. 125.
3. H. James,'West Germany's Green Imperialism', in H. James and M. Stone, *When the Wall Came Down. Reactions to German Unification*, New York: Routledge, 1992, pp. 227–9.
4. S. Wolle, *Die Heile Welt der Diktatur. Alltag und Herrschaft in der DDR, 1971–1989*, Bonn: Bundeszentrale für politische Bildung, 1998, p. 210.
5. See I. Hannover, 'Von Ost nach West und Umgekehrt', *Frankfurter Rundschau*, 23 September 1989, in Golombek and Ratzke (eds) (1991), pp. 65–72. See also the sardonic reports in J. Tilman, 'Grüsse aus der neuen Heimat', *Geo-Spezial DDR* 2, 11 April 1990: 39–49.
6. N.M.Alter,'Re/fusing the Past and Present. Cinematic Reunification under the Sign of Nationalism and Racism: Helke Misselwitz's Herzsprung', in K. Bullivant (ed.), *Beyond 1989. Re-reading German Literary History since 1945*, Providence: Berghahn Books, 1997, pp. 149–50.
7. See Alter, 'Re/fusing the Past and Present', in Bullivant (ed.) (1997), pp. 136–7. Actual rape as a metaphor for the west's takeover has featured in other post-unification accounts, notably Ingo Schulze, *Simple Storys. Ein Roman aus der ostdeutschen Provinz*, Munich: Deutscher Taschenbuch Verlag, 1999, pp. 24–30. Andreas Kleinert's television film, *Im Namen der Unschuld (In the Name of Innocence*, 1997), also features a West German raping (and murdering) a woman from the east.
8. P. Körte, 'DDR adé', *Frankfurter Rundschau*, 20 November 1992.
9. See A.S. Coulson, 'New Land and Forgotten Spaces: The Portrayal of Another Germany in Post-Unification Film', in O. Durrani et al. (eds), *The New Germany. Literature and Society After Unification*, Sheffield: Sheffield Academic Press, 1995, p. 216.
10. Alter, 'Re/fusing the Past and Present', in Bullivant (ed.) (1997), p. 138. Equally questionable is his association with superstition and magic, as suggested by a shark's tooth talisman he gives Johanna and the non-diegetic tribal percussion that accompanies their first meeting.

11. See B. Lubowski, 'Vom Herzsprung in Herzsprung', *Berliner Moregenpost*, 19 November 1992.
12. Hockenos suggests that the GDR's political legacy partly explains the sudden escalation of racist violence, with the fascist youth movement representing 'an active, albeit extreme extension of the authoritarian, petty bourgeois mindset that the state had nurtured'. P. Hockenos, *Free to Hate. The Rise of the Right in Post-Communist Eastern Europe*, London: Routledge, 1993, p. 103.
13. Nora M. Alter, 'Re/fusing the past and Present', 145 (footnote).
14. P.R. Ireland, 'Socialism, Unification Policy and the Rise of Racism in Eastern Germany', *International Migration Review* 31(3), 1997: 542. Others have suggested that racist attacks in the east are more likely to occur in rural areas and that the region's poor economic situation is not a contributing factor. See A.B. Krueger and J.-S. Pischke, 'A Statistical Analysis of Crime against Foreigners in Unified Germany', *The Journal of Human Resources* 32(1), 1997: 192–209.
15. Vanessa Jopp's debut received enthusiastic press coverage, where it was praised for a normalized representation of life in the east, i.e. one that did not foreground the region's social problems. See, for example, W. Höbel, 'Mach nur einen Plan', *Der Spiegel* 45, 2000: 360–2.
16. See also *Weltstadt* (*City of the World*), Christian Klandt's 2008 dramatization of the events leading up to the real life killing of a homeless man by a group of east German youths in 2004. For more on Borscht's film and other narratives charting lives of eastern teenagers see N. Hodgin, 'Marginalized Subjects, Mainstream Objectives. Insights on Outsiders in Recent German Film', *New Readings* 8, 2007. Retrieved 3 December 2009 from http://www.cf.ac.uk/euros/subsites/newreadings/volume8/articles/hodginarticle.pdf
17. Morley and Robins, in Carter, Donald and Squires (eds) (1993), p. 26.
18. See G. Kreutzner, 'On Doing Cultural Studies in Western Germany, *Cultural Studies* 3(2), 1989, cited in ibid., p. 16.
19. See M. Billig, *Banal Nationalism*, London and New Delhi: Sage, 1995. The term refers to the routinized 'flagging' of nationalism through subtle everyday reminders of the state's authority.
20. The east Germans' apparent interest in mysterious powers and superstition reflects also the (unexpected) decline in Church attendance and the loss of guidance to which they had been accustomed, albeit grudgingly, before 1989. For further details of continued secularization after unification, see L.K. Davidson-Schmich, K. Hartmann and U. Mummert, 'You Can Lead a Horse to Water, But You Can't (Always) Make It Drink: Positive Freedom in the Aftermath of German Unification', *Communist and Post-communist Studies*, 35, 2002, pp. 325–52.
21. Although the reasons differ, this delay between production and exhibition was depressingly familiar to the director. His previous (DEFA) film, *Jadup und Boel* (1980–81), did not meet with official approval and was only released in 1988.
22. The film's first draft, however, did involve greater geographical scope, stretching from Sachsen to Paris and eventually Marseille. The financial limitations meant that Simon's film does not stray beyond the German border. See H.-J. Rother,'Die Provinz als Reservoir der Utopie', *Film und Fernsehen* 4+5, 1994: 68–9.
23. Where one might have expected some contribution from the once politically-minded proponents of the New German Cinema, these remained strangely silent when it came to dealing with the complicated issue of unification. Wenders, Herzog, Jean-Marie Straub and Danièle Huillet, and Hans-Jürgen Syberberg have, in fact, shown little interest in the troubled dialogue of unification, preferring to make quirky documentaries, experimental films, or working in Hollywood. Sanders-Brahms and Margarethe von Trotta (whose GDR melodrama, *Das Versprechen*, was released in 1994) are among the few to have responded to unification. One might add Ulrike Ottinger, whose documentary film *Countdown* (1991) chronicled the last ten days before unification, to that list.
24. For a negative review of the film, see A. Simonoviecz, 'Gartenlaube', *TIP*, 1992: 12. P. Lee Parmalee, meanwhile, is more upbeat, praising the director's 'remarkably perceptive insights', whilst acknowledging that Ralf Schenk, the respected east German critic and

film historian, had listed it as one of the year's worst films. In P. Lee Parmalee, 'Movies Document a Turn', *German Politics and Society* 29, 1993, p. 132.

25. See 'Liebesgeschichte ertrinkt in DDR-Klischees', *Sächsische Zeitung*, 16 July 1992 (no author).
26. J. Plessis, S. Taubeneck, and P. Buitenhuis, 'Interview and Excerpts from a Master Class with Helma Sanders-Brahms', in J. Levitin et al. (eds), *Women Filmmakers. Refocusing*, New York: Routledge, 2003, p. 77.
27. Ibid. Hochhuth also railed against the clearance of east German apple orchards (here, a result of EU regulations). See R. Hochhuth, *Wessis in Weimar. Szenen aus einem besetzten Land*, Berlin: Verlag Volk und Welt, 1993, pp. 33–49.
28. J.W. Müller. 2000. *Another Country. German Intellectuals, Unification and National Identity*, New Haven and London: Yale University Press, p. 134. The left's post-89 crisis of faith has been closely explored in *Die Unberührbare* (*No Place to Go*, Oskar Roehler, 1999). Christa Wolf had already offered a melancholic view of the GDR as a lost opportunity. *Was Bleibt*, according to Huyssen (1995), 'articulates a radical critique of real existing socialism, a good-bye to the GDR as "the better half", a loss of confidence in the utopian promises of GDR socialism', p. 50.
29. P. Schlesinger, 'Sociological Scope of "National Cinema"', in Hjort and Mackenzie (2002), p. 20.
30. The phrase is taken from Peifer, who employs it to signify 'resonant symbols meaningful to the general public'. In D. Peifer, 'Commemoration of Mutiny, Rebellion, and Resistance in Postwar Germany: Public Memory, History, and the Formation of "Memory Beacons"', *Journal of Military History* 65, 2001: 1016.
31. P. Betts, 'The Twilight of the Idols: East German Memory and Material Culture', *The Journal of Modern History* 72, 2000: 739.
32. A.D. Smith, 'Images of a Nation. Cinema, Art and National Identity', in Hjort and Mackenzie (2002), p. 55. Smith gives a fuller account of the relationship between landscape and identity in A.D. Smith, *The Ethnic Origins of Nations*, Oxford: Blackwell, 1986. See also Richard Muir, 'Conceptualising Landscape', *Landscapes* 1, 2000.
33. See M. Howard, 'An East German Ethnicity? Understanding the New Division of Unified Germany', *German Politics and Society* 13(4), 1995. Pollack, meanwhile, claims that the east Germans are not treated seriously by those in the west but culturalized (and therefore dismissed) as an ethnic group. See D. Pollack, 'Modernization and Modernization Blockages in GDR Society', in K.H. Jarausch (ed.), *Dictatorship as Experience. Towards a Socio-Cultural History of the GDR*, Oxford, 1999, pp. 27–46.
34. D. Lowenthal, *The Past is a Foreign Country*, 3rd ed. Cambridge: Cambridge University Press, 1990, p. xxiii.
35. See A. Goodbody, 'Veränderte Landschaft: East German Nature Poetry Since Reunification', *GFL-Journal*, 2005: 2.
36. The green netting covering the socialist murals on many of the civic buildings throughout the east is an example of the present superposing the past.
37. I am suggesting, then, that the East Germans' relationship with their environment was identified and closely bound to an ideological purpose, with a strong emphasis on progress and development. 'A territory', as Smith notes, 'can also become sacred through a quest for liberation and utopia'. A.D. Smith, *Myths and Memories of the Nation*, Oxford: Oxford University Press, 1999, p. 153.
38. J. Habermas, *Vergangenheit als Zukunft*, Zürich: Pendo-Verlag, 1990b, p. 53.
39. P. Nora, 'Between Memory and History: Les Lieux de Mémoire', *Representations* 26, 1989: 22.
40. Ibid., p. 9.
41. The decision to stage a play that did not accord with SED ideology is not an indicator of the authorities' new-found openness. Away from the GDR epicentre, the authorities could afford to be moderate; and Anklam was, as one journalist noted, 'the penal colony at the end of the world'. M. Matussek, 'Rodeo im Wilden Osten', *Der Spiegel* 22, 1990: 195.
42. McGowan stresses the relevance of Beckett's play for the GDR when he asks 'how could a play about continually frustrated hopes fail to resonate in an Eastern Europe

characterized by restricted freedoms and arbitrary bureaucracies?'. In M. McGowan, 'Waiting for Waiting for Godot: Echoes of Beckett's Play in Brecht's Chosen Land', in *Brecht-Jahrbuch* 27, 2002: 133. Moran, meanwhile, notes that the east Germans became accustomed to waiting and even developed a different attitude towards time than those in the west. See J. Moran, 'November in Berlin.The End of the Everyday', *History Workshop Journal* 57, 2004: 220.

43. This is not to say that the play was randomly chosen. However, Dresen considered Beckett's text apposite because of its bearing on Fincke's situation (he decides finally to wait in Anklam) and not necessarily that of the GDR. See D. Hochmuth, 'Gespräch mit Andreas Dresen (1992)', in *Defa Nova-nach wie vor? Versuch einer Spurensicherung*, Berlin: Freunde der Deutschen Kinemathek eV, 1993, p. 310.

44. Dresen has expressed admiration for Soviet filmmakers such as Rjasanow, Iosseliani and Mittas, directors whom he admires not because of their particular formal style but because of a commitment to story-telling and authenticity. See Hochmuth (1993), p. 306. In an interview with this author (29 July 2004, Film Museum Café, Potsdam), he spoke highly, too, of the social criticism and realism in Ken Loach's work.

45. Though not confirmed by Dresen, it seems likely that the film was inspired by Matussek's report in *Der Spiegel* (1990). The script closely resembles features of the journalist's account, including an ambitious young director, actors who hope that certain contacts in the west will be able to support the provincial theatre ('and so they wait … for the west, for Godot', p. 198), and an ensemble comprising of disenchanted individuals or alcoholics. Unlike the magazine report, Dresen's film does not consider the theatre's Stasi members and avoids the details given by Matussek about the local drunks, whose drunken belligerence reveals extremist views, p. 200.

46. As Kellner and O'Hara noted, Bloch's 'critique of ideology … is not merely unmasking (*Entlarvung*) or demystification but is also uncovering and discovery: revelations of unrealized dreams, lost possibilities, abortive hopes – that can be resurrected and enlivened and realized in our current situation'. In D. Kellner and H. O'Hara, 'Utopia and Marxism in Ernst Bloch', *New German Critique* 9, 1976: 15.

47. Author's interview with Dresen.

48. Dresen made clear his objection to such retroactive heroism, commenting, 'it makes me sick when people make these claims'. See Hochmuth (1993), p. 302.

49. See, *inter alia*, R. Holloway's review of Kleinert's later film, *Wege in die Nacht* (*Paths in the Night*, 1997). Retrieved 22 August 2008 from http://www.filmfestivals.com/cannes99/html/quinzaine2.htm.

50. See Prof. Dr. Köhlert's 'Leistungseinschätzung', reproduced in K. Herold and J.Scherer (eds),*Wegzeichen. Fragen von Filmstudenten an Regisseure. Beiträge zur Film-und Fernsehwissenschaft*, Berlin: Vistas, 1998, p. 196.

51. Unlike the grotesque narratives which characterized a number of DEFA directors' first post-GDR work (Herwig Kipping's 1992 film, *Das Land hinter dem Regenbogen* (*The Country Behind the Rainbow*), or Ulrich Weiß's *Miraculi* (*Mirakuli*), released in the same year), the incomprehensibility of some images in Kleinert's film did not alienate critics. It is worth noting that *Verlorene Landschaft* brings together a number of other influences, including film noir, expressionism and, inevitably, Kafka, which combine to menacing effect.

52. Quoted in R. Schenk, 'Schattenboxer und Kinderspiele. Über einige neue deutsche Spielfilme während und im Umfeld der Berlinale', *Film und Fernsehen* 2, 1993: 25.

53. Nora (1989), p. 18.

54. See Kellner and O'Hara (1976), p. 29.

55. According to Maaz, east German families frequently mirrored the repressive tendencies of the state, resulting, ultimately, in a society of conformists, who from birth did not presume to question or criticize authority – whether of the parents or of the state. See H.-J. Maaz,.*Das gestürzte Volk, oder, die unglückliche Einheit*, Berlin: Argon, 1991, pp. 31–40.

56. E. Bloch, *The Principle of Hope*, trans. N. Plaice, S. Plaice and P. Knight. Cambridge, MA: MIT Press, 1995, p. 1376.

57. Kellner and O'Hara (1976), p. 16.
58. In an interview with E. Richter, 'Anarchie und Menschlichkeit', *Film und Fernsehen* 5+6, 1996: 54.
59. Ibid., p. 55.
60. See Helga Reidemeister's documentary film, *Rodina Heisst Heimat* (*Rodina means Heimat*, 1992), which follows the departure of a Soviet regiment from the German-German border back to Russia.
61. This special relationship between Germans and Russians was an official and never private matter. In fact, the soldiers stationed in the GDR had a poor reputation, even among Stasi observers, who recorded that rapes were high in those areas in which they were to be found. See J.C. Behrends, 'Sowjetische "Freunde" und fremde "Russen"'. Deutsch-Sowjetische Freundschaft zwischen Ideologie und Alltag (1949–1990)', in J.C. Behrends et al. (eds), *Fremde und Fremd-Sein in der DDR. Zu historischen Ursachen der Fremdenfeindlichkeit in Ostdeutschland*, Berlin: Metropol Verlag, 2003, pp. 75–98.
62. G. Seesslen,'Deutschland, Niemandsland', *Potsdamer Neueste Nachrichten*, 26 September 1996.
63. That the region has seen the return of wolves and an increase in the population of wild boar since the state's collapse appears to confirm the east's wild reputation. See S. Winter, 'Wölfe am Wasser', *Der Spiegel* 26, 2005: 56–9.
64. J. Rennie Short, *Imagined Country. Society, Culture and Environment*, Routledge: London, 1991, p. 8.
65. J.C. Witte and G.G. Wagner,'Declining Fertility in East Germany after Unification: A Demographic Response to Socioeconomic Change', *Population and Development Review* 21(2), 1995: 388.
66. Ibid., p. 390.
67. H. Blunk, 'Heimat und Vaterland in DEFA-Spielfilm', *Deutsche Studien* 26(103), 1988: 232.
68. B. van Hoven, 'Women at Work – Experiences and Identity in Rural East Germany', *Area* 33(1), 2001: 43.

Chapter 4

AT THE BACK OF BEYOND: HEIMAT EAST

The depiction of the east as a geographically remote and culturally stunted region, a ruined Heimat located at the edge of German culture and civilization, has proved to be an enduring one in post-unification films. This is not to say that the regional film boards were keen to continue financing the depressing representations of the east that characterized the films discussed in the previous chapters. While several of those films earned their directors critical kudos from international film festival panels, critics and film scholars, they did not fare well at the box-office. Inclusion on university syllabi may have assured some directors' reputations, but it was no substitute for the films' lack of commercial success. However, the films' repeated box-office disappointments did not dissuade producers from funding other post-unification narratives set in the region and numerous directors were able to secure financial backing, often drawn from generous public subsidy programmes as well as private investors, for their provincial east German stories.

Later filmmakers, mostly young, first-time directors, were similarly interested in the east, but the films made by this younger generation did not offer the critical approach evident in the earlier films. Bleak though the films' locations are, the narratives are of a lighter disposition than the morose productions discussed in the preceding chapter. Geographically, then, the films invite comparison with the provincial dramas already discussed, but there the similarity ends, for thematically the films mostly diverge from the kind of sustained critical engagement with unification discourse or earnest introspection offered in those earlier films. Instead, humour returns to post-unification discourse. Producers may have considered the combination of serious unification issues and comedy as a recipe for critical and commercial success, but the droll portraits of the east Germans' encounters with the west, which were central to the early comedies, were hardly tenable by the mid-1990s. The economic and political optimism had disappeared, as the reality of rebuilding the eastern economy and integrating the two populations became clear. Light-hearted takes on unification were no longer suitable given the continued disparity between eastern and western lifestyles and the east Germans' sense of inferiority. It would be a mistake therefore to categorize them as updated Wende comedies. The good natured, exaggerated comedy that was central to the witty, often sentimental take on unification and the two populations' idiosyncrasies gave way to a humour that was more cheerless than merry.

On the Road Again

Where Heimat had previously been an aestheticized landscape, offering a haven from the challenges of unification and providing east Germans with a collective niche existence beyond the real and the present, this vision of community success and old-fashioned good sense petrified, becoming a site associated with failure – the 'Arsch der Welt' (literally 'arse-end of the world' as a character in Nathalie Steinbart's film, *Endstation: Tanke* (*The Middle of Nowhere*, 2001) comments). In fact, this designation for the eastern Federal States has regularly been employed over the years, both ironically and judgementally. It served as a title for Claus Strigel's award-winning 'documentary western', *Die Siedler am Arsch der Welt* (*In the Back of Beyond*, 2004). In December 2008, Bündnis 90/Die Grünen (The Alliance '90/The Greens) held a conference titled 'Im Herzen Europas oder am Arsch der Welt?' ('The Heart of Europe or the Back of Beyond?'), at which the party highlighted some of the social, economic and environmental issues facing the region, and outlined some possible solutions. The filmmaker's and politicians' motivation for using this idiom, which in German suggests a place's geographical remoteness but may also refer negatively to the inhabitants' socio-cultural remoteness, their distance from centres of decision-making and authority, thus draws attention to the plight of those living in particular in the east's more isolated areas, and to the continuing economic decline, the related social problems and the inhabitants' feeling of neglect.

Like the directors of the previous chapter, these filmmakers search out similarly uncongenial and out-of-the-way locations for their narratives. The filmic vision often extends eastwards, not in an effort to explore any revanchist claims or to focus on the relationship between east Germans and their eastern neighbours (something that only began to be considered in recent years), but as a means of addressing regions that had ceased to exist in the national imaginary. Not that the films are indebted to any east German or eastern European filmmaking tradition. Indeed, what is most apparent about the films analysed in this chapter is the influence of western – specifically, Hollywood – filmmaking conventions.[1] And it is the road movie, in particular, that proves to be an enduring template for cinematic explorations of the new, still unknown eastern states in a number of later post-unification films. The genre was revived by Detlev Buck in his film

Wir können auch anders, by Peter Welz in *Burning Life* (1994), by Peter Kahane in *Bis zum Horizont und weiter* (*To the Horizon and Beyond,* 1999), by Jan Ralske in his deadpan *Not a Love Song* (1997), and in *Endstation: Tanke.* The east's reputation as 'the wild east' corresponds with the (Hollywood) road movie's traditional fascination for the badlands and wide open spaces of the American mid-west even if the region is hardly able to offer the geographical vastness of those films. But despite the geographical limitations, eastern Germany is able to mirror certain codified road-movie features. The genre's influence is clear in the way in which the region is profiled: panoramic shots of open fields stretch to the horizon and long, straight roads cut through the landscape allowing the viewer to imagine the east as similarly expansive. And just as road movies frequently represent the territories through which their protagonists pass as existing in a separate time and place, so the focus in these films is on the east as somehow separated from modern life. Territories in the road movie are traditionally portrayed as isolated and insular locations, associated with backward, hermetic communities who are suspicious of, and unreceptive to, strangers. Those passing through are not just excluded in these eastern road movies, but are marked as outsiders whose presence potentially threatens to upset the local way of life. Of course, the characters in these films are not searching for the security of Heimat within the communities through which they pass; the deserted homesteads and abandoned residences offer them no anchorage. Like most road-movie protagonists, they are either en route to a particular destination, or travelling as a means of escape.

For the most part, the directors, like Wenders before them, distort the American genre that they mimic.[2] Certain props initially connect the films to the road movie, but looked at closely the impression is often auratic.[3] In truth, the films amount to more than just the transposition of the Hollywood paradigm to east German soil, for the directors frequently subvert the genre by including certain subtle details that would register more deeply with audiences in the east. The protagonists' car in Peter Welz's *Burning Life* is such an example. Though it resembles the hulking 1950s models popular in Hollywood road movies, the GAZ Volga 'Tschaika' was an iconic Soviet car, a handmade luxury vehicle that was associated with the (male) party elite. The fact that the car's reverse gear does not operate is doubtless a satirical swipe at communism's self-proclaimed progressive tendencies. The choice of vehicle is not just important because its post-communist status now sees it serving the two heroines (any feminist triumph is, one should add, compromised by recurring gender stereotypes, among them the women's mechanical ignorance), but also because its eastern origin (Nizhny Novgorod) acknowledges the new states' old political and cultural orientation. In *Not a Love Song,* meanwhile, the disaffected hero stands apart from his friends with their Mercedes and BMWs, preferring an old Czechoslovakian car, the similarly admired Tatra T603. These hefty vehicles can be seen as replacements for the once ubiquitous Trabant, as if the ridiculed Trabi, symbol for a flimsy, inferior east German identity, had been exchanged for more staid vehicles, old-fashioned, but robust. Moreover, this alternative car problematizes the Trabi as a newly established signifier of a post-wall identity: not only does it displace it as the symbol of the east's ridiculed achievements as perceived by the west, it also rejects the popular (and uncritical) nostalgic function that it had come to serve for those in the east. The most important difference in these road movies, though, is the directors' refusal to comply with the fundamental dynamic of the genre they evoke, since the films are road movies whose roads lead nowhere. While this may, etymologically speaking, indicate some utopia (utopia literally meaning 'no' and 'place'), the desire to escape is, more accurately, the desire to be elsewhere. With escape the prime motive, the destinations named by those desperate to leave are often randomly chosen. Welz's heroines vaguely mention Africa – or Australia – as they escape the police in a stolen helicopter, while in Ralske's film the protagonists spontaneously opt for Italy. Only in Sören Voigt's graduation film, *Tolle Lage* (*The Perfect Site*, 1999) is there any realistic vision of a life elsewhere, with the film's principal character hoping to move to Hanoi, a plan, which though better arranged, ultimately fails.

The Occidental Tourists: *Wir können auch anders*

Unlike the previous unification comedies, Detlev Buck's 1993 film, *Wir können auch anders*, was both a commercial and critical success. It met with enthusiastic newspaper reviews, with the film's title frequently, if optimistically, interpreted as a declaration to break with the kind of banal commercial filmmaking that had heretofore typified German film culture in the 1990s.[4] There was little disagreement about the film's merits and the critics were positive about its refusal to engage in the kind of stereotyping that had become commonplace in unification comedies. The lack of east/west clichés in the film was widely attributed to Buck's talent as a director and scriptwriter, and offered further evidence of the young director's eye for detail and observational, down-to-earth comedy that had characterized his earlier films, *Erst die Arbeit und dann?* and *Karniggels* (*Rabbits*, 1991). Buck's ability to combine gentle humour and realism in his previous films had earned him plaudits from many critics. The comic, yet affectionate, accounts of life in the provinces had led some reviewers to refer admiringly to a new type of Heimatfilm, one that was both sentimental and authentic, with Buck's own background, a farmer's son from rural Schleswig-Holstein, often mentioned as if to contextualize and legitimize the apparent contradiction of this approach.

In *Wir können auch anders*, Buck continues his interest in the northern provinces and in ordinary, unassuming protagonists, only this time his attention shifts eastwards, towards the more remote regions of Mecklenburg-

Vorpommern. Essentially a road movie, the film follows two brothers' journey to the house they have inherited from their grandmother. Their illiteracy enables the film to avoid Germany's geographical limitations: the seeming endlessness of the journey, a convention of the road-movie genre, is made possible by their inability to read road signs or maps. But Buck's film is not just a reworking of the road-movie genre set among the back roads and lost highways of Germany's sparsely populated northeast. *Wir können auch anders* mimics other film genres, including the western, which is referenced throughout (the mock spaghetti-western musical score; the comic undertaker who must continually recalculate his coffin quota), and the road movie.[5] Buck's arrangement and subversion of these miscellaneous genres is a 'high-low self-reflexive' narrative strategy that avoids the paradigmatic tendencies discernible in other unification comedies.[6] The (domestic) road movie was a less established genre than its Hollywoood counterpart, though not entirely unknown (Wenders's *Im Lauf der Zeit* (1976) is perhaps the pre-eminent German road movie). The situation was, as ever, different in the east, where the strict travel restrictions placed on the East German population meant that it was not a genre much suited to GDR narratives. The genre was not completely unknown to DEFA, however, and Frank Beyer's much-admired *Karbid und Sauerampfer* (*Carbide and Sorrel*, 1963), which follows one man's journey to obtain the carbide that is needed if he is to resurrect his treasured factory, might be considered a rare example of the socialist road movie. After 1989, the genre quickly established itself as a useful template for unification narratives. *Go Trabi Go* had already made use of the genre, with the escape and (self-)discovery involved in the Struutzes' journey conforming to certain comic road-movie conventions. In charting his protagonists' route into the west, Timm's film was an exception to the rule. The majority of unification road movies attempt to offer a psychological and geographical map of the former GDR, effectively guiding audiences across the under populated regions of the east that remain largely unknown to those in the west and which had seldom served as a location in the DEFA films. The genre's relevance to unification narratives becomes all the more clear, given that the road movie provides, as Steven Cohan and Ira Rae Hark put it, a 'ready space for exploration of the key tensions and crises of the historical moment during which it is produced', and examples of the road movie are repeatedly found in more serious films and comedies alike.[7]

Buck resists the style of other unification films not only in his eclectic generic references, but also in his choice of protagonist. The brothers Kipp and Most variously described by critics as a modern-day Laurel and Hardy, or 'childlike figures from a fairytale', are certainly atypical figures in contemporary German film.[8] Kipp, a slight, endearingly affected figure in a suit and silk scarf, and the bulky Most, an equally gullible though less dapper figure, deny the standard representation of the prospecting Wessis venturing eastwards into the German hinterland. Most (Horst Krause) collects

Kipp (Joachim Król) from a psychiatric hospital with the immediate intention of driving to a house they have inherited in the east. Thus, despite their unsophisticated appearance and crude means of transport, their motivation for heading east is not very different from that of other west Germans, who travelled to the new states in the hope of reclaiming old family property. Their journey, however, is not a simple route to the old family home. They are hijacked along the way by Viktor, a Red Army deserter whom they eventually befriend despite the language barrier, and together they travel eastwards, a highly eventful journey during which they encounter con-men and bandits, a number of whom they unintentionally kill, forcing the trio to travel further east in an effort to escape the authorities.

Buck's film engages narrative motifs common to other unification comedies but it departs from the familiar characterization of the entrepreneurial west German figures found in other contemporary unification comedies like the *Trabi* films or *Der Brocken*. That they head into the east not in a huge Daimler but in a rattling pick-up was, as one critic noted, characteristic of Buck's feel for the realities of the post-unification period.[9] This praise of the film's realism may seem odd, given the film's far-fetched narrative and the bizarre characters that people the film. However, it is not the plausibility of the actual story or the various characterizations that is being commended here, rather the film's individual portrayal of the east, even if that depiction employs the topoi of diverse genres. Asked about his reasons for wanting to film in the east, Buck replied that he was motivated by the 'desire not to show the usual images', adding 'that irritates me. The east isn't just stifling, devastating, sad'.[10]

The director's aversion to conventional modes of representation had informed his previous portraits of country life, which similarly resisted the clichés associated with the milieu. His insistence that depictions of the east need not adhere to the narrative and visual codes typically found in such films hinted at an affinity with the east that can be attributed to the filmmaker's own rural origins and identity. Nevertheless, his rejection of the east as 'stifling, devastating, sad' is presumably not a comment directed at his generic stable mates, the unification comedies, since these, as we have seen, resolutely ignore the starker realities of post-unification life. Instead, one can infer that Buck's remark is aimed at those other representations of the east, films like *Apfelbäume*, *Herzsprung*, and *Jana und Jan*, which offer sober reflections of the Wende and may be seen as a correlative to the neo-Heimatfilme.

While Buck's dismissal of the bleak representations of the east may have been the motivation for his comedic take on the post-unification period, the result is not a superficial celebration of the new post-GDR opportunities. Nor is it a comedy that seeks to avoid any reference to the realities of the situation, even if the characters are often exaggerated, unrealistic figures. The film frequently acknowledges the expectations associated with unification only to subvert them. The house that Kipp and Most inherit is not the quaint, rural cottage that the viewer may have expected, nor is it the grand residence that the two illiterate brothers assume to be theirs, but a property so dilapidated that is barely standing. The brothers may be further examples of those west Germans who frequently made claims on old family property but, given the condition of the home, the claim is not a contested issue as it was in films like *Der Brocken, Cosima's Lexikon,* and *Das alte Lied,* which use such appeals to fuel their narrative. The inheritance, then, serves only one narrative function, namely to lead Kipp and Most into the east German hinterlands. Although the brothers fulfil the road-movie role of strangers in a strange land, little, in fact, is made of their west German origins. That they are from the west is only attributable to a vague remark Kipp makes as they cross the former border to the east, and to an observation made by two local women that they must be west Germans. This latter comment exposes precisely the way in which Buck's film subverts the usual stereotypes. The womens' assumption is clearly prompted by their 'otherness', the vaguely exotic, or western, appearance of the three. Such assumptions are not allowed to go unchallenged in Buck's film, and the associations prompted by the ostensible sophistication of the trio is quickly undermined by their speech difficulties and an artlessness not typically exhibited by western visitors in these films. Moreover, the scene reverses the familiar relationship between east and west, with the east German here ready to exploit the west Germans when they realize that the men before them are not the urbane westerners they supposed but unsophisticated nobodies. Buck's protagonists depart so radically from the prevailing representation of Wessis that some scholars have claimed Kipp and Most as surrogate Ossis. Naughton proposes that such a view is possible, even claiming that it 'rationalizes their movement further east with Viktor, because the brothers show their preference for what East Germans are familiar with: Soviet influences'. Mittman, meanwhile, suggests that 'their marginal awareness of the value of things in a market economy' makes them 'more 'Eastern' than the East itself'.[11] There are problems with these analyses. Naughton's claim is undermined by her attempt to ascribe a conscious disavowal of capitalist characteristics to the two brothers. Kipp and Most do not in fact 'eschew the westernized GDR with its fast-food kiosks, gas stations, twenty-four-hour convenience stores, thugs and con-men' as she claims.[12] These westernized locations and features provide key moments and actions in the narrative. The fact that the brothers' lack of social and commercial skills results in further mishaps is not to be mistaken with any ideological objections or a pronounced identification with the east. Ever the naïf, Kipp is happy to go to anywhere, east *or* west (he cheerfully mentions Scandinavia as a possible destination), whereas Most announces on several occasions that he will certainly not be going to Russia. The brothers themselves make little reference to the geographical and political space that they traverse during the course of their journey. No mention is made of east Germany's past or of its present situation. Though

Most is aware of the change in currency, his brother naively accepts an old GDR banknote during one transaction, a mistake that east Germans in particular would be careful not to make. The brothers' experiences at the hands of various hostile or exploitative characters may function as a reminder of the east Germans' own uneasy first contact with the market economy but Buck's film cannot be described as a simple allegory. Mittman's comment, that the pair is somehow more eastern than even the GDR community, reveals a degree of cultural essentialism in her reading of their behaviour; it also implies that their illiteracy, and Kipp's speech defects and learning difficulties are somehow eastern attributes. The brothers' en route vicissitudes as they negotiate their way across the north-eastern states might approximate the challenges faced by the east Germans, but it does not guarantee their assimilation into the east German community. Forced in the end to flee the country altogether, they are finally seen in Viktor's hometown, a small village on the Don, somewhere in Siberia. If not quite assimilated (as Naughton would have it), they are at least accepted by the local community, which seems mostly to consist of genial elderly peasants. No longer inhibited by his stammer or by the usual reactions to his manner, Kipp is able to regale the villagers with a typically muddled monologue, while Most pours and serves rounds of beer. Apparently at ease with this surrogate community, it is not Heimat that is regained, but rather its Russian equivalent, *Rodina*.[13]

Buck's film ultimately presents the integrative possibilities of unification as a fantasy that can only be realized outside the German context. His road movie is thus one that needs to transgress not only the conventions of the genre but also the borders and the culture of the original locations. Even the film's happy ending is conditional on the continued otherness of the protagonists; and, paradoxically, the implied harmony of the conclusion may only be sustained through difference. It is significant that the few east Germans who appear in the film – and their presence is limited to cameo roles – are not offered such comfort of community. They remain disendowed, solitary figures. In keeping with the road movie, it is passage that offers the hope of some redemption; those who are left behind are left in limbo, beyond the dynamic of the narrative. The film's only east German character, the barmaid who becomes the trio's willing hostage, is able to escape the dreary hamlet and finds happiness with the three fugitives in a distant Russian village.

Resisting Stereotypes

Wir können auch anders does not present the east Germans with ambitious schemes for resistance and cultural security found in unification comedies like *Go Trabi Go*, *Der Brocken* or Heiko Schier's 1992 film *Alles Lüge* (*All Lies*, discussed in the final chapter). The few east Germans in Buck's film are

disparate individuals who lack the organizational flair and cohesive identity found in the other films. There is no equivalence to the Struutz family
or the Rügen islanders, who participate in various micro-enterprises as part
of a collective strategy designed to safeguard their eastern identity against
the new economic and cultural hegemony. A group of would-be bandits,
who occupy a rarely used back road, waiting for someone to rob, epito-
mize the passive nature of the east Germans in Buck's film. Otherwise, the
local inhabitants are only seen in passing, or as lone figures walking along
country lanes or looking out of windows. Those who are seen in groups
are usually silent: the skinheads in the local bar; the older villagers on a
roadside bench. A wake offers the closest thing to community, but one
where little is said and no great community spirit evident.

One can see, then, why some critics described *Wir können auch anders* as a
film that is not about Wessis and Ossis at all. Not that this lessens Buck's contribution to unification discourse. As one critic observed, his film offered 'more
satiric potential than the well known reunification comedies.'[14] Yet the film is
not explicitly satirical. It does not directly address the problems of unification
by centring them within the narrative. Instead, life in the east is only inciden-
tally communicated, seen en passant. The ennui of small-town life is visible in
the children standing on the roadside, drinking beer and smoking cigarettes.
The skinheads who sit in the small town bar and the town sign that warns
'Follow our rules, stranger, or we'll follow you' reveal small town prejudice,
an inversion of the community values that typically constitute a sense of
Heimat. As with many other modern road movies, which 'produce visionary
images in place of the absent image of the people', it is the east German countryside rather than its inhabitants that is repeatedly the subject of the camera's
gaze.[15] The landscape is not just a mere backdrop, but featured in pseudo-documentary detail: the flat sweep of the north-eastern fields, the regions' long
straight roads, the dilapidated bridges and simple housing all appear to emphasize the rusticity of the region, its old-fashioned features and ways. Buck
introduces a tension between nostalgia and actuality, between the sentimen-
tally rendered vistas of the east German landscape and the economic torpor of
the rural east, home to the disenfranchized figures and those Wende opportunists who were ready to exploit – the road bandits, the garage attendants, the
second-hand car salesman. *Wir können auch anders* acknowledges these aspects
of life in the east but does not draw them too deeply into the narrative. Nor
does the film simplify or ignore the consequences of the GDR's collapse – as
represented by the Russian army's sudden loss of authority or the uneasiness
of the east's isolated communities – by presenting them as humorous subjects,
an approach that is more typical of the previously discussed comedies. Again,
one can assume that Buck's own experiences have some bearing on his representation of the rural east. The film is, in a sense, further proof of the director's
reluctance to resort to familiar depictions.

In *Wir können auch anders*, seemingly incongruent genres are made com-
patible: the topoi of the traditional Heimatfilme are variously fused with

Figure 4.1 *Wir können auch anders*
Resisting stereotypes: Buck's odd couple, the Brothers Kipp (Joachim Król, Horst Krause) in *Wir können auch anders* (Detlev Buck, 1993) © Boje Buck Produktion

the road movie, the buddy-movie and the western. These disparate influences problematize Naughton's proposal that Buck's film is a Heimatfilm reimagined in the context of the Wende. Though she correctly adduces certain Heimat motifs – the issue of inheritance, the tension between town and country, the itinerancy of the two 'bumpkins' and the conciliatory conclusion – Buck's film cannot be so easily classified.[16] Where westerns often involve the salvation of a rural community (the pueblo being the Hispanic Heimat) from hostile outsiders, here the protagonists' confrontation with bandits and their unwitting escape from the law takes place within a territory that is essentially foreign to them, a territory in which they are the transgressors. It is important, too, to recognize the brothers' outsider status. Road movies of course thrive on the otherness of their protagonists; this difference ensures their failure to be welcomed in as fixed members of the community or society. The brothers' apartness is not attributable to existential personas, however. They are not the disaffected wandering anti-heroes that people Wenders' road films; nor do they imitate the archetypal road movie nihilists. Instead, they are two innocents looking forward, as Kipp repeatedly says, to 'lovely times', and in search of a house that will never be a home.

The pursuit/escape motif that characterizes many road movies is likewise subverted by Buck, whose hapless heroes meander through the empty landscape of east Germany unaware that they have left behind them a trail of dead and are the focus of a major police hunt. Indeed, Kipp and Most are oblivious to most things. Their strange manners and trusting nature are evident throughout, and this childlike-innocence frequently makes them easy prey for the various swindlers and opportunists whom they encounter. Their innocence, which is compounded by their illiteracy, extends to their understanding of historical events and current affairs. Such ignorance is not necessarily disadvantageous. Their lack of historical and political knowledge unburdens them of the prejudices associated with the post-unification period and with other social situations, allowing them to travel undaunted into the east and to talk with everyone they meet. Unaware of the constraints that usually govern social behaviour, Kipp, in particular, is prepared to chat quite openly with strangers, regardless of their superior station and unsuspecting of any malevolent intentions. In trying to reach their destination, and here the film is both road movie and travel western, they come into contact with antagonistic individuals and pass through established communities, even if these are revealed as forlorn districts, where little happens and only death or murder brings the people together. The desire to return home is expressed by Viktor alone. In accompanying him home, Kipp and Most are thus able to discover Heimat by accident, where, though apparently welcome, they are and must remain outsiders.

Like *Der Brocken* and *Das war der wilde Osten*, *Wir können auch anders* promulgates localized social harmony through retrogression. Kipp's and Most's progress across the east begins in their old pick-up truck and ends on horseback (an acknowledgement of the tension between tradition and modernity that was often featured in the genres to which it refers – the western, the Heimatfilm and the road movie). After their travels through the neglected spaces of the east, ignorant both of the calamitous events of their wake and of wider contemporary events, the small Siberian village in which they finally come to rest is one in which their otherness is not determined by Most's old-fashioned outfit or Kipp's unmodern *politesse*. Here it is the cultural differences that distinguish but do not alienate them from the local populace, who, like its two new inhabitants, appear to exist in a state of historical and political abeyance, in a reality apart from the Wende and from glasnost.

Buck's film can be seen as a bridge between the faux utopias of unification comedies like *Der Brocken* and the *Trabi* sequel and the dystopian narratives of later films, which imagine the east as a site of indolence, petty crime, prejudice and violence. The eastern states that are depicted in *Wir können auch anders* are not the pastoral retreats of either *Der Brocken* or *Go Trabi Go II*; nor is the region represented as the physically and emotionally scarred Heimat that was to define many later films. Instead, the film counts as a rare example of a balanced mainstream unification narrative that is able to be comedic without resorting to crude stereotypes and is elegiac but never portentous.

On the Run

Welz's film, *Burning Life*, consciously references the key road movie of the 1990s, Ridley Scott's highly successful *Thelma and Louise* (1991), and the influence of American filmmaking is evident throughout, particularly in its bluesy, country-and-western soundtrack. Despite the similarity of the narrative structure to Scott's film – two women (played by Anna Thalbach and Maria Schrader) impulsively decide to leave their respected homes and together undertake a journey during which the two dissimilar characters become bank robbers and close friends – Welz's film does not transplant *Thelma and Louise*'s feminist concerns to an east German milieu. Given the discrimination facing east German women after unification, this absence is somewhat surprising. East Germans may have wondered at their marginalization from the process of unification that they had initiated, but if any group truly qualified as the losers of the unification, it was east German women. Birgit Meyer summarizes the situation for women in the east thus:

> the ideological and economic rejection of socialism, technological rationalization, capital restructuring, public savings plans, the dismantling of many government social programs and child care facilities, and the elimination of numerous jobs had a disproportionate impact on women in the East. Despite women having contributed in large measure, from the mid-1980s to the end of the decade, to destabilizing the system in the former GDR, they have become the losers of the unification process.[17]

Once active members of the GDR workforce, women suffered the highest proportion of redundancies after unification and struggled more than their male counterparts to find employment in the new system whose policies did little to promote women's return to employment. Their new status did more than put them at a financial disadvantage. The workplace had not just been a scene of labour and productivity for women in the GDR but a place of vital social interaction, providing a close community, one that many women were subsequently unable to replicate within their private/domestic spheres.[18] Nor did women find themselves well represented at policy-making levels, despite, as Birgit Meyer indicates, their previously active engagement with grass-roots organizations before and during the Wende.

Beyond mirroring Scott's subversion of the gender roles that traditionally define buddy-movies, Welz's film, like many post-unification films, avoids any specific critique – or even mention – of relevant gender issues. The narratives' ascription of strong and affirmative roles to women seldom advances any feminist cause but provides further evidence of the east German men's relative loss of power and authority in gender relations and emphasizes their social, political and (occasionally) sexual impotence. In contrast to their ineffective male counterparts, the east German women are the stronger, more confident characters. The presence of confident women is

Figure 4.2 *Burning Life*
The east's own Thelma and Louise? Lisa Herzog (Anna Thalbach) and Anna Breuel (Maria Schrader) in *Burning Life* (Peter Welz, 1994) © antaeus-film

reminiscent of *Thelma and Louise* but it also recalls East German cinema. DEFA, unlike Hollywood, had a tradition of self-assured heroines, though their attributes were often ideologically determined and did little to further the cause of female emancipation which, according to the state's ideology, was a *fait accompli*.[19] Despite its English title and generic derivation, *Burning Life* is primarily concerned with wider east German issues rather than universal gender politics. Though clearly indebted to Scott's film, the anti-capitalist, pro-communitarian impetus of Welz's protagonists, Anna and Lisa, connects them with this latter tradition, even if it lacks the relevant ideology. Although the women assume roles that are traditionally associated with men, exploits that combine bank robber with Robin Hood, their east German heredity is at least as important as their gender categorization. Their rebellion constitutes a politically motivated act, an attempt to undo the effects of the new administrations' policies: robbing the banks that they believe are robbing the east and redistributing the proceeds to needy local residents.[20] Mitigating factors explain (and are intended to justify) their deeds. Stefan Kolditz's script provides an emotional validation for Lisa's actions: she finds her father, who has committed suicide after discovering that his plans to regenerate the small town by selling land to developers (a site, as in *Das war der wilde Osten*, that is destined to be a golf course, the defining symbol of a self-indulgent western lifestyle that sacrifices place and people to minority pleasures) have resulted in forced evictions. *Burning Life* therefore aims to provide relevant details that absolve the women of any moral crime, even if the women's legal guilt is unequivocal. Their popularity with the east German population, who cheer them on and ask for autographs, represents a wish projection by people forced to accept the policies of a new political order. *Burning Life* clearly presents the east as a colonized territory, whose inhabitants have come to accept their subjugated roles.

The film contextualizes the east Germans' plight, showing them (the population as a whole and not women in particular) to be victims of the west, which is represented by unsympathetic institutions, property developers, and western security forces. Importantly, the characterization of the east Germans distinguishes Welz's film from the early comedies: the solidarity that was previously aroused by inspired individuals is absent. While the early unification films found solutions to the threat from the west through a revitalized eastern solidarity, Welz's film advances no such strategy for collective action. Resistance remains an individual (or rather double-act) endeavour, and does not provide a transferable scheme for defending regional identity, as did the pro-active but non-aggressive tactics employed in other films. Instead, *Burning Life* echoes the leftist criticism of the east Germans' gullibility and their irritation that the population has (again) come to accept their subordinate role. Their passivity suggests that the east Germans' essentially submissive disposition did not disappear with their old political masters. As if to emphasize their innate obedience and perplexed identity, the hostages, when asked to sing the national anthem as the robbers make their escape, are unsure whether to sing that of the GDR or that of the new, united Germany, resulting in chaotic, polytextual renditions.

Like Welz, Peter Kahane chooses to focus on individual, rather than collective, acts of rebellion in his later film, *Bis zum Horizont und weiter*. Avoiding the community altogether, Kahane's film concentrates on individuals (notably the ever popular Wolfgang Stumph in the role of Henning Stahnke) who reject the apparently submissive role adopted by their compatriots and attempt to wrest control of their lives away from the new administration. The east/west antagonisms in Kahane's film shows some continuity with the simplified characterization of the east and west Germans as unification's winners and losers that was central to the Wende comedies. The west is represented by an impassive bureaucrat – a wealthy and conceited judge (Corrina Harfouch) – while the east Germans are presented as the more human and sympathetic figures – emotional, disorganized and dispossessed (Stahnke, the film's hero, sleeps in his car, while the judge, who he will kidnap, pads about in her luxury villa). Stahnke's decision to abduct the judge is never questioned; and though it is not motivated by the altruism that guides Welz's protagonists, the narrative's supplementary biographical details qualify his decision – as they do his fiancée's prison escape. The action swiftly relocates from the Berlin courts to the open road, taking in a number of visually striking sites, the most symbolic of which is Stahnke's former place of work, a disused, open-cast mining district in the north east.

Unlike the early east/west narratives, which pit east German individuals against faceless institutions, the establishment is individualized in Kahane's film in the form of the west Berlin judge. The abduction results in her transformation from hard-hearted civil servant to affectionate sympathizer. Her experiences on the road with her abductor finally allow her to understand and empathize with the east Germans as victims. Stahnke's motivation for the abduction is not to acquaint the hostage with the realities of the life in the east, but to secure the release of his girlfriend whom the judge has sent to prison.[21] Oliver Bukowski's script makes little allowance for the judge's actual victim status, which is largely disregarded and of minor importance compared with the generalized victim status of the east Germans.

Again, the landscape is analogous to the east German psychological state: the deserted mines offer a bleak impression of the east, an uncanny vista that shows no sign of vegetation, let alone human activity. These barren surroundings, which provided the backdrop to an earlier TV satire in which east and west Germans collide and in which Harfouch also starred, *Wer Anhält Stirbt* (*Who Stops, Dies*, Olaf Kaiser, Alexander Ris, 1995), serve to remind the viewer of the east's once active industries and, by implication, its once active community. The kidnapper's maternal home, a lone house, presided over by his mother, another veritable Mother Courage figure (Gudrun Okras, a celebrated stage actress) appears to be the last inhabited building in the district. The landscape and locations may be etched with the memories of the past, but it is a past that is understood differently by the characters. For the east Germans, it symbolizes an idealized past that was associated with progress and the collective. For the west German judge, the lonely house with its orchard and wizened owner engaged in traditional Heimat activities – knitting, making Schnapps, preserving fruit – represents an older past and briefly offers an ersatz existence that compensates for the implied vacuity of her metropolitan lifestyle. But the envisioned Heimat is unable to resolve the post-unification problems as it did in the earlier, more positive comedies. The space offers neutral ground – being neither quintessentially eastern (as with the abandoned state mines), nor typically western (as with the judge's designer home) – on which to reconcile the immediate differences between the characters. The mutual understanding that develops may hint at a happy ending, but Kahane's film presents a resolutely downbeat conclusion. Surrounded by a heavily armed police unit dispatched to rescue the judge, the reunited lovers finally choose to commit suicide and step in front of an approaching train.

The film's combination of melancholy and comedy did not find much critical or commercial favour. Reviewers attributed the narrative's uneven tone to the odd pairing of a director known for his serious dramas with the popular cabaretist.[22] The response to Stumph's performance was revealing: most journalists commended his attempt at gravitas but found that the former cabaret star was unable to separate himself from his earlier screen personas, which had made him a national star after unification. Stars are often prone to such categorization (and Stumph had exploited this guise not only in the *Trabi* films but also in the television comedy series, *Salto Postale* and *Salto Kommunale,* which ran to fifty episodes during the mid-1990s), but the ambivalent reception to his most serious role arguably revealed the public's disappointment with a narrative in which the loveable east German underdog was unable to prevail.[23]

The Community as Mob

The prognosis of the east Germans' future is less optimistic in these films than it had been in the earlier comedies. The tragic ending in Kahane's comedy was perhaps the clearest indication that east/west encounters were no longer considered the laughing matter that they had once been. The shift in mood from light comedy to dark humour became increasingly common in later productions. The rivalry between east and west was not always the films' essential ingredient. Over the decade, the camera's gaze would also turn inward, finding similar conflict among the east Germans themselves, with inner strife as much a feature as the tensions between east and west Germans. In Sören Voigt's ironically titled debut, *Tolle Lage*, a shabby east German campsite provides the location for a number of conflicts ranging from the domestic (family strife) to the regional (east/west tensions).[24] Where comic one-upmanship had previously characterized the competition between east and west, it is in Voigt's film defined by acrimony and the threat of violence. This balance between tension and comedy owes more to the bittersweet social realism of directors such as Mike Leigh (an influence acknowledged by the young director) than the slapstick and sentimentality on offer in films such as *Superstau* or *Der Brocken*. Like Leigh's films, the social criticism in *Tolle Lage* operates on a number of levels, highlighting various unification issues (property claims, cultural antipathy, unemployment, and economic exploitation) through a cast of grotesquely realized characters. These range from the ridiculous – petty bourgeois campers, who tend their barbeques in their socks and swimming trunks; drunken campsite inspectors, who don formal jackets over their Hawaiian shirts when reprimanding the negligent owner – to more odious figures (a husband with poor personal hygiene who mistreats his wife and daughter), who lack the sympathetic qualities that had been present among even the villains in the earlier comedies.

While Voigt makes use of essentialized cultural differences – simple east Germans opposing devious west Germans – his film refuses to represent the locals as sympathetic victims attempting to defend their identity against hegemonic impulses. The community spirit that provided a safety net in *Der Brocken* and *Das war der wilde Osten* has all but disappeared; not even the family unit is able to offer any security or comfort. Perhaps the most important break with the earlier comedies is the representation of the east Germans. Without anyone to motivate them or to re-kindle the community values that offered a foundation for resistance, they remain isolated and unengaged individuals.

Economic decline was, as I have indicated above, a catalyst for assertive, often criminal, enterprise in Kahane's and Welz's films. Here, too, an east German robs a bank in an attempt not just to improve his financial situation but in order to regain some pride by besting the bank's security. But the crime counts as an individual reckoning and is not a symbolic gesture or matter of regional defiance. The additional detail that the criminal enjoyed abusing the bank manager, together with the character's disagreeable personality and habits, confirms the bank robbery as an act of personal revenge. Moreover, the successful bank raid worsens the robber's situation, further alienating him from his family and neighbours. The campsite's west German owner (Paul Faßnacht) is similarly alienated from his family, whom he bullies and exploits, particularly his son-in-law, the east German-Vietnamese, Pit (played by German music channel host, Ill Young Kim). Disillusioned and dysfunctional, the east and west Germans are, then, increasingly similar, though their mutual prejudices ensure continued hostility, with the campsite owner representing exploitative western business, and the campers, who are frequently characterized as dreary provincials, economically restricted and emotionally retarded.

There are few winners in Voigt's film. The western entrepreneur's business prospects are routinely sabotaged – the campsite is subjected to anti-west graffiti and vandalism (ironically by his daughter who is ashamed of her father's exploitative methods). Those who oppose the western manager are only able to perform crude acts of defiance – driving a herd of cows through the campsite, refusing to pay their rent. There is no framework for any positive, collective opposition, no sense of communal motivation directed to securing some future autonomy, as in the earlier comedies, nor the heroics and/or philanthropy found in Kahane's and Welz's films. Only when the east Germans are drunk on free beer do they unite, suddenly asserting collective authority through mob rule. Looting and wrecking the camp shop, the synecdoche of western exploitation, they suddenly display communal strength under the guise of anonymity.

Such revenge without personal responsibility also emerges as the east German response to their apparently intolerable situation in *Endstation: Tanke*. In Steinbart's film, the locals are mostly presented as narrow-minded provincials, united only in their outrage and bigotry. *Endstation: Tanke* clearly identifies brute hostility as the defining characteristic of the provinces, which in turn is manifest in the transformation of a group of villagers into a drunken mob, determined to hang from the village sign a western interloper, an escaped convict mistaken for the financial advisor who has deceived the community. Numerous generic features are included – the landscape is shot to resemble the level, open plains of the mid-west, while the remote petrol station, is staffed by a young woman in baseball cap and worn dungarees who is harassed by a local 'redneck' in a pick-up truck – but their inclusion is not simply a question of pastiche or homage, for they also allude to the post-unification frontier mentality and to the region's 'wild-east' reputation. Such recourse to the western has, as previously discussed, been a recurring feature in post-unification comedies. Its influence is evident in the film's thematic as well as its visual scheme: Steinbart for instance reworks one of the genre's enduring narratives, in which spirited villagers resist marauding bandits (representing the community versus outsiders). In Steinbart's and Voigt's films, the western does not act as a model for such small-scale community opposition as it did in the earlier films, but provides a generic paradigm for the east Germans' mob justice. Significantly, the portrayal of the locals as a mob ready to take their revenge on those apparently responsible for their miserable situation reveals a new version of the east German community that is no longer associated with the positive communitarianism evident in the earlier films. And the sight of a crowd demanding justice refers not to the demonstrators of 1989 but to a darker past, with the lynch mob reminiscent of Hitler's malevolent squads. That their wrath is directed at two individuals, one of whom has a Polish name (Marek) and another who is disabled, offers further parallels with NS activities. The only member of the crowd to voice an objection is a homosexual, who is routinely, and often violently, dismissed by his neighbours. Similar scenes of mob rule are to be found in Norbert Baumgarten's *Befreite Zone* (*Liberated Zone*, 2002), in which the residents of a small east German town squander their recent economic successes and finally reveal themselves as a community of unreconstructed provincials unable to escape the narrow minded provincialism that west Germans believed defined the eastern zone.

Unique among post-unification films, *Tolle Lage*'s main protagonist is a non-ethnic German, the (east-)German-Vietnamese, Pit Sun. His presence extends the familiar east/west tension even further eastwards, and relativizes the east Germans' self-perceived 'minority', second-class citizen status.[25] Pit himself mentions his 'otherness' (from both east and west Germans) as the reason behind his plan to escape to Hanoi with his son and wife. Prejudices towards the Vietnamese are acknowledged, but the film examines the issue of prejudice as a matter of cultural and historical antipathy between the east and west Germans. Ironically, the character's distinctiveness allows him to act as mediator between the west (his boss and father-in-law) and the locals, since he is exempt from any historical rivalry. In fact, Pit's hybridity problematizes the notion of an unalterable east German identity. That he is viewed as an outsider despite his GDR biography (many

Figure 4.3 *Tolle Lage*
Pit Sun (Ill-Young Kim) and Anita Skiernitzki (Henriette Heinze) dreaming of
escape? (Henriette Heinze) in *Tolle Lage* (Sören Voigt, 1999) © Mediopolis Film-
und Fernsehproduktion

Vietnamese emigrated to East Germany) is a fact not considered by the 'real'
east Germans, while his father-in-law's hostility towards him could be
based as much on his South East Asian origins as his east German social-
ization. The enlarged photo of his German passport, which he hangs in the
camp shop where he works, serves to remind the locals that, despite his
physical appearance, he too is an east German. *Tolle Lage* casts several characters in a similar mould to those found in the unification comedies but the
qualities that were previously considered charmingly backward are in
Voigt's film further proof of an unappealing and occasionally malignant
provincialism. Although the east German Heimat is once again associated
with chauvinism and rivalry, Voigt's film does not imply that the prejudices
that are aired are in any way a consequence of unification.

Tolle Lage is concerned with a contemporary east German identity that
references and reworks the GDR past. A decade after the state's collapse,
the GDR past continued to be the key reference point for their identity. But
reference to the past was no longer a matter of working through thorny
issues of collective guilt or personal accountability. Remembering the past
had also begun to facilitate the personal celebration of GDR life and history
from below. The focus on individual experience resisted the historicizing
of the personal and its inclusion within the wider political context, which

had earlier defined east German *Vergangenheitsbewältigung*. It was the cultural rather than historical references that had gained currency in the process of remembering the east. While Ostalgie partly ushered in a bathetic reappraisal of commodities once reviled for their ordinariness, it was not, as the final chapter will argue, simply a question of resuscitating good old GDR brands. Though not an Ostalgie film (in the sense that *Sonnenallee* and *Good Bye, Lenin!* are seen to be), *Tolle Lage* does acknowledge certain nostalgic impulses. The east German campers reconnect with their past in a number of scenes. One resident, in particular, is seemingly unable to forget the past, and builds a Heath Robinson-like contraption that allows him to replicate Jürgen Sparwasser's goal which secured the East German team's 1974 World Cup victory over its western neighbours (a triumph that mattered more to the east than the west, who eventually won the title). The invention once again demonstrates the east Germans' knack for resourceful invention, born of a time when materials were at a premium, while underlining the paradox of applying such aptitude and innovation to a project used only to celebrate past victories.

Such impulses have no useful purpose, according to Voigt's film, which ends on a surprisingly positive note – for the only non(ethnic)-German. Pit transcends regional prejudices and historical enmity between east and west and assumes ownership of the site, which is restored with friends from diverse backgrounds, displaying a kind of harmony that may not be possible between the Germans themselves but which is able to exist among ethnic communities on the fringe of German society.

Borderland/Bored Land

The east German backwater continued to be the favoured location for many filmmakers throughout the 1990s. Among them was Jan Ralske, whose debut *Not a Love Song* earned him several awards at international film festivals but hardly caused a stir in Germany, where it fell victim to distribution problems. The film's English title is perhaps more understandable than is the case with most other post-unification films with English names, given its references to American iconography (and the director's American background).[26] Unlike the other films, it is not Hollywood's influence that is visible in Ralske's film, but the smaller lo-fi cinema of the American independents, particularly Jim Jarmusch's early work, whose 'gently ironic, dedramatized, barely generic narratives' the film echoes.[27] In contrast to the mainstream style that shapes most of the other early post-unification comedies (in terms of colour, dialogue, common narrative patterns), Ralske's film opts for long takes, spare dialogue and, like early Jarmusch, forgoes colour for monochrome. Though Ralske is indebted to a film language that is unmistakeably American in origin, neither the film's east German location nor its context is downplayed.[28] *Not a Love Song* acknowledges the region's economic decline and its depressed residents but avoids apportioning any blame or enquiring into the social and economic reasons behind the circumstances, preferring instead to look at the effects on the inhabitants. Ralske's style, then, is observational rather than analytical; the tendency towards social realism celebrates the ordinary and the mundane, seeking to bring an additional stamp of authenticity that counterbalances the melodrama: briefly, a love triangle between three friends (Bruno, Luise and Karl). A documentary-like approach is apparent in the forensic focus on locals and imbues the film with a degree of authenticity that was new to unification comedies. In one long shot (of almost 30 seconds), the camera concentrates on a man downing his beer, while his bored girlfriend watches with a look of tired disapproval. These documentary touches also balance the mannered behaviour of the three protagonists who are quite unlike their fellow villagers. Such formal inconsistencies are not uncommon in the later comedies, which compensate for their rather atypical (east German) protagonists by including realistic snapshots of the east German *Alltag*, usually focusing on disaffected individuals suffering from small-town ennui and shots of the landscape that confirm the region's decline.

Central to the narrative is Bruno (Lars Rudolph), the film's antihero. Coolly nonchalant, the character's swagger and poise was intended to resemble that of James Dean, but the role is arguably closer to the central character played by Martin Sheen in Terence Malick's acclaimed *Badlands* (1974). Certainly, the latter offers a more direct comparison, given the similarities of the two protagonists' environments – the Dakota Badlands in Malick's film and Germany's north-eastern badlands in Ralske's.[29] As a young man from the provinces keen to escape his environment, Bruno is equal to Malick's hero. Yet this desire to escape does not become the starting point for a road movie/crime spree through the hinterlands as in *Badlands*, since Bruno's Tatra fails to convey him even beyond his hometown. With its businesses closing and its insolvent locals attempting suicide, the village conforms to the dismal portrait of the east German provinces that had become the staple of many unification dramas. But the humour in Ralske's film distinguishes it from those dour studies and aligns it instead with the other films in this chapter. Suicide, for instance, is a darkly comic motif throughout, affecting not only the human population but, according to Bruno, even the animals. One character repeatedly tries to end his life without success. The catalytic converter on the newly purchased BMW that he cannot afford thwarts one suicide attempt. Later, Bruno finds his depressed friend sitting on the train tracks, where again his attempt to end his life cannot succeed, since the trains no longer run on that line. Only when told that, 'there's no point your waiting here until at least July', does he reconsider his plans.

This eastern Heimat could hardly be further from that envisioned in the early comedies. Drunkenness and boredom typify village life, a mood that is emphasized by the film's slow pacing. Enervated by their provincial lives, the locals only come together as a community with the promise of free beer. Little remains of the east German Heimat in Ralske's film; nor is there much evidence of the new society. The Berlin Republic is an abstract concept, as distant as the capital itself which is made even more inaccessible by the train station's closure. Other than the high speed trains that pass through, there is no sense of the outside world, the world beyond the village itself. The west's influence is only evident in the effect it has had on Karl (Matthias Freihof), the optimistic local who takes on not just the principles of western venture capitalism but its tactics too, suddenly treating Lisa (Anna Thlabach), his wife, and Bruno as subordinates and threatening to dock their pay. His plans for recreating the area as a fashionable spa resort, together with the investment jargon learned at business seminars, stand in contrast to Bruno's pessimistic evaluation of local prospects and his disgruntled demeanour. Where Bruno is a would-be James Dean, with quiff and sunglasses, Karl is the would-be high-flyer, the pro-active entrepreneur. Like Udo's unconvincing conversion from parochial local to snappy businessman in the second of the *Trabi* films, Karl is ill-suited to this new role. This inability effectively to mimic the new political and economic masters reaffirms an essentialized view of the east Germans as lacking the ability to escape their innate provincial simplicity – which is reinforced in Ralske's film when Karl's plans fail and he suffers a breakdown, and is evident, too, in other later films.[30]

Figure 4.4 *Not a Love Song*
The provincial dreamers, Bruno (Lars Rudolph) and Luise (Anna Thalbach) in *Not a Love Song* (Jan Ralske, 1997) © Jan Ralske

The realities of life in the provinces inevitably weigh heavily on the characters and none is finally able to succeed in their aspirations, a disheartening conclusion that is typical for many of the post-unification dramas and indeed accurately represents the fates of many small businesses that opened after unification. Karl's grand scheme inevitably fails, as does Luise's newly-opened café at the redundant train station.[31] Bruno, too, proves less spontaneous than his attitude first suggests and he abandons both his dreams of escape and the girl of his dreams. Stranded at a motorway service station when their (stolen) car has been stolen, he decides, with evident relief, to return to Ketschdorf, telling Luise 'I haven't even packed any shirts'. Only Luise, who is never wholly convinced by either Bruno's or Karl's visions, succeeds in her (ad)ventures. Mistreated by her egotistical husband, and finally disappointed by Bruno's inability to commit, she is the most determined of the three, showing willingness in her café project, and then eagerness in the flight to Italy (a further example of empowered east German women taking the initiative in post-unification film).

Where unity and resourcefulness were central to the survival strategies conceived by the community in comedies made at the beginning of the decade, Ralske is one of several directors to propose escape as the only chance of survival for those in the east German provinces. The proposal bears some correlation with fact, given the migration of significant numbers of people from the rural east. Beyond the rather skewed comedy, the final scene does not offer any happy ending: walking directly up to the camera, Bruno adopts the pugilist's posture, before dropping his raised fists and muttering 'shit', as if only then realizing that he has wasted the one real opportunity to escape his Heimat.

One of the few films to allow its protagonist an escape from the depressing east German provinces was Michael Schorr's *Schultze gets the Blues* (2004), a well-received study of one man's attempt to adjust to his early retirement after a lifetime working in the mining industry in provincial Sachsen-Anhalt.[32] Though Schorr had written the screenplay in the early 1990s in response to the mass redundancies then facing the west's mining and steel industry, he later rewrote his script in order to reflect a similar situation in the former GDR.

Like *Not a Love Song*, Schorr's film is a laconic, poignant film that strives for authenticity through its documentary approach, which is evident in the static camerawork and an economy of dialogue. Unusually for the films of this period, *Schultze gets the Blues* reflects not on the region's youth but on the older generation forced into early retirement. Despite the difference in age between the characters in Schorr's film and the generation portrayed in the other films, the narratives converge in articulating the anxieties and frustrations that appear to be symptomatic of the provinces. Schorr's film, too, reflects on Heimat and on identity. The narrative exposes the provincial prejudice and intransigent conservatism of the east German Heimat.

The locals' resistance to outsiders is not concentrated on any non-natives; there are no west Germans to imperil or exploit the community, no strangers passing through. The cause of hostility is more subtle but no less threatening to local identity: when Schultze (Horst Krause) decides to substitute the traditional polka that he always plays at the annual Heimat club celebration for the unfamiliar rhythms of a Cajun melody, members of the audience are outraged and accuse him of playing 'Negermusik'. While Schorr references the insularity and chauvinism of small town life, his film is not an indictment of the east German provinces. Indeed, Schorr's interest in regional identity and community values extends far beyond Sachsen-Anhalt to Texas and finally to Louisiana. In the Texan town of New Braunfels, where Schultze is sent to represent his hometown at the annual accordion festival, he is disappointed to discover that the event, organized by the American-German community, is equally narrow in its musical focus. Ironically, Schultze, coded as the epitome of the provincial German (evident in his eating habits, his old-fashioned clothing, his home and allotment, which even features that ridiculed ornament, the garden gnome), is even less comfortable in these self-consciously German surroundings – a perfect example of a constructed and self-perpetuating identity – than he is on his home territory. In search of the authentic music and community that has captured his imagination (the Cajuns of the Louisiana bayous), he escapes this faux Heimat and heads downriver.[33] More riverine than road movie, *Schultze gets the Blues* nevertheless observes generic convention as Schultze travels deep into the marshlands of the southern states, encountering eccentric characters and narrowly avoiding disaster. But Schorr's

Figure 4.5 *Schultze gets the Blues*
Schultze (Horst Krause) searching for a Cajun Heimat in *Schultze gets the blues* (Michael Schorr, 2001) © filmkombinat / Christian Stollwerk

film avoids clichéd storytelling and, contrary to expectation, his protagonist does not, after all, find a home among the Cajuns or return to his Heimat the experienced traveller. Schultze's escape provides no salvation: temporarily taken in by a sympathetic African-American woman and her daughter, Schultze finally dies aboard her houseboat.

Community Undone

In an article published sixteen years after the collapse of the GDR, Thomas Bulmahn offers an analysis of the relationship between modernity and happiness in Germany that counters the generally held (Durkheimian) proposition that modernization and rapid social transformations inevitably result in 'anomic reactions' amongst those affected.[34] Bulmahn remains sceptical to other studies of modernity and anomie, saying doubtingly of a study by Hans Hartwig Bohle et al., 'structural crises, they believe, "lead to innovation, ritualization, withdrawal, protest and criminality"'.[35] Bulmahn argues that in east Germany, 'the subjective well-being of the people has improved considerably' and that accelerated modernization 'does not perforce lead to a permanent increase in anomic reactions'.[36] Bulmahn's is a lone voice. Other articles may not specifically address east German anomie, but the evidence presented in many other studies contradicts his cheerful diagnosis. Reißig, who draws on a wider range of reports and surveys than Bulmahn, talks for instance of 'an identity crisis in east Germany, a vacuum that has emerged'.[37]

Certainly, many of the films made during the 1990s confirm Reißig's point; there is scant evidence in their narratives of the happiness to which Bulmahn refers. Unlike the Heimatfilme that were made soon after unification, the majority of comedies made since the mid-1990s present narratives whose protagonists are no longer constituent of the east German community. Sympathy lies with those individuals who stand apart from the mass and who do not, therefore, embody the community and its values. Struggling to find some footing in the post-unification society, some of the protagonists eventually rebel against its values and regulations, directly challenging the authority of the new establishment – the banks and the courts in Kahane's and Welz's films, the police and immigration control in Hebendanz's film. Rather than accepting their marginalized status and general disempowerment, they opt for a forceful rejection of their colonizers, engaging in practices intended to sabotage their authority. The two bank robbers in *Burning Life* donate their money to poor locals yet remain emotionally and physically distant from their compatriots. In Kahane's film, Stumph's character voices grievances that were common in the east, but his act of defiance is motivated by personal issues and lacks the sense of indignation and integrity (leading to a re-energized regional loyalty) that guided his characters in previous films. The motivation for their rebellion has various causes – redundancies, property claims, and other financial woes – but the criminal strategies they employ provide neither a suitable blueprint for future resistance nor an incentive for collective action.

Although the characters' dismal economic situation is a recent development, that is post-unification, unification is seldom mentioned and there is rarely any reference to the GDR. Occasional details provide visual reminders of the East German state but these are, for the most part, subtly inscribed. In an attempt to present a more authentic vision of the east, these filmmakers often eschew those relics of the state that had subsequently acquired cult status (the Trabis, the SED mementoes, etc.) and avoid the quaint Heimat images that characterize the earlier comedies, focusing instead on the east as a forlorn territory – from the coast's deserted lunar landscape in Welz's film to the barren fields captured by cameraman Hans Fromm in *Not a Love Song*, and the empty vistas of Sachsen-Anhalt in Schorr's film. The depressing environment may provide some context for the inhabitants' grievances, but sympathy for the region's population has, surprisingly perhaps, ceased to be unconditional despite, and this is the important difference between the early and late comedies, the similarity in their circumstances. The economic and social situation remains bleak, yet the portrayal of the east Germans as victims of unification has diminished. Indeed, several of these later films imply that it is the east Germans who are, in part, responsible for their situation.

The east Germans who people these films are not, then, the cognates of those characters typically found in the comedies made soon after unification. The previous representation of the east Germans as either loveable naïfs, inveterate provincials whose old-fashioned guile proves a match for the sophisticated tactics of the west, or slow-witted ex-Stasi operatives, had, it seemed, exceeded its shelf life, as had the schematic vision of the east German province as some quaint, pre-industrial Heimat. Like the films discussed in the preceding chapter, the rural provinces, re-presented in more authentic accounts, constitute a depressing post-industrial Heimat often associated with indolence, drunkenness and insularity. The protagonists, meanwhile, do not try to mobilize the community and reawaken its inherent integrity and solidarity but surrender community to individual self-realization – often manifested in the attempt to escape. This countered not just the post-unification version of the east German community, but denied the socialist values that underpinned many DEFA narratives. For the most part, then, the characters' responses to the structural crisis that followed unification do in fact support some of the claims that Bulmahn dismisses, with withdrawal, protest and criminality replacing the buoyant diligence and common sense that had defined the earlier post-GDR communities.

Notes

1. Hollywood does not of course have the copyright on road movies; but it is primarily Hollywood's conventions that are referenced in the films discussed here. For more on European road movies and travel films see E. Mazierska and L. Rascaroli, *Crossing New Europe. Postmodern Travel and The European Road Movie*, London: Wildflower, 2006.

2. Wenders stands out as the most individual proponent of the genre. Most German road movies, however, are unashamedly American in terms of plot, direction and dialogue. Consider the American sounding *Knockin' on Heaven's Door* (Thomas Jahn, 1997), whose tagline reads 'a fast car, a million Marks in the trunk and only a week to live'. See also Sönke Wortmann's *Mr. Bluesman* (1993).

3. I refer to 'auratic' according to Benjamin's description: 'as a unique phenomenon of distance, however close it may be'. Here the genre's (cultural) distance is mitigated by its appearance within a recognizably German context. See W. Benjamin, 'The Work of Art in the Age of Mechanical Reproduction', in *Illuminations*, London: Fontana, 1992, p. 216.

4. See for example Reif (1993), p. 28.

5. The western theme was noted by a number of critics. See, *inter alia*, the review by Frank Arnold, *epd Film* 4, 1993: 40. Naughton considers the issue in more detail (2002), p. 160. Mittman, meanwhile, identifies the influence of genres as diverse as the 'sci-fi and the Soviet agricultural epic'. See E. Mittman, 1991, 'Fantasizing Integration and Escape in the Post-Unification Road Movie', in R. Halle and M. McCarthy (eds.), *Light Motives. German Popular Film in Perspective*, Detroit: Wayne State University Press, 2003, p. 338.

6. Hutcheon's original refers to 'high-low self-reflexive fiction'. Cited in S. Mamber, 'In Search of Radical Metacinema', in A. Horton (ed), *Comedy/Cinema/Theory*, Berkeley: University of California Press, 1991, p. 85.

7. S. Cohan and I. Rae Hark, Introduction', in S. Cohan and I. Rae Hark (eds), *The Road Movie Book*, London and New York: Routledge, 1997, p. 2.

8. See the review by S. Lux, *Film Dienst*, 1993, 6. See Mittman, 'Fantasizing Integration', in Halle and McCarthy (2003), p. 339. Only Bruno S., who appeared in a number of Herzog's films (*Kaspar Hauser*, *Jeder für sich allein und Gott gegen alle*, 1974 and *Stroszeck*, 1977), surpasses Buck's characters in simple eccentricity.

9. M. Hanisch, 'Eine lustige Reise zum stillen Don', *Neue Zeit*, 1 April 1993.

10. In M. Worthmann, 'Dann setzen wir eben eine Kalaschnikow ein', *Berliner Zeitung*, 1 April 1993.

11. See Naughton (2002), p. 140, and Mittman, 'Fantasizing Integration', in Halle and McCarthy (2003), p. 339. Naughton bizarrely mentions the Polish etymology of Joachim Król's surname by way of suggesting a further 'eastern affinity', p. 161.

12. Ibid.

13. Mittman makes a similar point when she says that the film evokes the agricultural epic of Soviet cinema in scenes where the brothers' old truck steers through the expansive rural landscape of Mecklenburg-Vorpommern, commenting that it offers a vision of Heimat: 'Heimat, yes – but German, no', in Mittman, 'Fantasizing Integration', in Halle and McCarthy (2003), p. 341.

14. Lux (1993).

15. B. Schaber, '"Hitler can't keep 'em that long"', in Cohan and Hark (1997), p. 31.

16. See Naughton (2002), pp. 158–9.

17. B. Meyer, 'Much Ado about Nothing? Political Representation Policies and the Influence of Women Parliamentarians in Germany', *The Review of Policy Research* 20(3), 2003: 417.

18. See van Hoven (2001).

19. For further discussion of women and GDR film (in later DEFA productions), see A. Rinke, 'Images of an Extinct State: Heroines in the GDR Cinema', in P.M. Daly et al. (eds.), *Images of Germany. Perceptions and Conceptions*, New York: Peter Lang, 2000, pp. 73–85.

20. Numerous armed hold-ups did in fact take place after the Wende, as robbers took advantage of the east's poorly defended safes storing newly stocked Deutschmarks. There

is, however, no evidence to suggest that these raids were motivated by anything other than private need/greed. See D. van der Vat, *Freedom Was Never Like This. A Winter's Journey in East Germany*, London: Hodder and Stoughton, 1991, p. 39.

21. Kahane's film conforms to the road movie sub-genre, the en route hostage comedy – particularly in the antagonistic relationship ('Stockholm Syndrome'), according to which the antagonistic relationship between abductor and abducted is resolved as a bond develops between them, with the victim finally recognizing, and even supporting, the kidnapper's motives.

22. See for example B. Galle, 'Das mit uns geht so tief rein', *Berliner Zeitung*, 28 January 1999.

23. In fact, Stumph has now widened his scope with his highly popular role as a detective in the ZDF television series *Stubbe – der Mann für jeden Fall* (*Stubbe. A Man for Every Occasion*, which has also reunited him with Kahane), though the new character hardly constitutes a complete reinvention. A later television comedy, *Das Blaue Wunder* (also by Kahane, 2004), set in Dresden, capitalized on Stumph's everyman figure, this time as an Elbe riverboat captain trying to keep his business afloat.

24. The success of the RTL series, *Die Camper* (*The Campers*, Peter Lichtfeld and others), which had a following of over six million viewers and originally ran to more than ninety-one episodes from 1996 to 2005, demonstrated the Germans' fondness for the comic deprecation of particular German mores – fastidiousness, petty rivalry, parochialism. The campsite had already briefly featured as a location for ridiculing certain regional and class differences in a number of post-unification films (in *Go Trabi Go* and also in *Superstau*, where one of the regional traffic jams becomes an impromptu caravan park in which Germans from all over the republic, including the FRG's newest members, come into contact with one another).

25. The only other post-unification film to feature a non-ethnic German as the main character is Branwen Okpako's television drama, *Tal der Ahnungslosen* (*Valley of the Innocent*, 2003), in which an Afro-German returns to her home in Dresden.

26. This is common to many post-unification films, from *Go Trabi Go* in the early 1990s to *Kleinruppin Forever* (Carsten Fiebler, 2003), made more than a decade after. Although it is tempting to see this juxtaposition as a deliberate reference to the films' application of American genres or Hollywood storytelling to specifically German narratives, in an industry that is largely defined by US cinema, the reason may be more a matter of commercial appeal rather than a self-referential gag. Ralske's original title, *Fata Morgana*, could not be used as another film bearing the same name was released at the same time. Unimpressed by the suggested alternatives, the director eventually chose an English title that the film's producers 'couldn't debate on linguistic grounds'. From correspondence with Jan Ralske, 29 July 2005.

27. G. Andrew, *Stranger than Paradise. Maverick Film-makers in Recent American Cinema*, London: Prion, 1998, p. 164.

28. A fact that is made less surprising given the director was born in Texas (1959), though he has lived and worked in (east and west) Germany since the 1980s.

29. In fact, Ralske's intention was to 'make the Uckermark look like Texas' (from correspondence with Jan Ralske). The area's tourist website prefers the sobriquet 'The northern Toscana'. Retrieved 19 May 2008 from http://www.uckermark.de

30. Only in *Sumo Bruno* (Lenard Fritz Krawinkel, 1999) does an east German succeed in mimicking an 'other'. In Krawinkel's film, a timid, overweight east German is encouraged to train and enter for the Sumo World Championship in provincial Riesa. Bruno struggles to adapt to this foreign sport, but does finally qualify for the tournament, though Krawinkel does not offer any fairytale ending. Like these other films, the portrayal of the east is uninviting and confirms the region's intolerance of outsiders and of those who would attempt somehow to deny their 'easternness'.

31. Their plans exhibit a naive understanding of business that corresponds with a general view of the east Germans as financially naive. Consider also *Vergiss Amerika*, in which one of the characters living in a depressed town opens a garage selling American imports.

Of the 1.3 million businesses that opened between 1990 and 1995, 600,000 did indeed close. See L.K. Davidson Schmich et al. (2002), p. 329.

32. See, for example, M. Ranze, 'Schultze gets the Blues' (review), *epd Film* 5, 2004: 22. Schorr's film, a low-budget production which, like numerous post-unification films, was part funded by ZDF for its series, 'Das Kleine Fernsehspiel', did reasonably well at the box-office and earned an award at the Venice Film festival.

33. See N. Hodgin, 'Eastern Blues, Southern Comforts: Searching for *Heimat* on the Bayous', *Mississippi Quarterly* (forthcoming).

34. T. Bulmahn, 'Modernity and Happiness – The Case of Germany', *Journal of Happiness Studies*, 1(3), 2000, 375-400.

35. Bulmahn is referring to a chapter by Hans Hartwig Bohle et al., 'Anomie in der Gesellschaft. Bestandsaufnahme und Kritik eines klassischen Ansatzes', in W. Heitmeyer (ed.), *Bundesrepublik Deutschland. Auf dem Weg von der Konsens- zur Konfliktgesellschaft. Vol. 1. Was treibt die Gesellschaft auseinander?*, Frankfurt am Main: Suhrkamp, 1997, p. 59, cited in Bulmahn (2000), p. 383.

36. Bulmahn (2000), p. 391.

37. See Reißig (1999). It should be added that others accused the media of disproportionate reporting, and of exaggerating the level of dissatisfaction felt amongst east (and west) Germans. See H.M. Kepplinger, 'Wie sehen sich die Deutschen?', in E.J.M. Kroker and B. Dechamps (eds), *Die Deutschen auf der Suche nach ihrer neuen Identität?*, Frankfurt am Main: Frankfurter Allgemeine Zeitung GmbH, 1993, 45–61. A lengthy cover article in *Der Spiegel*, ('Jammertal Ost'), 39, 2004, would also seem to reject Bulmahn's thesis.

Chapter 5

BERLIN:
DISORIENTATION/REORIENTATION

One can say that the city itself is the collective memory of its people, and like memory, it is associated with objects and places. The city is the *locus* of the collective memory.[1]

After Unification: *Lapsus memoriae?*

In contrast to the provinces, which were represented as geographically and historically distant, existing outside time, the city – or at least Berlin – came to define the times. Short notes that the city is invariably 'a metaphor for social change, an icon of the present at the edge of the transformation of the past into the future', adding that 'attitudes about the city reflect attitudes about the future'.[2] It comes as no surprise, then, that directors have frequently turned to Berlin as the setting for their post-unification dramas. The reasons are self-evident: Berlin provides the symbolic expression of the country's recent history, the location where east meets west, the vortex of change. Despite the freedom of access, movement between the two Berlins has not proved as effortless as the post-unification maps would suggest, and for much of the 1990s was weighed down not by bureaucratic procedure but by cultural baggage. This has allowed filmmakers to explore the east/west conflict as a condition naturally arising within the city. Since the end of the city's bi-polar status in 1989, directors have often focused on Berlin's constituent elements. Neither the opening of the border nor the federal government's relocation to the city after its forty-year residence in provincial Bonn has resulted in a unified civic identity. Berlin's political profile as the seat of German power may have been restored (to the consternation of a good many west Germans), but the city has witnessed the re-emergence of localized identities and neighbourhood pride, which have been the focus of a number of *Kiez* ('hood) dramas. Films such as *Wedding* (Heiko Schier, 1990), *Heidi M.* (Michael Klier, 2001), *alaska.de* (Esther Gronenborn, 2001), *Status Yo!* (Till Hastreiter, 2004), and *Kroko* (Sylke Enders, 2004) attempt to capture the current atmosphere of particular city districts and largely avoid framing them within a historical narrative.[3]

This is not to say that Berlin's regeneration has been ignored. Documentary filmmakers in particular have chronicled the architectural changes taking place, especially those involving the grand designs for the city's former commercial centre, Potsdamer Platz. An empty space for decades, the site was considered a tabula rasa after 1989, a blank canvas for competing architects desperate to showcase their talent. The area was not a place untouched by history, however, but a void haunted by the ghosts of the past.[4] The city's history repeatedly resurfaced in post-unification dialogue, especially where there were proposed changes to the city. The heated quarrelling that accompanied proposals to change the urban nomenclature was often an extension of the architectural and town planning disputes. A number of west German politicians (mostly Christian Democrats) took issue with the continued use of street signs bearing names associated with the East German regime, which they provocatively likened to the honorific practices that had existed under the National Socialists, and proposed restoring them to their original names. Their objections may have stemmed from genuine discomfort with certain dubious GDR figures but a degree of political triumphalism was also at play.

This discomfort with the past only focused on particular pasts, however. The authorities were not quite ready to remove all those markers of the previous regimes (the Olympia stadium, for example, re-opened in July 2004; the road that had once borne the names of Stalin and later of Marx was protected by a preservation order, a decision that not only acknowledged its historical significance but also their relegated status). Above all, it is the Weimar period that has been reified by contemporary architects with the modernism of the 1920s informing new architectural schemes (including the designs for former urban centres in and around Potsdamer Platz and the Reichstag) in an attempt to circumvent the city's 'more recent and disquieting assaults on tradition'.[5] Interestingly, the (admittedly much smaller) debate surrounding some of the films of the period similarly makes claims for the influence of Weimar aesthetics, which is seen as evidence of a more engaged and dynamic film culture. But successful documentaries such as *Berlin – Sinfonie einer Großstadt* (*Berlin Symphony*), Thomas Schadt's 2002 film, which reconceptualised Walter Ruttmann's 1927 classic, *Berlin. Die Symphonie der Großstadt Berlin* (*Berlin Symphony of a Great City*), and *Berlin Babylon* (Hubertus Siegert, 2001) have also been accused as lacking the critical impetus of the period's earlier documentaries – Jürgen Böttcher's *Die Mauer* (*The Wall*, 1991), Heide Reidemeister's *Lichter aus dem Hintergrund* (*Lights from Afar*, 1998) and Hito Steyerl's *Die leere Mitte* (*The Empty Centre*, 1998) – and for failing to present a sustained, historically specific reflection of developments within the city's urban space.[6]

In an effort to consolidate Berlin's film history, journalists and scholars have gone to great lengths to establish links between post-unification films and the city's pre-war film tradition. Mila Ganeva, for instance, claims that 'in consciously avoiding engagement with recent history and politics, recent Berlin films inevitably tap into some highly effective and productive aspects of past traditions' and that the return of 'the outsider, the underdog, the marginal character' shows some continuity with narratives of the New German Cinema.[7] In fact, figures such as these have a long tradition in urban narratives and are by no means a construct unique to the critical reflections of the directors associated with that period. Tracing the influences of these films certainly continues to be a task to which scholars apply themselves, resulting in considerable divergence. Andreas Dresen's celebrated *Nachtgestalten* (*Night Shapes*, 1998) is a case in point. His film has variously been claimed as a film that operates 'in true Film Noir style', one that employs 'Weimar-era aesthetics for specifically German identity-forming purposes', and as a film that also follows the critical tradition of the New German Cinema. Others, still, have linked Dresen's work to Soviet film culture.[8] Of course, Dresen's film may be all (or even none) of those things. Certainly, the director, who counts as one of the most cine-literate directors working in Germany today, will be aware of these traditions and genres and indeed his film may consciously reference a number of incongruent styles. In interviews, Dresen has also acknowledged the work of British directors Mike Leigh and Ken Loach (and there are certain similarities between Leigh's 1993 film, *Naked*, and *Nachtgestalten*, though his protagonists are less prone to the nihilism that guides Leigh's anti-hero).[9]

Figure 5.1 *Nachtgestalten*
Two of Dresen's outsiders, Peschke (Michael Gwisdeck) and Feliz (Ricardo Valentim) in *Nachtgestalten* (Andreas Dresen, 1998) © Rommel Film

Nachtgestalten offers a view of the city that is analogous to the *flâneur*'s roving observations, with Dresen's interest in the motley characters that people his film (all of them outsiders – punks, the homeless, junkies, refugees) corresponding with the 'eccentric and despised representatives' that so fascinated Benjamin.[10] Dresen's narrative avoids obvious east/west references; the city is, overall, not thematized in terms specific to the east German experience. But his interest in Berlin's marginalized figures offers a view of the city from the bottom up, a sub-urban perspective that aligns it with other films of the period (from the comedy-drama of Wolfgang Becker's *Das Leben ist eine Baustelle* (*Life is All You Get*, 1997) to Susann Reck's bizarre 1998 documentary-like feature, *Alle der Kosmonauten* (*Cosmonauts' Alley*). Dresen says his intention is 'to describe life in its full, with humour and a lot of pain', an approach favoured also by Leigh.[11] *Nachtgestalten* foregrounds the depressing side of metropolitan life (drugs, prostitution, homelessness, violence, theft) in a manner close to documentary realism – a realism that is reinforced by the city's authentic locations, by the hand-held camerawork and the desaturated film stock – but does not investigate the causes and origins of addiction, cultural hostility or social disintegration. Despite this joyless portrait of the urban environment, Dresen's film includes some unexpectedly positive moments: a homeless couple is reconciled and allowed a night of brief luxury; an irascible businessman is softened by his brief guardianship of a young Angolan, while a farmer and addict/prostitute each experience unanticipated acts of kindness. As with so many of the characters in post-unification films, their circumstances are improved, albeit briefly, by chance and not by design (or perhaps providence, given that the film is set at the time of the Pope's visit). The urban environment never ceases to be intimidating, but respite and contentment may occasionally be found in the most unexpected of places.

No-Man's Land

The energy and tension fuelled by the protestors on the streets of Berlin in the cold, autumn days of 1989 did not dissipate once the people had returned home but was manifest in the passionate discourse and frenetic building activity. The no-man's land, which had once been the location of Berlin's bustling Potsdamer Platz, did not remain empty or go unclaimed for long. The debates that ensued went beyond the aesthetic differences of ambitious architects, for any discussion about building and rebuilding at such historical locations could not but acknowledge the city's problematic pasts if they were to draw up plans for a city of the future. Although not the true centre of Berlin, it was regarded as the heart of the city and reconstituting the area was considered an operation that was necessary if the real Berlin was to be brought back to life. The discussions concerning the centre's new urban scheme were analogous to those regarding Germany's new identity: both demanded careful handling of the past and sensitivity to the present if they were to offer a dependable and appealing foundation for the future capital of a united Germany. As ever, the decisions taken tended to indulge the investors and not the local population and the reactions to the final building projects have not been upbeat. For many, the designs failed to live up to expectations, while others (principally Berliners) feel that the area now exudes a corporate rather than a civic identity.

The construction of Potsdamer Platz attracted documentary filmmakers throughout this period. Directors such as Hubertus Siegert were eager to capture the process of architectural transformation as city planners, together with major corporations and their architects, sought to fill the void. The few feature film directors who chose to set their narratives against the reconstruction of the city's centre considered the development from the viewpoint of the city's marginalized figures, as in Eoin Moore's *Plus-minus-null* (*Break Even*, 1998), whose protagonists are drawn from society's edges (refugees, prostitutes, petty criminals, illegal workers) and positioned in the heart of the city.[12] However, the majority of the post-unification films set in Berlin tended towards a decentred portrait of the city. Thus, several of the films consider the post-unification experience in Berlin's (eastern) outskirts amid those 'residential silos', the massive prefabricated housing estates, or in the old, dilapidated districts, which were slowly transforming as investors moved in and rents rose.[13] It was in these areas, away from the touristic routes, that directors could focus on the people displaced or marginalized by unification.

Orientations

The eastern orientation of Michael Klier's narrative was evident in the title of his film, *Ostkreuz* (an important train station in east Berlin). Made in 1991, *Ostkreuz* (*East Crossing*) presented the city at a time between times, between the GDR past whose legacy is apparent in the architectural references, and an unknown future – implied in the as yet empty spaces. Berlin exists as a place of urban decay, an unremittingly grim world of housing estates, vacant plots and lifeless waste grounds. These gaps in the city's urban makeup have been evaluated by others. The Spanish architect Manuel De Sola-Morales has described Berlin as a city marked by clear distances, 'a city in which the recurrence and sequence of the buildings counts for less than the recurrence and sequence of the spaces between them'. The 'urban structure of East Berlin', he adds, 'thus appears as an exercise in keeping things apart, as a spatial separation of buildings according to various different activities and purposes'.[14] With the state departed, the open spaces are emptied of their original meaning – whether as points of public interaction (according to some utopian socialist town planning), or sites designated for some future project. That the ideology that had once brought people together within these open spaces no longer existed was evident in the plinths symbolically denuded of their statues and the more unyielding effigies of once revered socialist heroes, whose imposing demeanour was repeatedly compromised by graffiti assaults.

Berlin has, according to Andreas Huyssen, been characterized by voids of one sort or another for much of the twentieth century. They are represented by the craters and cavities left in the city after the war, the cartographic void that replaced West Berlin on East German maps, and the open space between east and west Berlin that after unification was to become Europe's biggest building site.[15] The voids in Klier's film – the expanse of land surrounding the angular *Plattenbau* (prefabricated apartment blocks) estates, the disused premises of former businesses – suggest the incompleteness of the GDR without indicating whether plans were curtailed by historical events or by the state's financial shortcomings. Voids are implied also in the absence of any emotional connections between the film's characters (as in the teenage protagonist, Elfie, or the petty criminal, Darius, or the homeless Edmund).[16] The lack of a home and of possessions reflects the characters' transient status and aligns the east Germans with the city's other refugees, represented here by the eastern Europeans also housed at the centre in which Elfie and her mother live, and by the disenfranchised Polish community. Elfie's efforts to earn the deposit needed for one of the apartments constitutes an attempt to recover some material and emotional security; in short, to fill the voids. Paradoxically, the newly opened city is all the more difficult to access and Elfie is just one of several characters caught in a no-man's land between the society she has left behind and the society that seems to deny her admission. Life for the displaced characters in *Ostkreuz* is thus a matter of existing rather than living. With the demonstrators long gone and many east Berliners emigrating, the Berlin that Klier explores is an abandoned environment. Even the imposing apartment blocks seem little more than facades and give no indication of any human activity. The many empty spaces in Klier's film, the vacant buildings, the near-motionless streets, accentuate this lifelessness and the lack of hope. Berlin is thus imagined not as the centre for a new beginning but as a ghost city, the dilapidated buildings in the east as the tombstones of the former state. Yet Klier's young protagonist is not haunted by the past. Elfie's movements across the city do not prompt a remembrance of things past, as they do for the (older) protagonists of other Berlin films; instead, her energies are focused only on surviving the present in order to establish a foundation for the future. Uprooted from her home and environment, she is cast into an unfamiliar territory that she must learn to navigate. This poses both a geographical and psychological challenge: Elfie must identify and comprehend a new set of coordinates if she is to survive. Klier uses Elfie's geographical confusion as a metaphor to highlight the east Germans' problems of direction in the new society; her experience of the city, meanwhile, is a rude introduction to predicaments that have arisen in the absence of accommodation, of state control and, importantly, community.

It is clear that Elfie must learn to overcome the obstacles she encounters – by whatever means – if she is to make her way in the new Germany.

Elfie's fortitude is essential, for Berlin proves a demanding, frequently hostile and disorientating environment. In one scene, she comes across one of the city's many empty spaces. Out in the open, she momentarily appears to have lost her bearings. Filmed at long distance, she is made small against the rising urbanscape, one of many visual compositions in the film that emphasizes the isolation of the subject. Dressed in black, Elfie appears silhouetted against the uniform apartment blocks, a fragile specimen framed by the massive concrete towers. The camera focuses on her temporary bewilderment as she struggles to recognize some landmark – the television tower, piercing the grey sky, is the only recognizable pointer. The emptiness is emphasized by the long takes and the static camera, which characterizes Klier's distanced relationship to his subjects. Characters thus photographed are dwarfed by the surrounding brutal architecture. Shots of buildings and of austere rooms and corridors are suddenly interrupted as people move in and out of the frame, the camera remaining motionless, 'cutting only when it seems each shot has exhausted itself'.[17] The unnaturalness of the ghostly city is intensified by the audiovisual techniques used by Klier. The eerie soundtrack, a score consisting of echoed discordant instrumentation (composed by avant-garde composer Fred Frith) imbues the scenes with a tension that emphasizes the city's alienating effect. The film's aural arrangements, from

Figure 5.2 *Ostkreuz*
One of unification's victims: the vulnerable but resourceful Elfie (Laura Tonke) in *Ostkreuz* (Michael Klier, 199) © Filmgalerie 451

the echoes and electronic howls of the score to the diegetic sounds, fill the void left by the minimal dialogue (consisting of little more than staccato questions and challenges, demands and threats). The spare communication and restrained camerawork in *Ostkreuz* again recall Jarmusch's work, to whose work Klier's earlier film, *Überall ist es besser wo wir nicht sind* (*Things are Always Better Elsewhere*, 1988), had been favourably compared. The film shows Klier's continuing interest in this audiovisual approach and in the relationship between the environment and the individual, which is filmed in a detached manner, avoiding both drama and exposition.

Ostkreuz was more than just an opportunity for Klier to study the displaced and marginalized. The director was determined to capture the images and the mood of a city on the brink of change: 'time has stood still there, and I was determined to film there before this "time" had vanished'.[18] The film's locations, together with the struggles of his protagonists to negotiate the transition, led some reviewers to speak positively of a new 'rubble film', a comparison that rather overstated east Berlin's material condition.[19] Nor is *Ostkreuz* a film that advocates the reconstruction of the city or provides its characters with the kind of redemption offered in the post-war films. Others pointed to Italian neo-realism as a more likely source of influence, and though Klier's film does not emulate the poetic drama and sentimental pathos of the neo-realists, there are certain thematic parallels. In Elfie's desire to acquire the money for the unseen flat, upon which all her hopes and future seem pinned, there are echoes, for example, of De Sica's *Bicycle Thieves* (1948) and its protagonist's desperate search for the bicycle that will guarantee him the job that he needs. *Ostkreuz* is equally concerned with documenting the uncertainties of a society in transition (*Bicycle Thieves* of course focuses on Italian society in the aftermath of the war), though Klier does not emulate the liberal humanism of De Sica. Nor does Klier promote the family as an inviolable refuge as does De Sica, since Elfie is finally abandoned by her mother, who leaves the city for the small town comfort of Duisburg in the west. There are parallels, too, with Rossellini's neo-realist masterpiece, *Germany Year Zero* (1946), an influence acknowledged by the director, who likewise names one of his leads Edmund.[20] As with the young protagonist of Rossellini's film, Elfie drifts through Berlin trying to earn money on the black market. Interestingly, the children in both films come to the conclusion that they are a burden to their families. Rossellini's film ends tragically with the young protagonist unexpectedly committing suicide in order to relieve the pressure on his family. It is perhaps surprising, given that Elfie overhears her mother conceding that 'it would be easier without her', and that, statistically speaking, young women were most prone to suicide during the period, that Klier's film resists a similarly tragic conclusion.[21] Nevertheless, some future tragedy cannot be wholly dismissed, since the film ends with Elfie and her friend, Edmund, cold and alone in an empty, windowless building, smoking cigarettes and sharing their meagre food supplies.

Haunted by the Past

Klier's characters uncomfortably occupy a space that represents a threshold between two worlds; though desperate to establish herself in the new society, Elfie is inevitably drawn back east. When she is stranded at an abandoned Polish border train station during a botched black market deal, she is, ironically, even further east than she was at the beginning. That she is there fulfilling a role as a translator in a stolen car deal between Russians and Poles is evidence of her 'in-between' status: unable to participate in the new opportunities of market capitalism, she is forced to make use of her school Russian for illicit transactions. But these returns to the east and to the past carry no emotional significance for Klier's heroine, a fact that is emphasized when she purloins her grandfather's Meissen porcelain, not for its emotional significance but for its black market value. The past simply equips her with the resources for surviving the present.

Ostkreuz imagines Berlin not as the frenzied metropolis but as a ghostly, dehumanized city; in other urban dramas the focus is on individuals haunted by the past. The transience emphasized by the vacant plots and temporary housing units in *Ostkreuz* is echoed in these films, and though the characters (primarily middle-aged men) are more firmly rooted in their milieus – not the transitional no-man's land of *Ostkreuz* but a more identifiable east Berlin – they are no less dislocated than Klier's young protagonist. The architectural makeup in films such as *Der Kontrolleur* (*The Border Guard*, Stefan Trampe, 1994) and Kleinert's *Wege in die Nacht* plays a similarly symbolic role, with the crumbling facades and demolished buildings of east Berlin corresponding to the protagonists' emotional state, their dispossession and loss of stability. Just as the city appears to be disintegrating, so all relationships are ruptured: there is no evidence of neighbourhood identity; gone is the niche society, the professional camaraderie and private, social friendships; families no longer exist and marriages barely function.

Where Elfie resourcefully attempts to assume some control over her situation and her future, the male protagonists in these later films respond to their post-unification anxieties by reverting to the past. Regression becomes a coping strategy, an attempt to restore some order to lives that have lost all constancy and whose impermanence finds its apotheosis in the ruins and the rubble. The effects of the social, architectural and cultural transformations do not so much arouse a fear of what is to come than a dread realization of what has been lost. As Marc Augé notes:

> It is only the idea, partially materialized, that the inhabitants have of their relations with the territory, with their families and with others. This idea may be partial or mythologized. It varies with the individual's point of view and position in society. Nevertheless, it offers and imposes a set of references which may not be quite those of natural harmony or some 'paradise lost', but whose absence, when they disappear, is not easily filled.[22]

Erasure of the GDR past does not constitute the loss of paradise (none of the characters actually eulogizes the former state) but represents the disappearance of a way of life that provided coherence and direction. Whether or not such principles were enthusiastically embraced is immaterial; it was the sense of collective purpose in following the regime's rallying call or in rejecting it that was important. The reaction to the loss of structure and to the certainties that the GDR provided, as fragile as these were, is explored in a number of post-unification films. It is central to Trampe's and Kleinert's films, which consider the post-unification experiences of men of authority – Hermann, an ex-border guard in *Der Kontrolleur*; and Walther, a former director of one of the state-owned factories, in *Wege in die Nacht*. The narratives' uncritical focus on individuals who are identifiable with the state apparatus and who remain unapologetic about their former roles marks a significant departure from the majority of post-unification films. The period's comedies tend towards apolitical everyman figures, while the rural dramas centre their narratives on ordinary individuals with no official connection to the state. Those associated with the Party tended to be portrayed as crude caricatures, as with the bumbling bullies in *Das war der wilde Osten* or the sinister bureaucrats in *Apfelbäume*. Both Trampe and Kleinert eschew such characterization, refusing to judge their characters because of their past allegiances. While neither Hermann nor Walther is specifically linked to the Party (Walther distances himself from a secretive network of the former elite whom he accuses of opportunism), they are close to the previous administration, a relationship that in other films is contiguous with the crimes of the state (Lienhard Wawrzyn's 1993 film, *Der Blaue* (*The Blue One*) for instance). Paradoxically, their dubious past makes them the more sympathetic. As once-loyal servants of the state, they feel the pressures of the new society more keenly and struggle to maintain some equilibrium between the past and a new society that operates according to different rules of conduct and behaviour.

The films portray a city that is in transition. A new Berlin emerges between the ruins and the architectural remnants of the previous administration. The openness of the city is often acknowledged in the characters' movements around the metropolis. With the exception of Gwisdek's chamber-film, *Abschied von Agnes*, which limits its views of the city to the protagonist's peregrinations around central Berlin, most of the characters in the films are seen passing through the urban landscape at various stages in the films. This mobility is ultimately limiting, however, for rather than leading to any positive resolution, the characters' increased exposure to the city only reinforces their displacement and anxieties. The locations in which they find themselves are often the city's 'non-places', places of transition (the subway system, the airport, for example), or sites that are the loci of bureaucracy and administration (the job centre, the defunct border station). Although the protagonists are occasionally in places that offer some opportunity for interaction – bars, restaurants, etc. – they each remain separate from the people there, resistant to any conviviality or camaraderie.

The freedom of movement and the release from the strictures of a closely monitored society introduces the inhabitants to new problems, not least the problem of orientation. Since the environment's physical structures are bound up with the social activity and urban identity of the east Berliners, their collective past encoded by place, the disappearance of particular landmarks necessarily requires considerable physical and psychological readjustment, a process that is especially applicable to the protagonist in Hannes Stöhr's film, *Berlin is in Germany*.

For Heiner, the central character in *Abschied von Agnes*, it is exposure to the past, in the form of an unwanted guest (played by a maniacal Sylvester Groth), that threatens to disrupt his fragile existence. The former Stasi operative's intrusion disturbs Heiner's efforts to systematize his memories of the past in general and of his late wife in particular. Gwisdek's understated psychological drama focuses on Heiner as he struggles to cope with the intrusion into his personal (physical and mental) space. *Abschied von Agnes* – the title refers to the protagonist's deceased wife – considers the relationship between victim and antagonist, which is transformed by evolving mutual dependencies – with the victim dependent on his visitor's knowledge about his past, and the antagonist reliant on his host for shelter. The visual composition heightens the film's claustrophobic mood, with Gwisdek's rangy frame frequently enclosed by doorways, window frames and narrow corridors. This claustrophobia is not simply a reaction to physical containment but also to the city's generally oppressive atmosphere. Surveillance, an act in which all of the characters engage, adds to the film's sense of paranoia and unease. Although surveillance is most closely aligned with Stefan, the former Stasi agent who appears to know every detail of Heiner's life, Gwisdek's film reveals a society given to voyeuristic tendencies, be it the nosy neighbours or unappeasable journalists, who follow the fugitive to Heiner's door. Heiner, too, surveys and scrutinizes the city around him. Initially, Gwisdek's character is reminiscent of the *flâneur*: apart from the crowd, he observes and records the city around him in a manner that is 'inquisitive, anecdotal, ironic, melancholy, but above all voyeuristic'.[23] However, Heiner is not the detached observer to whom Benjamin refers in his writings on the *flâneur*. His record of the events happening around him is not prompted by dispassionate observation but by an existential desire to make sense of developments (the material and social changes in Berlin, and the changes within his private, domestic space) that threaten his identity. His surveillance signifies a need to organize his memories: he tapes his thoughts and conversations, and documents his experiences, casting himself as a detective in his own story. He attempts to decipher the clues that he is given by his visitor/tormentor, whom he also continually monitors. In trying to organize his understanding of the past he becomes dependent on the interloper who exploits his position and knowledge, a situation that echoes the real-life encounters between Stasi employees and those they persecuted.[24]

Heiner's rehabilitation is possible only once he has rid himself of the intruder, thereby symbolically exorcizing the past: in a shock ending, he throws Stefan from the window – a scene filmed so casually that the viewer is momentarily unsure as to what has actually happened. Although the film ends with the disturbing revelation that Heiner dispatched his wife in similar fashion, Gwisdek's hero (played by the director himself) looks to have settled an account with the past and emerges from his ordeal revitalized and confident, ready to face the present.

Disorientation

The past is not so easily resolved in Trampe's and Kleinert's films, whose characters are less willing to disengage from their memories than Heiner. This is understandable, given the characters' changed fortunes – a decline in circumstances that refutes Kohl's assurance of a brighter future. Trampe's protagonist, in particular, is a disenchanted, wretched figure. Demoted from border officer to security guard at the same site, premises now overgrown with weeds, Hermann (played by Hermann Beyer, the east German stage actor and brother of DEFA luminary Frank Beyer) counts as one of the losers of unification. By focusing on a former member of the security forces, Trampe employs an extreme agent of GDR authority and thereby maximizes the conflict between the order of the GDR and apparent disorder of post-unification society. But the observations that Hermann

Figure 5.3 *Der Kontrolleur*
Facing an uncertain future. Herman Beyer as the former border guard in *Der Kontrolleur* (Stefan Trampe, 199) © Stefan Trampe

makes, mostly spat out in near incoherent disgust, are not unrepresentative of attitudes in the New Federal States. Principal among these is a perceived breakdown in civil behaviour and the fear of increased criminality. These sentiments awaken a paradox: while those surveyed confirm their anxieties about these threats, the safeguards that existed in the GDR would hardly be wished for since these were one aspect of the regime's repression. Still, this paradox does not diminish the unease many east Germans feel about behaviour that they associate with the west. The vandalism that Trampe's character witnesses results in violent agitation and when Hermann struggles to find an appropriate label for the kids who have broken his window, his final cry is 'traitors!' The inappropriate and now obsolete description reveals both his fundamental despair and sense of betrayal. Not the children are the traitors, but the society that allows such antisocial behaviour. His later comment, 'fucking crime – they wouldn't have dared before', echoes the idealized memories of the GDR as a near crime-free society (naturally disregarding the state's own crimes) and reveals a yearning for the harsh punitive measures that previously existed.[25]

Trampe's film is one also defined by voids and ellipsis. Hermann's memories of the past shape his experience of the present, from the corporeal absence of his wife, who is present only in photographs and when resurrected in frequent flashbacks, to the emptiness of the sprawling border complex that he alone monitors.[26] His continued attachment to this site of memory goes beyond taking refuge in the comfort of the past, as he soon becomes incapable of distinguishing between past and present. While GDR uniforms had been dusted down for Ostalgie parties, the official livery is for Hermann a last vestige of individual authority and identity. His decision to wear it once more does not signal nostalgic fancy-dress but an attempt to re-engage with the past. Believing himself to be a border guard once again, he begins conducting an absurdly officious interrogation of two strangers he has forcibly detained as intruders. Once he realizes his mistake, Hermann tries to rid himself of the past by burning the uniform together with the contents of his office. Realization brings no happy resolution for the protagonist: finally aware that the role that has defined him no longer exists, he bricks up the spy holes in the narrow watchtower, thus sealing himself inside. Hermann's final response to the events around him literally results in his being walled in. By entombing himself within the watchtower, he invokes the two rationalizations of the Berlin Wall, for this last desperate act can equally be seen as (self-)imprisonment and as a means of protection against the influences beyond.

Like *Der Kontrolleur*, Andreas Kleinert's *Wege in die Nacht*, whose distinctive visual style delighted critics and film festival jurors alike, focuses on one man's difficulties in accepting his diminished post-unification status (an intense performance by the expatriated DEFA veteran, Hilmar Thate). Although the characters differ in terms of their professional profile and social standing, both figures are marginalized and divested of their previous responsibilities. The changes in the men's individual circumstances amounts to a kind of emasculation, since their new responsibilities are reduced to domestic roles typically associated with women, whose absence is acknowledged in each of the films (they exist only as photographs and as memories in Trampe's and Gwisdek's films; Kleinert's film, meanwhile, makes obvious the reversal of traditional gender roles in Walther's and Sylvia's marriage: he cooks and cleans, she goes out to work). Kleinert's protagonist experiences a similarly profound loss of self – so profound that, according to Kerstin Decker, he may already be dead – and struggles to regain the order and authority that defined his pre-wall role.[27]

Huyssen's remark that 'Berlin as text remains first and foremost historical text, marked as much, if not more, by absences as by the visible presence of its past', is borne out in Kleinert's film.[28] Walther's frequent visits to his former factory, an ethereal location of deserted and partially demolished buildings, demonstrate the past's mesmeric hold. Though he is unable to re-establish his professional base and authority, he is able to restore order to the world around him. Perceiving a breakdown in civil society, Walther reinvents himself as a vigilante, a new out of hours role that compensates for his passive daytime existence. Accompanied by a young couple, he patrols Berlin looking to administer justice of a very rough kind to any transgressors who they encounter on their nocturnal tours of duty. Belligerent racists are targeted, as are gangs who torment S-

Figure 5.4 *Wege in die Nacht*
Role reversal: Walter (Hilmar Thate) takes brief comfort from his wife (Cornelia Schmaus) in *Wege in die Nacht* (Andreas Kleinert, 1998) © Robert Paris/öFilm Filmgalerie 451

Bahn passengers and abuse the homeless. But Walther is no heroic figure and certainly not the positive socialist defending the rights of others. The 'insecurity of existence' in this new society does not become, as Bauman previously proposed, a communal affair, but remains a matter of personal righteous anger.[29] His form of justice exposes a deeper rage, as Walther seeks to resume his original authority, resulting in brutal acts of aggression in which the antagonists themselves become victims. Just as Hermann's re-immersion into his former role hastens his own downfall, retrieving some semblance of his previous influence does not mark the beginning of Walther's psychological rehabilitation, but the beginning of his demise, which ends in suicide at the site of his former factory.

For some critics, *Wege in die Nacht* was further evidence of Kleinert's debt to Tarkovskian composition and narrative organization; others began to refer to Kleinert as an auteur – a description seldom heard since the decline of the New German Cinema. Regardless of the accuracy of such claims, *Wege in die Nacht* certainly counts as one of the most distinctive films of the post-unification period. The city had been made to look suitably austere and unappealing in most other Berlin films, which tended to film in dreary locations in a pallid winter light. In Kleinert's film, the cinematography (by erstwhile Fassbinder collaborator Jürgen Jürges) transforms the city into something more sublime. Berlin is made to resemble a noir location, a shadowy world of subterranean passages, half-lit streets where and mists that drift across abandoned buildings. The visual reference to film noir is apposite, since Walther, the determined solitary figure at odds with society around him and determined to see justice done, is driven by impulses that typically guide film noir's troubled antiheroes. The black and white photography adds a chiaroscuro quality that deepens the contrast between light and dark and gives expression to Walther's inner division.

New Cartographies: *Berlin is in Germany*

Hannes Stöhr's debut film *Berlin is in Germany* charts a convict's return to Berlin after a decade's imprisonment during which time the GDR has fallen and the two states unified. Readjusting to freedom is doubly problematic for Martin (Jörg Schüttauf), the film's hero, since his release introduces him both to a life outside prison and to life outside the erstwhile containment of the GDR. Berlin's palimpsestic quality is emphasized in Stöhr's film, as his protagonist attempts to find his way in the new metropolis using co-ordinates that have been superseded during his incarceration. Martin experiences the city as if for the first time: the film focuses on the wide-eyed innocent, a latter-day Rip van Winkle, as he encounters, and is confused by, the banal features of the modern city: ticket machines, mobile phones, the ephemera of everyday life. In postponing Martin's exposure to western modernity by a decade, Stöhr's film imaginatively re-engages with the image of the unreconstructed Ossi so popular at the beginning of the decade.[30] This is not to say that *Berlin is in Germany* revives the crude stereotypes of *Der Superstau* or *Go Trabi Go*; nevertheless, there is a degree of continuity in the characterizations, a nostalgia even for the optimism of the early days of the Wende, before such portrayals had taken on more hostile signification. Martin's belated exposure to the peculiarities of the modern city initially allows the viewer a repeat enjoyment of the east Germans' cheery bewilderment with the objects of the everyday, that pays little attention to the developments of the intervening years, the increased antagonism and disillusionment.

Nevertheless, Stöhr's film is not an uplifting and updated version of the east–west encounters. Berlin is frequently depicted according to familiar modernist anxieties: home to vice and corruption (represented by pornography and prostitution), a city in which individuals lack community and remain isolated from one another. Importantly, Stöhr's film implies that these features and the angst and social dislocation that they generate are the by-product of life in the new post-socialist city. The envisaged life in the *Plattenbau* estates is far removed from DEFA's predominantly rosy portraits of city living. No longer proof of the state's provision, the east's mass housing estates are now synonymous with social problems associated with a new economic underclass (xenophobia, unemployment, suicide) that were unimaginable, or at least, unrepresentable, in the GDR. If the commercialization and corporate redevelopment of Berlin bear the influence of (western) market capitalism, a seamier entrepreneurship in the form of the sex industry is linked to the arrival of eastern Europeans, a link that is also implied in Eoin Moore's Berlin film.

Stöhr's film emphasizes Berlin as existing in a state of flux. This is evident not only in its physical regeneration, the architectural developments that are observed en passant, but in its changing values and new modes of behaviour. In contrast to the staid, predictable pace of life that characterized the city under the former political masters, those elderly cadres whose prescribed plans never allowed for spontaneity (as the reactions to the demonstrations in 1989 clearly showed), life in post-wall Berlin is one in which the old certainties have been swept away. But while this release from the previous regime denotes new freedoms (independence, individuality), it also signifies the end of certain securities that its citizens later often missed (even if they were the result of economic and political stagnation). Few securities are evident in the open city – though a similar, if less malign, level of bureaucracy exists, as represented by the police, the judiciary and the parole agency. No longer controlled, protected or regulated by the state, the east Germans have apparently been set adrift in the new society.

Martin's place in this strange environment is therefore not assured. His discharge hardly amounts to a homecoming, since the defining aspects of his home – on a personal level, his domicile, his family (in an Odyssean twist, his wife is remarried and his young son a stranger to him), his social

Figure 5.5 *Berlin is in Germany*
Martin (Jörg Schttauf) rediscovering his home city in *Berlin is in Germany* (Hannes Stöhr, 199) © Hannes Stöhr

world; and in a more general sense, the state in which he was socialized – have all but disappeared. A late arrival in the new Berlin, Martin struggles to establish himself in a society that he barely recognizes. Yet in contrast to the protagonists who remain imprisoned by the past in Kleinert's and Trampe's films, Martin understands the need to disengage from his former co-ordinates if he is to gain some footing in the new Germany. The film traces his movements around the city that is both familiar and unknown to him with numerous shots positioning him in trams and subway trains as he travels across the ever-changing landscape. In *Berlin is in Germany*, the city's pasts are intricately layered; mastering Berlin's new codes and signs is essential for Martin's successful adjustment. This is symbolically under-lined in his decision to train as a taxi driver in the new capital, a process that poses an anamnestic dilemma, as he struggles to acquaint himself with Berlin's new map while simultaneously trying to forget the co-ordinates that previously existed.[31] His willingness to familiarize himself with the new system (via its signage) in effect acknowledges the new administrative order but it also demonstrates a resolve that is apparently lacking in the other east Germans.[32]

Made at a time when the east Germans' selective retrieval of their past had become commonplace, Stöhr's film offers a counterpoint to such nos-talgic processes. *Berlin is in Germany* seems to privilege the elision, not the celebration of memory. Remembering to forget, 'active forgetting', as Huyssen calls it, is therefore the key to survival.[33] Stöhr's film even out-lines the dangers of failing to break with the past. While Martin embodies the preferred east German characteristics (a positive stereotype of the honest, unpretentious proletarian), his friend, Peter (Thomas Jahn, sometime director and, more recently, an actor frequently called on to play depressed blue-collar east Germans), exhibits the worst traits of the post-unification Ossi – or the Jammerossi (moaning Ossi). Emerging in opposition to the Besserwessi (the east Germans' neologism for arrogant west Germans), the Jammerossi encapsulated the western view of those indolent and ungrateful east Germans who apparently preferred to complain about their situation rather than actively improve it. Resentful, timid and self-pitying, Peter thus personifies the stereotype. His is a wretched account of life in the post-socialist republic, a jeremiad that admits no personal responsibility for his failures and disappointments and explains his suicidal tendencies, a fate from which his friend rescues him. Conversely, Stöhr makes plain the benefits to be had from divesting oneself of such rudimentary east German thought and behaviour. Unlike Peter, the *Plattenbau* resident and Trabant driver, Martin's ex-wife, Manuela, is one of the few east Germans in post-unification cinema to have successfully transformed into a west German. Having shaken off all vestiges of her east German past she is rewarded with a comfortable apartment in Pankow (the leafy Berlin suburb that was once home to loyal SED functionaries), a partner from the west, and all the trappings of a bourgeois lifestyle that includes a Mercedes, bijoux home furnishings, dinner parties and international cuisine.

Stöhr's hero oscillates between these two worlds, between the familiar environment of the past and the unfamiliar and exotic surroundings of the present but remains detached from both, reluctant to mimic his wife's assimilation to western codes and practices, and alert to the dangers of Peter's recidivism. Martin's restlessness causes his friends to evaluate their own lives: in acknowledging her long-absent husband, his wife rediscovers a connection to the east, and is suddenly aware of her partner's cowardly and ineffectual side. Peter, meanwhile, is prompted out of his torpidity by Martin's reappearance, and renews his efforts to find work. Despite the positive influence that he brings to bear, Martin does not seek to revive any east German community in the way that the protagonist of the early Wende films did, though his reappearance does reunite former east German friends. His personality appears to stir affirmative east German traits (co-operation, initiative, resilience) which have been dormant in others in the years since unification, without invoking SED ideology or expressly valorizing the collective/community. Unlike the protagonists of *Wege in die Nacht* and *Der Kontrolleur*, Stöhr's protagonist is certainly not of the Party fold, a point that is confirmed in a flashback sequence that explains Martin's incarceration (attempted escape from the GDR and the accidental killing of the man who threatened to betray him to the authorities) and draws attention to his opposition to the GDR.

Martin therefore symbolizes an idealized, depoliticized east German – a humble figure whose motivation for finding work is principally to provide for his family (in this case his son) and not to secure the material comforts favoured by his ex-wife. Though Martin's lack of enthusiasm for the new culture of untrammelled consumerism does not amount to actual critique (his suspicion towards electronic toys for example reflects his age rather than any ideological or pedagogical objection), his indifference to such materialism at least indicates a lack of pretension that distinguishes him from the west Germans and the new eastern materialists, whose sudden consumer fervour so disheartened left-leaning critics. Stöhr's hero therefore offers substance rather than style. His interest in Russian literature conveys some seriousness and depth that is absent in his western hosts, but in case the point is somehow misunderstood as an attempt to extol the GDR's Soviet orientation, Martin qualifies his literary tastes (writers who in any case either pre-date the Bolshevik Revolution or opposed its ideology), emphasizing 'they don't have a clue about politics. But write – that's something they can do'. Despite his reading habits, which suggest a sensitive and introspective reader, Martin does not resemble the emasculated figures found in other post-unification films. A number of scenes stress his masculinity, be it his romance with Ludmilla, a Serbian prostitute (a relationship that at the same time emphasizes his broad-mindedness) or in aggressive confrontations with bullies who express racist and homophobic sentiments (a reaction that emphasizes his active rejection of prejudice).[34] Displaced though he is from his traditional gender role as paterfamilias, his masculinity is never in doubt. Certainly, it is not, as some have suggested, compromised by his western rival. Lacking Martin's humility and physical presence, he is an effete poltroon to Martin's sturdy proletarian, and his status is weakened as Martin's wife and son each identify with the true husband/father.[35]

The post-unification portraits of Berlin looked at in this chapter do not endorse the grandiloquent discourse of Berlin's new start or the speechifying of the architects, politicians and city-planners intent on re-energizing the capital. The city's architectural rebirth is occasionally acknowledged in the films but it is the demise of east Berlin that is foregrounded. The city's renaissance is clearly a project that will not extend to all, that is, to the losers and other marginalized figures who are typically the focus of the urban narratives. For all the political rhetoric of integration and inclusion, disorientation, isolation and exclusion are the dominant characteristics. These brooding chronicles of metropolitan life are by no means unique to post-unification representations of the city. Berlin has long served filmmakers as the quintessential German city. These films have their antecedents; scholars have sought to analyse the films diachronically, expending much energy in tracing their influences. However, contemporary filmmakers' continued interest in the city's underbelly – sub-urban Berlin – must also be considered synchronically, that is in terms of their specific post-unification, context. Just as writers were using the city's 'symbolic landscape … to find spatial correlatives for their experience', so the filmmakers also explore and fix on images of a city in decay, or a city that has been abandoned and consigned to a history of failed dreams and lost communities.[36]

A number of the narratives suggest that the new freedoms that unification offers are no less isolating and constrictive than life in the closely regulated East German state. The tangible certainties and assurances that the GDR offered have been replaced by intangible freedoms – abstract notions such as autonomy and freedom of choice. Similarly, the security previously provided by families, close professional groups and social circles, the constituent features of an east German community, has all but eroded. The early Wende narratives demonstrated that reviving a dormant community was essential to the east Germans' success. The urban dramas allow for no such continuity. The focus, instead, is on individuals struggling to find their way in an urban environment that is ever changing and in which nothing can be certain. The ensuing disorientation was, in part, spatial, but the energetic redefinition of the city, as much a question of erasing as defining, corresponded with the wider social confusion following unification. Disorientation is the result of the east Germans' general (that is social, ideological and political) loss of direction since the state's collapse as much as it is a problem of spatial bearing. Excluded from policy-making (unless high-ranking SED members), much of the population had adapted to the Party's chosen course – whether in opposition or in support. The east Germans thus require new mental and geographic cartographies, if they are to navigate the city and society successfully.

In their separate ways, the protagonists in Klier's and Stöhr's films each recognise this and set about learning how to read the city anew. Importantly, they show no desire to be fully assimilated, a course of action that is associated with other self-effacing characters. The challenge of adjusting to the new city looks more likely to succeed in *Berlin is in Germany* than *Ostkreuz*, whose heroine is likely to remain a victim of the new geography. In his own insular way, Gwisdek's protagonist is also ready to relinquish the past. Less hopeful are Trampe's and Kleinert's films whose characters are unable to escape their past. Like the obdurate Ossis in films such as *Der Brocken* and the *Trabi* series, there is some opposition to the new changes, though resistance is not of the sentimental, apolitical kind favoured in those narratives. Unlike the characters in those films, Hermann and Walter are too shaped by the GDR's political and ideological culture to be able to adapt. Recourse to the past, to its values, its ideology, can only result in one's undoing, as *Wege in die Nacht* and *Der Kontrolleur* unequivocally demonstrate.

Against these narratives, the city functions as 'both a physical site and a pathological state'.[37] Architects have a fondness for seeing their work as a means of treating some urban disorder and certainly the metaphor of architecture as surgery was frequently used in the literature. Architects Volker Fischer and Anna Mesure, for example, were among those who felt that their designs could go some way to addressing the city's pathology, referring to the question of renovation as a surgical process, and recommending that 'the tissue needs to heal again'.[38] The symbolic use of glass in many of the prestigious building projects implies an openness and transparency that distinguishes the Berlin Republic from the opaque SED regime and the shadows of the NS dictatorship. However, the directors of these films do not concur with the optimism inherent in these constructions, which they mostly avoid, and keep instead to the city's darker recesses, its alleys and abandoned plots. There, in the shadows, protagonists suffer from claustrophobia, paranoia and melancholia, symptoms of a new pathology for which unification has, as yet, offered no cure.

Notes

1. A. Rossi, *The Architecture of the City*, Cambridge, MA, and London: MIT Press, 1982, p. 130.
2. Short (1991), p. 41.
3. The city's heterogeneous constitution has also been manifest in a number of metropolitan novels, or *Kiezromane*. See W. Kaminer, *Schönhauser Allee*, Munich: Goldmann, 2001, and Sven Regener, *Herr Lehmann*, Frankfurt am Main: Eichborn Verlag, 2001.
4. See A. Huyssen, *Present Pasts. Urban Palimpsests and the Politics of Memory*, Stanford: Stanford University Press, 2003, pp. 52, 78.
5. Ladd (1997), p. 125.
6. See E. Preuss, 'The Collapse of Time: German History and Identity in Hubertus Siegert's *Berlin Babylon* (2001) and Thomas Schadt's *Berlin: Sinfonie einer Großstadt* (2002)', in C.A. Costabile-Heming et al. (eds), *Berlin. The Symphony Continues. Orchestrating Architectural Change in Germany's New Capital*, Berlin and New York: Walter de Gruyter, 2004, pp. 41, 123. It should be noted that numerous filmmakers, including several foreign directors, were attracted to the city during its transformation, resulting in some highly individual (and seldom screened) accounts, among them the film essays by Jean-Luc Godard (*Allemagne Neuf Zero*, 1991) and Jan Ralske (*Vergangen, Vergessen, Vorüber*, 1994).
7. M. Ganeva, 'No History, Just Stories. Berlin Films of the 1990s', in Costabile-Heming et al. (2004), p. 263.
8. S. Simon, 'Weimar Project(ion)s in Post-Unification Cinema', in Costabile-Heming et al. (2004), p. 302. In the same volume, see also Mila Ganeva, 'No History, Just Stories. Berlin Films of the 1990s', pp. 261–77. See also P. Cooke, *Representing East Germany since Unification. From Colonization to Nostalgia*, Oxford: Berg Publishers, 2005, p. 110, and Alexandra Ludewig, 'Heimat, City and Frontier in German National Cinema', *Debatte* 9(2), 2001: 181.
9. This author's interview with Andreas Dresen. The director has also acknowledged the importance of Gianni Amellio and the Dogme filmmakers. See C. Ziesche, 'Gespräch mit Andreas Dresen (Drehbuch und Regie)', in A. Dresen, T. Schulz and A. Leusink, *Nachtgestalten*, Berlin: Aufbau Taschenbuch Verlag, 1999, p. 112.
10. G. Gilloch, *Myth and Metropolis: Walter Benjamin and the City*, Cambridge: Polity Press, 1996, p. 9. Vidler holds that 'a fondness for the marginal and the forgotten: these are the traits of flâneur and filmmaker alike', in A. Vidler, *Warped Space: Art, Architecture and Anxiety in Modern Culture*, Cambridge, MA.: MIT Press, 2000, p. 116.
11. Ziesche, in Dresen et al. (1999), p. 112. The director's interest in outsiders can be traced throughout his oeuvre, from the young Turkish German who relocates to east Berlin as soon as the wall has opened in his debut film (*So schnell es geht nach Istanbul*, 1991) to the naive political candidate desperately campaigning in an east German town that is unreceptive to the CDU in his documentary film, *Denk ich an Deutschland – Herr Wichmann von der CDU* (2003).
12. See D. Sannwald, '"Ich heiße Alex, wie der Platz." Berlin-Film der anderen Art: "Plus minus null" von Eoin Moore', *Der Tagesspiegel*, 30 March 2000.

13. M. Mönninger,'Growing Together Again', in A.C. Papadakis (ed.), *Berlin Tomorrow. International Architectural Visions*, London: Architectural Design, 1991, p. 17.
14. M. de Sola-Morales, 'The Abstract City', in Papadakis (1991), p. 85.
15. Huyssen (2003), p. 54. See Rogier, who also refers to the 'vacuous intersections' left by certain post-Wall developments: F. Rogier, 'Growing Pains: From the Opening of the Wall to the Wrapping of the Reichstag', *Assemblage* 29, 1996, p. 45.
16. The biography provided by Edmund is in fact that of the lay-actor, Stefan Cammann. Abandoned by his parents, he was found drifting the streets by the production crew and invited to participate.
17. Coulson, in Durrani et al. (1995), p. 223.
18. Quoted in I. Meißner, 'Die neunziger Jahre'. Retrieved 25 August 2008 from http://www.deutsches-filminstitut.de/sozialgeschichte/dt105a.htm
19. See W. Wiegand, 'Anpassung als Katastrophe. Ein ungewöhnliches "Kleines Fernsehspiel": "Ostkreuz"', *Frankfurter Allgemeine Zeitung*, 25 July 1991.
20. See Meißner (2000).
21. According to one study, 'death rates for girls aged 10–14 ... were up by nearly 70%' during the *Wende*. In N. Eberstadt, 'Demographic Shocks in Eastern Germany 1989–1993', *Europe-Asia Studies* 46(3), 1994: 528. It should be noted that studies of suicide in the east since unification have not resulted in consistent conclusions. A later report, for instance, stresses that the number of people taking their own lives did not increase after 1989. In S. Straub, 'Der Suizid und "die Wende" in der DDR. Zur Tragfähigkeit von Durkheims Konzeption des (anomischen) Selbstmords am Beispiel Thüringens', *System Familie* 13, 2000: 68.
22. M. Augé, *Non-Places. Introduction to an Anthropology of Supermodernity*, London: Verso, 2000, p. 56.
23. See W. Benjamin, *Charles Baudelaire: Zwei Fragmente: ein Lyriker im Zeitalter des Hochkapitalismus*, Frankfurt am Main: Suhrkamp, 1969, p. 58. See E. Wilson, 'The Invisible Flaneur', *New Left Review* 191, 1992: 96.
24. A strange psycho-sexual tension develops between the two men. This is perhaps not as contrived as it may appear, given the curious relationships that did sometimes develop between Stasi operatives and their targets. See C. Epstein,'East Germany and Its History since 1989', *Journal of Modern History* 75(3), 2003: 652. See also the discussion of *Das Leben der Anderen* in the following chapter.
25. East Germans certainly felt that the life in the east was safer before unification. What is more, statistics show that the general fear of an increase in crime in post-unification society has proved justified. See D.E. Clark and M. Wildner,'Violence and Fear of Violence in East and West Germany', *Social Science & Medicine* 51, 2000: 377.
26. Trampe had previously worked as assistant director to Gwisdek on *Abschied von Agnes*.
27. K. Decker. 2000. 'König im Niemandsland. Hilmar Thate', in K. Decker and G. Decker, *Gefühlsausbrüche oder Ewig pubertiet der Ostdeutsche. Reportagen, Polemike, Porträts*, Berlin: Das Neue Berlin, p. 192.
28. Huyssen (2003), p. 52.
29. Z. Bauman, *Community. Seeking Safety in an Insecure World*, Cambridge: Polity Press, 2001, p. 112
30. The innocent east Berlin resident struggling with the challenges of the city is also explored in Helke Misselwitz's Berlin film *Engelchen* (1996).
31. See N. Hodgin, '*Berlin is in Germany* and *Good Bye Lenin!* Taking Leave of the GDR?', *Debatte: Review of Contemporary German Affairs* 12(1), 2004: 30–34.
32. Martin's fortitude also distinguishes him from the east Berlin taxi driver in Christa Wolf's essay, who does not dare head west for fear of being mocked by impatient fares. See C. Wolf, 'Wo ist euer Lächeln geblieben? Brachland Berlin 1990', in *Auf dem Weg nach Tabou. Texte 1990–1994*, Köln: Kiepenheuer & Witsch, 1994, pp. 39–40. In a scene in Tykwer's hip Berlin film *Lola Rennt*, the eponymous heroine complains that a taxi driver has misunderstood her Grunewald Strasse destination for an eastern address (presumably a joke about the general problems of orientation in post-wall Berlin since no such street exists in the east). As for the

taxi business, it had its own share of east/west problems and, like many other East German businesses, had undergone fundamental changes to its organization and administration after 1989. The west German takeover was signalled by the arrival of the substitution of the standard West German taxi, the Mercedes, for the trademark East German taxis, the Wolgas. See 'Mercedes statt Wolga', *Der Spiegel* 3, 1990: 124 (no author).

33. Huyssen (1995), p. 34.
34. It should be noted that Martin's permissiveness does know its bounds. He expresses his contempt for hardcore pornography when he briefly works in the peep show run by a former prison acquaintance, in whose dealings with the paedophile market he is unwittingly implicated.
35. See D. Clarke,'Representations of East German Masculinity in Hannes Stöhr's *Berlin is in Germany* and Andreas Kleinert's *Wege in die Nacht*', *German Life and Letters* 55(4), 2004: 438.
36. K. Leeder, *Breaking Boundaries. A New Generation of Poets in the GDR*, Oxford: Clarendon Press, 1996, p. 57.
37. Vidler (2000), p. 26.
38. V. Fischer and A. Mesure, 'Ideals for the Heart of a Great City', in Papadakis (ed.) (1991), p. 13.

Chapter 6

GOOD BYE, OSTALGIE?

The crusade for cultural amnesia coincided with the rise of nostalgic time travel and the manipulation of history as a commodity; all three trends converge in the impulse to preserve.[1]

Perhaps the most significant development within unification discourse and in the discussions about east German identity was the rise of Ostalgie. As outlined in the first chapter, this neologism originally described a simple, localized nostalgia for the GDR that enabled some east Germans to guard their experiences from post-unification histories of the GDR. It later developed into a lucrative industry (for retailers and television and film producers alike) in which enterprising individuals provided nostalgic east Germans with material reminders of their past, a profitable business, given that 'most people', as John Gillis observes, 'find it difficult to remember without having access to mementoes, images, and physical sites to objectify their memory'.[2] Many of these markers were under threat in the post-communist east as the incumbent administration set about removing not just the obvious political totems but other signs that were of cultural significance to the local population. The ensuing rescue of East Germany's discontinued products thus came to serve an important mnemonic function, with these 'talismans of continuity' helping to perpetuate memories of life in the GDR.[3] The east Germans' memories, too, could also serve a dual function: not only did they connect them to the past as a way of barricading themselves against the present, they could also function as a secret handshake, one that was able to identify those without a legitimate claim to east German memory.

Ostalgie is not simply a matter of defiant regionalism. The east German past has become a commercial venture that is open to all. T-shirt sellers specializing in 'original' GDR fashions obviously do not restrict sales to those with genuine east German postcodes, just as the television Ostalgie Shows of recent years (discussed below) are not broadcast only within the territories formerly constituting the GDR. Nevertheless, the rediscovered materials from the past have become central to many east Germans' sense of identity, corresponding with what Eric Hobsbawm refers to as an 'elaborate language of symbolic practice and communication'.[4]

In a culture obsessed with quality and excellence, the east Germans' celebration of unremarkable GDR products, whether condiments or chocolates or films, has also introduced an antagonistic counter value of modesty and simplicity (characteristics that had also been attributed to the east Germans themselves), which is often intended as a snub to the west's assumed superiority. The actual quality of the products (in truth, often mediocre, though appealingly so) is of less significance than their provenance. At first, some commentators were reluctant to see the resurgent interest in the once commonplace as anything other than a whim, a harmless fashion that would soon be replaced. But Ostalgie's appeal throughout the 1990s and into the new millennium is not evidence of a superficial attachment to the GDR, even if the importance of appearance (in the guise of GDR ephemera) is one of its defining features. The interest in surface authenticity – the genuine GDR labels, the original east German clothes, provisions, furniture – has not lessened its significance for a deeper post-communist east German identity. Nor has the west's subsequent embrace of old east German products proved that Ostalgie is simply part of a modern fascination with and ironic celebration of retro-authenticity. What is ironic is that an east German identity previously predicated on socialist ideology is now largely based on the remnants of its material culture. The economic principles that were behind the uncomplicated packaging and basic commodities have disappeared, leaving behind tins on supermarket shelves that may be branded as *Ostprodukte* but which are now firmly established within the ethos of a capitalist market economy.

It was perhaps inevitable that Ostalgie's counter-narratives would find favour among those east Germans exasperated by a reductive post-unification account of the GDR, which considers the east German state principally in terms of its dictatorial character and its many flaws and which, as Dieckmann has noted, were often penned by west Germans.[5] According to these reports, issues such as pollution, political extremism and the region's economic decline are the legacy of forty years of corrupt and incompetent rule. While some east Germans may be sensitive to accounts that blame post-unification troubles on the pre-unification administration, their main indignation has been reserved for other, more generalizing claims. A number of gaffes and disputed research by public figures and academics has ensured that the east Germans' perceived inferiority continues to be a source of debate. The different attitudes to work and the challenges facing the east German economy resulted in numerous contentious publications. Thomas Roethe's 'Arbeiten wie bei Honecker, verdienen wie bei Kohl'('Work Like under Honecker, Live like under Kohl'), a controversial study that pointed to the east German workforce's inveterate indolence, did little to dispel mutual suspicions and recriminations.[6] The inflammatory claim by Jörg Schönbohm (a west German politician in an east German seat) that a serial infanticide in the east was attributable to a regional moral degeneracy borne of the communist regime offered further evidence of a colonizer's view of the east as a region in need of civilization. Although these are among the more extreme examples of the kind of prejudice directed against the east (and were roundly criticized in the press), they give some sense of the hostility and suspicion that has come to characterize post-unification discourse.

Commodifying the Past

The resurgence of east German products can be attributed to a number of facts. Regional identification partly explains the unexpected consumer loyalty: recognizing the dismal economic consequences for the province, many east Germans initially looked to support eastern businesses which had come under threat from western interests – 'the colonial goods dealers', as one *Spiegel* report described them.[7] Buying east German products was not an exclusively east German matter. The need to support old and new east German business was both politically and economically necessary, and investment in *Ostprodukte* was encouraged by, among others, the German President, Richard von Weizsäcker. It was ironic, considering the significance of regional products for an eastern identity, that the east Germans partly had their western neighbours to thank for the products' revival, for it was often western entrepreneurs who established shops specializing in east German goods. Moreover, at a time when many east Germans were rejecting anything 'Made in GDR' [sic], as their products were traditionally branded, be it ideology, consumer goods or cultural products, it was western supermarkets that offered customers the opportunity to assist their eastern neighbours by carrying contemporary eastern products which were clearly highlighted as such. Specialized Ossi stores in the west do good business in eastern products that continue to be marketed in original GDR packaging, though the important difference between these products and those marketed as 'from the new federal states' standing on national supermarket shelves is that these consumer goods are advertised in terms of GDR heritage as well as their eastern production. Lucrative though the Ossi products are, no politician has yet sought to endorse retro-GDR produce as the answer to the considerable economic problems facing the region. Government interest in national heritage may often encourage nostalgic reflection but nostalgia seldom underpins policy.

Although some scholars have suggested that Ostalgie may be a useful tool in helping the Germans deal with the past, it is probable that continued reference to and use of GDR realia will sustain division, since these function as beacons of different pasts. Nostalgia is, as Steven Ostovitch has pointed out, a dangerous aspect of memory, a 'refusal to let the past be simply past while resisting its incorporation into the present'.[8] For some, the east Germans' nostalgia appears, therefore, as a threat to a post-unification identity. Nostalgic practices blur the line between simply remembering the GDR and actively missing the GDR. The desire to save east German biographies from a generalized narrative that appears not to recognize the nuances of experience has proved contentious and has led to accusations of selective amnesia, an allegation that echoes the delayed post-NS discourse in the west that only began to take place in the late 1960s. Central to the criticism of east German nostalgia is the charge that a refusal to acknowledge the crimes of the former state ultimately excuses the perpetrators and disregards the regime's victims. For its critics (including civil rights campaigners and conservative politicians), Ostalgie does exactly that. It encourages east Germans to wallow in memories of their past, and sanctions self-indulgent recollection at the expense of other truths. It reinforces a post-unification identity that may (indirectly) encourage a mentality of exclusion and cultural segregation. In re-establishing old co-ordinates for a newly defined east German community, Ostalgie rejects the modern, politically correct plea for integration and pluralism.

Though the GDR no longer exists, East German culture continues to be accessible through various archives and museums. The socialist past is readily available, too, in the form of its cultural products and anyone can build up an extensive collection of genuine GDR curios which are offered for sale at diverse locations from flea market stalls to vintage boutiques and online market places. DEFA films are routinely broadcast on regional public service stations in the east and old GDR rock bands are on tour once again, promoting reissued albums. In terms of its commercial manifestation, Ostalgie is no longer an exclusively east German practice, since anyone can buy into GDR culture. But the one thing that remains elusive, and exclusive to the east German community, is their memory of the past, their personal experience. Those from the west may cherish the period's features or myopically envy certain comforts that the east enjoyed (western directors certainly envied eastern directors' fixed salary and generous studio support), but they cannot miss what they never had. And yet, this paradox also informs many east Germans' nostalgia.[9] Regardless of the frustrations of 'real existing Socialism', these east Germans harboured a utopic yearning for a model socialist state (as indeed did many socialists in the FRG). The collapse of the Eastern Bloc signalled the end of the communist system (with a few exceptions) and the end, too, of the east Germans' dreams for a credible socialism. For some, then, there is more to Ostalgie than exuberant performance or the accumulation of socialist paraphernalia. Ostalgie also offers a means of remembering unrealized aspirations.

Disneyland GDR

The first film to engage with post-communist nostalgia, and one routinely overlooked by scholars (and largely dismissed by reviewers and audiences), was a low-budget satire by a young west German filmmaker, Heiko

Schier. Made within a year of the GDR's disintegration, *Alles Lüge* antici-
pates many features later associated with Ostalgie that in 1991 were considered grotesque exaggerations but in hindsight have proved remarkably
perceptive. Like other directors in those early days after unification, Schier
drew inspiration from the cabaret, casting the popular comedian and
satirist, Dieter 'Didi' Hallervorden (who had fled the GDR in 1958, and
later become known to audiences in both the GDR and FRG as a result of
various television shows), in the lead role as Günther Kasulke.[10] Schier's
film follows Kasulke, an ex-GDR cabaretist formerly engaged, as he says,
in the 'development of the people's owned humour' as he attempts to
locate his daughter in Berlin, a quest that involves a series of comic encounters in the recently unified Germany and offers a satire whose good-
natured humour barely masks the film's deeper distrust of unification's
positive outcome for the east.[11] Kasulke's admission that he would rather
have been united with Switzerland foreshadows the east Germans' disenchantment with unification and echoes the director's own considerable
scepticism towards the process of unification, which closely echoes the east
German sense of betrayal and disappointment.[12]

> Everything that we were told about reunification is a lie. That goes from the
> unnecessary tax rises, the promise to have achieved blossoming landscapes
> in three to four years right to the myth that the Germans are one people and
> will now finally grow together because they belong together. This whole
> politicians' pathos is a complete lie.[13]

Schier is among the few west German directors to criticize Kohl's supervision of unification so directly. Other west German directors, such as
Sanders-Brahms, had their misgivings, too, but the qualms of the 1968 generation often gave rise to a regret at the passing of the east Germans' unrealized socialism, something that Schier is not willing to countenance.

Though Schier's film is critical of unification and ridicules many aspects
of the free-market society, which its protagonist discovers to be a breeding
ground for treachery and vice, it also targets the GDR. *Alles Lüge* happily
satirizes east as well as west Germans, and not just those entrenched SED
supporters who show no signs of relinquishing their allegiance to the SED-
state. Indeed, this is one of the few unification comedies in which east
Germans are as proficient in the art of exploitation as their western neighbours. Portmann, Kasulke's former cabaret partner, displays a profiteering
spirit normally associated with the west in these films. The one-time comedian has changed his act and now inveigles sponsors to invest in a series
of 'guaranteed' ventures, ranging from Swiss oysters to Finnish wool, a
swindle whose success depends on the greed and gullibility of investors,
which the new, open Berlin apparently attracts like the Klondike. When
Kasulke, who is innocent to the various cons, finally asks his friend, 'so it's
about deception?', Portmann reassures him, answering, 'that's Capitalism'.
Kasulke lacks the confidence trickery of his friend and his few attempts to

dupe potential investors prove unsuccessful. Apparently incapable of exploiting others, he draws instead on his experiences and does what comes best to him – he improvises. But Kasulke does not use his talents to cheat or deceive; recognizing the opportunities available in this new market economy, he prefers a more legitimate enterprise. Rebranding himself a 'Rent-a-Comic', he hires himself out as GDR fool, a jester whose wild antics and pre-arranged irreverence provide executive stress relief. This is more than an opportunity for Hallervorden to showcase his comic talents. It satirizes a post-unification tendency to view the east Germans as figures of amusement (the reverse side of which saw them as criminals).

Unlike the majority of early unification comedies, Schier's film does not eschew the features of the GDR past in its portrayal of life in the post-wall period. The director makes use of the kind of details that would generally appear only in more sober reflections of the east, with Schier's protagonist making fun of subjects, that in the early 1990s were still taboo. The Stasi are among the once unmentionables to be mocked; so, too, the Party adherents, seen here clinging on to vestiges of the recent past. Buoyed by his success as GDR clown-for-hire, Kasulke recognizes the further potential in mining the past and proposes that the defunct Palace of the Republic, which accommodated the East German parliament and doubled up as a cultural venue, become a 'Socialist Disneyland'. Schier's film shows some acuity in focusing on a new role for 'the Ballast of the Republic' as it was known locally. Plans for the building's demolition after unification immediately roused consternation among some east Germans. Their indignation was prompted as much by the detractors' apparent disregard for the building's cultural significance for east Germans as by the determination to rebuild the Berlin City Palace, the former Royal Prussian and Imperial residence, which had previously stood on the site. The final scene shows the enterprise up and running, complete with mock *Volkspolizei* (VoPo – People's Police) supervising entry to the museum-cum-entertainment park, where children sing FDJ songs and Portmann is already planning a similar scheme for the Cuban people – when the time comes.

Schier's film imagines a perfect solution for unification woes. Kasulke's inspired project allows wistful east Germans to re-engage with the GDR, albeit on a micro-scale. The 'Socialist Disneyland' offers east Germans a re-acquaintance with their Heimat, one that is not compromised by the exigencies of the actual SED-state. West Germans, meanwhile, are also given the opportunity to satisfy their curiosity. In the limited space of the Palace of the Republic they are also able to experience a miniaturized GDR, which observes the health and safety guidelines of a theme park. In re-imagining the GDR past as a source of future income, *Alles Lüge* offers a foretaste of the later Ostalgie trend. But significantly, Kasulke's motivation for restaging the obsolete state is not a wish to restore the past. He is as derisive of his wife's attachment to the former regime as he is indignant at the swindles that appear to be a consequence of unification. His business strategy does not rely on duplicity but capitalizes on the east Germans' bond to the GDR and the west's posthumous interest in their former neighbours in an honest fashion. In a bizarre case of life imitating art, the unthinkable seemed likely to become real: among the more dubious schemes to have been proposed was that by Massine Productions, whose directors in 2003 sought approval for an east German Disneyland in a disused warehouse in the Berlin district of Oberschöneweide, a project that ultimately failed due to lack of funds.

Reimagining the GDR

Nostalgia is, as previous chapters have indicated, a sentiment that suffuses many of the post-unification narratives. Under threat from a modern western lifestyle, the east German communities frequently look to secure a way of life that is firmly rooted in past traditions. Reference to the past is generally not politicized, or made to shore up a distinct ideology. In the post-GDR Heimatfilme, for example, community and solidarity were coded as traditional ways of being rather than rooted to any (socialist) ideology. The films may have centred on the conflict of interest between east and west, but they also addressed contemporary concerns about globalization and connected with a general yearning for simpler times. From the mid-1990s, however, nostalgia, or rather Ostalgie, was a malaise borne of post-unification frustrations and expressed a more precise loss, a longing that focused its desire specifically on the GDR past, thereby excluding the west Germans from participation.

Although films such as *Der Kontrolleur* engage with the memory and nostalgia for the past, these are not considered Ostalgie narratives. They may focus on individuals who regret the passing of the GDR state, but they do not echo the cheerfully defiant mood with which Ostalgie has come to be associated. The protagonists' memories of the past are specifically linked to those GDR features that are largely absent from Ostalgie discourse. This might explain the films' failure to resonate with the wider east German community (along with the general principle that socially-critical filmmaking seldom performs well at the box-office). Audiences may have been able to identify with the protagonists' helplessness but the antisocial behaviour and biographical details made any emotional attachment to the characters problematic. What is more, the films' tragic endings – death, suicide, murder – indicated that east German nostalgia could in fact prove fatal.

Late autumn of 1999 is significant to this discussion of Ostalgie, for it witnessed the release of two films, one of which, *Sonnenallee*, has come to be seen as a key Ostalgie text, while the other, *Helden wie Wir*, is an adaptation of Thomas Brussig's novel of the same name, which many critics regarded as the first significant reunification novel. The release of each film was timed to coincide with an important anniversary. Released on 7

October 1999, *Sonnenallee* coincided with the fiftieth anniversary of the founding of the GDR; *Helden wie Wir*'s release, some weeks later on 9 November 1999, coincided with the anniversary of the opening of the Berlin Wall. The films' release dates were not the only coincidence. Like *Helden wie Wir*, *Sonnenallee* was based on a book (and script) by Thomas Brussig, and each film marked the debut of its young director (Haußmann had come from a background in theatre; Peterson had just graduated from the Film School in Potsdam). Most importantly, each film offered a narrative of the GDR that ran contrary to post-unification accounts – although in what ways remains to be seen.[14] Despite these similarities, it was Haußmann's film that resonated with cinema audiences and not Peterson's. *Sonnenallee*'s success was considerable. With over 2.4 million viewers, it was one of the biggest domestic films of the decade, and seemed to suggest that, ten years after unification, what east German audiences were most interested in seeing was not films that chronicled their current difficulties but a film that celebrated their past.[15] At least, this is what many of the film's reviews appeared to imply, for *Sonnenallee* was seen by some critics as a hagiography of the GDR. While some reviewers were sympathetic to a vision of the GDR that challenged the standard media representation, others expressed misgivings about the film's tame depiction of the GDR authorities, claiming that the film showed little respect for the victims of the regime or that the rosy view of the GDR was, as one reviewer claimed, a long advert for the 'party of dissent and nostalgia', the PDS, which that year had finally gained a seat in Berlin's regional parliament.[16] Where the film came under attack, it was the comic representation of those figures symbolizing the state that provoked the strongest criticism. The film even faced a court case for defamation (under Paragraph 194 of the Criminal Code, a law that is better known for its use in prosecuting Holocaust deniers) brought by HELP e.V., a support organization for the victims of political violence in Europe, which considered the film an affront to the victims of the wall. While Brussig criticized the organization's misuse of funds (for a case that they would not win), the director dismissed their objections, impudently claiming that he had understood the accusation to be a practical joke.[17]

The film's irreverence was arguably a crucial reason for its success, for *Sonnenallee* is a film that, ostensibly, refuses to recognize any authority, be it the authority of post-unification history, which invariably views the GDR with reference to its politics and distorted ideology, or the agents of East German authority, who are lampooned throughout. The portrayal of the state's agents as little more than bumptious bureaucrats and goonish careerists, as exemplified by Detlev Buck's interpretation of the humourless *Abschnittsbevollmächtigter* (akin to a voluntary policeman), was frequently understood by the film's detractors as an attempt to make light of the state's well-known iniquities and not seen as a long-delayed opportunity to ridicule on screen those who had once intimidated the East German pop-

Figure 6.1 *Sonnenallee*
East German self-deprecation: the primitive Ossis encounter technology in
Sonnenallee (1999, Leander Haußmann) © Boje Buck Produktion

ulation. No less important to the film's success, though, was the film's
timing. Haußmann's film capitalized on Ostalgie and a general enthusiasm for retro-fashion, specifically the 1990s' interest in 1970s' culture. Set
in and around Sonnenallee, a road divided by the Berlin Wall, the film
follows a group of East Berlin teenagers in the mid-1970s. The film therefore offered a generation that had been socialized in the GDR the opportunity of indulging their reminiscences. Despite *Sonnenallee*'s attention to
period detail, the various GDR in-jokes and the presence of former east
German actors such as Henry Hübchen, Katharina Thalbach, and later
Winifred Glatzeder, whose cameo references DEFA's one true cult 1970s
film, *Die Legende von Paul und Paula* (*The Legend of Paul and Paula*, Heiner
Carow, 1973), *Sonnenallee* is more indebted to western filmmaking than it
is to DEFA. Observing the thematic and stylistic conventions of the western
teen genre – sex, drugs, friendships threatened; a pop soundtrack, a wistful
voiceover – the film is closer in spirit to the nostalgic high school films that
have been popular since George Lucas's *American Graffiti* (1974) and bears
little resemblance to the DEFA films of the day, thus making it accessible to
western audiences (though anecdotal information tends to emphasize their
incomprehension at many points in the film). The 1970s' voguish appeal
also satisfied a younger audience that had no memory of the period.
Haußmann's decision to set the film during the 1970s actually deviated
from the original script, which began the action during the 1980s, finally

culminating in the collapse of the wall. Setting the film a decade earlier may have created narrative difficulties (solved by an alternative ending in which it is a song and dance routine that finally undoes the barrier between East and West), but it undoubtedly contributed to the film's overall appeal, even if the director was less inclined to acknowledge the fascination for that decade, claiming instead that 'in a sense, the GDR was always in the 1970s'.[18]

This indifference to historical fact, together with the film's kitsch take on the GDR, irritated a number of critics, whose reading of the film revealed a remarkable lack of irony. Claus Löser, who thought the film an egregious production, highlighted its numerous anachronisms and inaccuracies, as if the jumble of clothing styles from various decades or the inconsistency of the soundtrack lessened the film's worth.[19] Such incongruities are intentional, of course. Though a novice filmmaker, Haußmann was an experienced theatre director and well aware of presentation. In *Sonnenallee*, he favours a look that substitutes artifice and theatricality for realism. The director claimed that the unconventional, non-realistic style was simply the only satisfactory course open to him when dealing with the memory of life in the east. To do otherwise was clearly not an option he was willing to entertain: 'that people try to make this utterly surreal situation in which we used to live realistic is a disagreeable thought'.[20]

This allows him certain freedoms, as with the physical layout of the street in which most of the action takes place. The Sonnenallee that is recreated here (a set on the edge of the Babelsberg studios) offers a microcosm of GDR life and is not concerned with factual accuracy. According to this account of East Berlin life, grocers sold their cabbages yards from the border crossing; Micha (Alexander Scheer) and the other teenage protagonists are apparently able to dance in front of the border control, occasionally exchanging jeers with the curious western tourists peering over from a viewing platform that rises over the wall. The mise-en-scène is deliberately artificial; the visual composition of the interior scenes, especially, supplies a mass of period details, the inclusion of which is more a nod to the lucrative rehabilitation of that era's fashion in our own than an attempt to recreate an authentic GDR. This is not to say that *Sonnenallee* is intended as a surreal account of life in the east, but is instead a 'hyper-real simulation' which initially panders to nostalgic east Germans.[21] On the one hand, the film's inclusion of so many East German signifiers offers an inventory of souvenirs (ungainly furniture, unsophisticated packaging) intended to stimulate (eastern) audiences' memories but the film also reminds audiences that it was western products that were fetishized in the GDR, particularly by the young. Micha and his friends are self-styled pop music aficionados whose focus is on western bands. The quest for a prohibited Rolling Stones record both highlights the cultural similarities between teenagers on both sides of the wall and serves as a reminder of the state's unsympathetic cultural policy.[22]

Asked by one interviewer whether he had been unwilling or unable to present a more critical response to the SED-state, Brussig explained, 'I didn't consider that necessary since the book makes no attempt to illuminate the real GDR but occupies itself instead with memories of the GDR'.[23] There is, then, a distinction in the author's mind between the GDR state and the memories of having lived in it. This distinction is alluded to also in the cheerful voiceover with which the film closes: 'Once upon a time there was a land and I lived there. And if you ask me what it was like, it was the best time of my life. Because I was young and in love.' *Sonnenallee* is an attempt to present an alternative account of the GDR, one that defiantly supports the east Germans' right to individual recollection without recourse to the assumed GDR differentia.[24] However, a number of devices – the accentuated artificiality of the recreated GDR, the occasional fairytale-like quality of the voiceover, the rapidly rewritten diaries with which Micha hopes to persuade Miriam of his opposition to the state – reveal memory to be unreliable, disjointed and malleable. It is doubtful that such reflexive caution was central to the film's success, which was more pronounced in the east than in the west. Viewers' online comments suggest that the film was appreciated as a straight comedy and as an uncritical celebration of East German adolescence rather than as a wry look at GDR society and a subtle warning about the perils of memory.

Given that the second Brussig adaptation that autumn was based on his fêted Wende grotesque, 'Helden wie Wir', and that the film met with critical approval, with some reviewers praising it above the original novel, it seemed likely that Peterson's debut film would at the very least match the success of *Sonnenallee*. That was not to be. Not only were the film's box-office returns disappointing, it has been all but ignored in the critical literature on post-unification film, where it is mentioned only in passing, and usually as an addendum to discussions of Haußmann's film. This seems strange given that the novel has received so much critical attention and that, formally, *Helden wie Wir* is (for the first half at least) one of the most inventive films of the period.

Though the adaptation does not remain faithful to the novel's more grotesque caricatures or its psychosexual aspects, the Oedipal turns and the alleged misogyny, the film (which was co-scripted by Peterson, Brussig and Markus Dittrich) keeps to the novel's picaresque tale of Klaus Uhltzscht (Daniel Borgwardt), a young, prurient east German who becomes a Stasi employee in the vain hope that his role will involve sex-espionage. His professional work is as unsatisfactory as are his sexual experiences (the penis complex that results in a number of comic, if humiliating, sexual escapades in the source text is mostly omitted), and he is only rescued from anonymity when, following a blood transfusion for Honecker, he is left with what he proudly refers to as 'the biggest member that you've ever seen'.[25] This side effect, and not Günter Schabowski's famous press conference blunder, is ultimately the reason for the breach of the wall: distracted by the hero's tumescent organ, the border guards allow the swelling crowds to pass through.[26]

This new piece of historical evidence is emphasized at the beginning of the film, which opens with footage of people crossing the border accompanied by the soundtrack of Louis Armstong's 'What a Wonderful World'. In a voiceover that adapts one of the novel's closing lines, Uhltzscht asserts the accuracy of the account that is to follow: 'I'm under no illusions. Those who don't believe my story will not understand what is up with Germany. I, Klaus Uhltzscht, opened the Berlin Wall.' The editing of this opening scene reflects Peterson's attempts to capture the novel's unfilmable irony. The use of Armstrong's utopian ballad, a song that has become a byword for sentimentality, simultaneously engages and deflates nostalgia for those days. Uhltzscht's claim, meanwhile, which could not be more preposterous, mocks historical fact and parodies those east Germans who were quick to rewrite biographies after 1989.

No attempt, then, is made to present a conventional or realistic picture of the GDR past. Rather, *Helden wie Wir* re-invents the GDR throughout, drawing from an image bank of east German documentary footage, animation, and period advertising, and juxtaposing these dissimilar styles in order to create a portrait of the past that reflects the constructiveness of memory. Like *Sonnenallee*, the film's artificiality therefore consciously undermines the supposed reliability of its own account. The protagonist's birth, in 1968, as the Russian tanks head towards the Czech capital, is shot in black and white stock and in a manner that recalls the DEFA films of the period. In other sequences, GDR footage, accompanied by an upbeat muzak soundtrack, documents the state's parades, the building projects and sporting events, a reminder of the state's more optimistic self-image. Other sequences demonstrate an irreverent take on GDR icons, as in the story concerning Ernst 'Teddy' Thälmann, the communist leader and hero, who Uhltzscht imagines as a giant bear agitating for the socialist cause in a film style reminiscent of early agitprop, complete with simulated aged film stock and an old time piano score.

Despite its artifice, this postmodern collage of East German details was admired as a credible representation of the GDR. Indeed, a number of critics claimed that this Brussig adaptation offered a more accurate portrayal of the GDR than had Haußmann's. For the celebrated east German satirist, Peter Ensikat, the film was 'authentic and therefore the opposite of Ostalgie'.[27] Initially the film appears to be edging towards a nostalgic representation of the GDR. Like *Sonnenallee*, it offers a series of recognizable symbols and details with which east German audiences in particular might connect, from television shows to cartoons, interior décor and vintage clothing. But *Helden wie Wir* does not indulge in any performative nostalgia in the way that *Sonnenallee* does – or at least was seen to. While it appears to approximate nostalgia films – images of the protagonist's childhood amid the Berlin high-rise estates are shot to resemble the period's super8 home movies and are accompanied by a breezy melody – Peterson's direction routinely disrupts all sentimentality, either exaggerating the sentiment beyond all plausibility or introducing elements that frustrate any nostalgic expectations.

It may seem inconsistent that one Brussig text should appear to validate positive memories of the GDR while the other satirizes them, but this 'cognitive dissonance' is commonplace among east Germans, as we have already seen; indeed, such contradictions are central to the nostalgic turn, which, as Svetlana Boym has noted, 'can be homesick and sick of home, at once'.[28] Brussig has tried to clarify his ambivalent attitude to the past in a number of articles.[29] In these, Brussig supports and explicates the east Germans' nostalgia and the author is clearly sympathetic to Ostalgie as a means of balancing an uneven view of the GDR that denies the specificity of its citizens. But he is critical, too, of those east Germans who, after 1989, altered their biographies as a means of compensating for their own failures – in this case, the failure to oppose the state – a practice that he likens to the hastily constructed resistance biographies that surfaced after the Wende and after the war.

While *Sonnenallee* provides a less seductive vision of the East than many critics imagined (focusing on the film's comedic representation of the authorities, most of the reviews fail to acknowledge the film's general criticism of the GDR, evident in the dialogue about the poor quality consumer goods, the state's travel restrictions and the rigid ideology), it does commemorate East German adolescence, showing that high spirits and youthful capers existed in the shadow of the wall. *Helden wir Wir*, by contrast, is less interested in a celebration of youth than it is in ridiculing the SED-state, epitomized by the farcical Stasi agents with a penchant for meaningless departmental jargon, and the obsessiveness of Uhltzscht's parents. The film's sceptical approach distinguished it from *Sonnenallee*'s take on the GDR, which both indulged and teased nostalgic east Germans, and the unambiguously ironic tone may account for its disappointing returns at the box-office.

Recycling the Past: *Der Zimmerspringbrunnen*

A couple of years after *Helden wie Wir*, Peter Timm released *Der Zimmerspringbrunnen* (*The Indoor Fountain*, 2001), his adaptation of Jens Sparschuh's much-admired and best-selling satire which had been published the same year as Brussig's novel. Unlike Peterson's film, *Der Zimmerspringbrunnen* lacks inventiveness and relies on the kind of clichéd representations that had dominated early Wende comedies, with the west represented by superficial businessmen looking to conquer the eastern market, and the Ossis fulfilling the role of unification's unlucky bystanders.[30] Though the film engaged with Ostalgie, Timm's film was mostly ignored and enjoyed neither the critical success of the novel, nor the commercial success of his Trabi film.

Der Zimmerspringbrunnen follows its luckless protagonist, Lobek (former DEFA actor Götz Schubert), who finally manages to shake off his post-unification lethargy to become a regional sales representative for a particularly kitsch product, the indoor water feature of the title. Although mainly set in east Berlin, Timm's film travels briefly to the west, where he is required to attend an induction day. Lobek is temporarily transformed by newly practised marketing jargon and mission statements, and is soon repeating absurd management-speak, phrases as hollow as were the old socialist slogans routinely uttered in the GDR and which Lobek randomly repeats in the hope of sounding apposite. This is not the first film in which an east German attempts to undergo some form of social ecdysis, shedding their old east German skin in an effort to adapt to their changed environment. Such metamorphoses are rarely successful; whatever external changes the characters may undergo (and these are seldom credible), they remain, at core, east Germans who will never be quite like their western compatriots, and whose makeover even risks alienating them from their own community (as with Karl, the would-be entrepreneur in *Not a Love Song*). Some scholars have considered the east Germans' imitation of their western neighbours – invariably characterized as colonizers – in terms of Homi Bhabha's influential reading of mimicry.[31] At first glance, the east Germans' attempts to mirror the west Germans seems to echo Bhabha's theory, according to which the result is an exaggerated replica, a parody that exposes the absurdity of the original.[32] However, one has to be cautious not to make too much of Bhabha's concept of mimicry in the German context. On no occasion does the overstated impersonation in any way truly threaten or subvert the authority of those mimicked, i.e. the west. What it does do, however, is reveal a fundamental inability to be assimilated or even to evolve into some hybrid composite, thus highlighting the deep-rooted differences between east and west and reaffirming the east Germans' distinctiveness. There is, in any case, a sense of relief when the characters, self-conscious and awkward in their act of imitation, are able to return to type. Certainly, this is the case when Papa Struutz is able to get out of his suit (a costly but ill-fitting item) and back into his workaday clothes. Lobek's transformation into a western salesman is similarly unconvincing and, like Udo before him, he reverts to his original, apparently 'natural' behaviour soon after. Importantly, it is only when the characters revert to type, that they are able to remedy their situation. As with many other post-unification narratives, Timm's film suggests that the east Germans know best how to overcome their problems and this either involves mobilizing the community or, in this case, applying the east Germans' well-known ability to improvise (a talent witnessed throughout in films as diverse as *Superstau*, *Das war der wilde Osten*, *Alles Lüge*, and *Bis zum Horizont und weiter*).

Figure 6.2 *Der Zimmerspringbrunnen*
A rare moment: Lobek (Götz Schubert), one of the east German underdogs,
experiences success in *Der Zimmerspringbrunnen* (Peter Timm, 2001) © senator film

Timm's satire fails to convey the ironic tone of Sparschuh's novel and,
in keeping with the director's oeuvre, it settles instead for the exaggerated
characterization of east and west Germans that had proved so successful in
his earlier film, though *Der Zimmerspringbrunnen* lacks the clowning that
had been a factor in *Go Trabi Go*'s success. Timm's film is closer to *Alles Lüge*
than it is to the Brussig adaptations. Like Schier's film, it targets western
business strategies and unreformed Ossis alike, though neither is unsym-
pathetically treated. At a basic level, *Der Zimmerspringbrunnen* parodies the
kind of east German nostalgia that *Alles Lüge* had anticipated. As with the
virtual GDR that Kasulke assembles within the walls of the Palace of the
Republic, the water fountain that Lobek secretly adapts for his east German
clientele – the 'Atlantis', which features a model of the east German television tower rising to the tune of the GDR's national anthem – allows each
teary-eyed owner to observe a symbolic resurrection of the east German
state. Atlantis' success, evidence once again of the east Germans' ability to
improvise, is Lobek's success. It signifies his financial independence from
his wife, the state and the west German parent company. Lobek's market
triumph revitalises him in other ways, too. He overcomes his sexual impotence, which is a consequence of his low self-esteem and general indolence, and wins back his estranged wife, a plot development that echoes the
Trabi sequel, if not the grotesque ending of Sparschuh's book. Unlike the
two Brussig adaptations, which both exploit and undermine Ostalgie,
Timm's treatment of Ostalgie is not ambiguous. The film targets the re-

gressive desires of the east Germans, who are mostly presented as unsophisticated plebeians in Berlin's high-rise estates, but also the commodification of their nostalgia.

Reconstructing the GDR

The box-office achievement of Haußmann's film was as nothing compared with the international success, some four years later, of Wolfgang Becker's film, *Good Bye, Lenin!* For most critics, *Good Bye, Lenin!* counted as the unification film par excellence, with several suggesting that the film went some way to burying the GDR. Few saw it as an exercise in nostalgia, or one that sought to sacrifice the GDR's more uncomfortable features for a relaxing trip down memory lane. That Becker's film does engage with Ostalgie is undeniable. Like the Brussig adaptations, it views the GDR through the eyes of a teenage protagonist, something that connects the film with the autobiographies, fictional biographies and 'egodocuments' of East German adolescence that had become increasingly common.[33] *Good Bye, Lenin!* is not just a nostalgic account of life before 1989. A film that simply pines for the GDR would hardly have gained the official support that it did. Like *Alles Lüge*, whose title would have been equally appropriate for Becker's film, *Good Bye, Lenin!* satirizes the east Germans' nostalgia for their pre-unification lives whilst simultaneously indulging that very nostalgia.

In contrast to the simulacrum of the GDR offered by Haußmann and by Peterson, *Good Bye, Lenin!* strives for a degree of authenticity that distinguishes it from these other films and connects it instead with Becker's earlier Berlin film, *Das Leben ist eine Baustelle* (1997), which was much admired for its realism and which is subtly referenced in the later film. At heart, *Good Bye, Lenin!* is a tragic-comic family drama set in East Berlin during the Wende. It follows the attempt of Alex Kerner to convince his ailing mother, Christiane, a recovering coma patient who collapsed on the eve of the state's downfall, that the GDR is still extant, a charade that becomes increasingly complicated as the son, fearing that the truth will prove fatal to his mother, tries to explain away mounting discrepancies with assistance from friends, family and neighbours. Children are hired to sing old FDJ songs, GDR television shows are recreated with amateur equipment, and discontinued East German groceries are frantically collected. Finally, even recent historical events are manipulated as Alex contrives to explain that the images his mother sees of people crossing the wall are of West Germans escaping the FRG for the safety of the East.[34] Like the films above, *Good Bye, Lenin!* engages with the construction of the east German past. However, the GDR that Alex is determined to recreate is not the recently deceased state but one that, in retrospect, he would have preferred, a position made clear in Alex's voiceover: 'the GDR I created for her increasingly became the one I might have wished for'. This sentiment

reminds the audience that the GDR Alex recreates is illusory, a safe reproduction as unreal as the *Sonnenallee* sets and the flat-pack GDR of *Helden wie
Wir*, and that there was more to the GDR than the décor and comfort foods,
more, perhaps, than the east Germans care to remember. Should this point
be missed, it is repeated in another voiceover towards the end, shortly after
his mother's death: 'The country my mother left behind was a country she
believed in ... A country that never existed in that form'.

Good Bye, Lenin! is not a succession of melancholic utterances warning
of the pitfalls of nostalgia. Becker's deft directorial hand works these issues
into a rather tender portrait of a family that suffers several tragedies, beginning with the loss of a father and ending with the death of a mother.
Though it offers a gentle critique of Ostalgie, it also recognizes the reasons
for the east Germans' nostalgia. The elderly neighbours who participate in
Alex's complicated deception may do so out of respect for Christiane, but
their collusion is also motivated by an understandable sense of loss, for the
freedoms of the new republic are presented as the extravagances of youth
and have less meaning for this generation than they do for Alex and his
sister, Ariane. For the latter, the open border to the west offers an introduction to an unknown and exotic lifestyle, associated here with drugs, sex and
fashion. Their wide-eyed view of the west distinguishes Becker's film from
many other post-unification films, which seldom record the east Germans'
post-1989 experience of the west in a positive light. Not just the west is the
unknown and exotic location. The difficulties Ariane's western boyfriend
has in playing his assigned role as Ossi in Alex's deception underlines the
otherness of the east and serves as a reminder that differences between the
two cultures exist. Differences are not insurmountable and *Good Bye, Lenin!*
is the first film since unification in which the union between east and west
is given a symbolic reward: by the end of the film Ariane and her boyfriend
are expecting a baby, while Alex's new Russian girlfriend suggests the possibility of a new, ideology-free 'German-Soviet Friendship'.

Unlike *Sonnenallee*, Becker's film is not intended to resonate with the
eastern audience in particular, and this may account for the film's international success. It largely avoids a partisan account of events, managing to
appeal to various sides simultaneously.[35] It shows moderation in its depiction of the GDR past, paying reference to both the state's achievements, in
particular the Cosmonaut Sigmund Jähn's space launch, and its iniquities
(the Stasi, the VoPo). This endorses east German pride and, through the
space flight motif, acknowledges the GDR's utopian projections but also
cautions against nostalgia's asymmetry. At the same time, *Good Bye, Lenin!*
does not vilify the west. Though it sets its sights on the usual representatives of global capital (banks, Coca-Cola), Becker's film is not a criticism of
the west. *Good Bye, Lenin!* frequently touches on pertinent unification issues
– among them, currency reform and unemployment – but their brief inclusion hardly amounts to a strident critique of unification. Equally important to the film's success (in Germany at least) was the film's symbolic

farewell to the GDR. Other films had chronicled the dying days of the GDR but these narratives were caught between a unloved past and an uncertain future, as exemplified in the final frames of Dziuba's film *Jana und Jan*. *Sonnenallee*'s repossession of the GDR past, meanwhile, was limited in its appeal. Its success was localized and it failed to make an impression on audiences beyond Germany. *Good Bye, Lenin!* goes so far as to allow the GDR a fond farewell, since a distinction is made between Christiane Kerner's principles and the distorted ideology that informed East German politics, therefore conceding that a *good* socialism, associated with a belief in true solidarity, kind deeds and neighbourliness, was ultimately suppressed in the GDR. The state to which Alex finally waves goodbye is, as he acknowledges, 'A country that, in my memory, I will always associate with my mother', and not the SED-state of unpopular memory.

Between Ostalgie and Westalgie

Good Bye, Lenin! naturally had its imitators; the success of Becker's film confirmed that Ostalgie had not exceeded its shelf-life, as had previously been predicted. The productions that sought to capitalize on the film's brand of nostalgia were, however, not feature films but television programmes, 'Ossi-Shows' such as *Meyer & Schulz – Die ultimative Ost-Show*, *Die DDR Show*, the *Ostalgieshow* and *Ein Kessel DDR*. Programme-makers may have offered alternative explanations for their show, variously claiming that they served some educational purpose or that they aimed to address unknown aspects of daily life in the GDR, but they were primarily interested in a new variation on the successful nostalgia shows of the period – a winning formula on television in Germany and abroad. The resulting programmes were mostly light-hearted retrospectives that failed to live up to these (unconvincing) declarations of intent. Seldom straying from anything but a narrative of GDR consumerism, with the east's poor quality (but in hindsight much cherished) goods the principal focus, they succeeded in attracting sizeable audiences, who regularly tuned in to watch east German celebrities reminisce about growing up in the GDR.[36] Critics of the shows argued that they were part of a bathetic move to substitute a politically deterministic account of life in the GDR with one that verged on the comedic.[37] The east German psychoanalyst and media commentator Hans Joachim Maaz was one of several high-profile personalities to write disapprovingly of the shows, claiming that these portrayals of life in the east were neither accurate nor honest.[38]

The critical aversion to the programmes and the ensuing misgiving towards Ostalgie did not discourage filmmakers from quickly issuing similar films. Carsten Fiebeler's *Kleinruppin Forever* (2004) was the first attempt to capitalize on the success of Becker's film, though the producers were naturally keen to point out that the film had been conceived long before *Good Bye, Lenin!* (though Lichtenberg, too, claimed to have written his treatment soon after 1989). *Kleinruppin Forever* synthesizes the interest in the 1980s that, by the millennium, had already begun to displace the 1970s as the preferred retro fashion, the continued interest in the GDR and a newly expressed nostalgia for the west that had been established with the publication of Florian Illies' bestseller *Generation Golf*.[39] Offering a corrective to the east German nostalgia, these *Westalgie* texts, as they came to be known, proved popular and several were adapted for film. Of these, the most successful was Leander Haußmann's *Herr Lehmann* (2003), adapted from Sven Regener's milieu comedy set among West Berlin's counter culture.[40] In *Kleinruppin Forever*, audiences are once again presented with a scenario in which a protagonist is immersed in an unfamiliar environment to which he must quickly adapt if he is to survive. This was, by now, a tried and tested plot and had been used with increasing inventiveness since the earliest Wendefilme. It had been used more recently in *Berlin is in Germany* (Martin's delayed confrontation with a strange new world) and *Good Bye, Lenin!* (Christiane's post-operative adjustment to a new Germany). Fiebeler's film requires a greater suspension of disbelief: identical twins separated at birth and each brought up in the other state unexpectedly meet one another when Tim, the western brother, visits the GDR on a school trip from Bremen. Knocked unconscious by Ronny, his brother, who assumes his identity and returns to the West in his place, the West German is forced to adjust to life behind the wall.

Figure 6.3 *Kleinruppin Forever*
Western teens about to go on safari in the unknown East in *Kleinruppin Forever* (Carsten Fiebeler, 2004) © Akkord Film, Volker Roloff

Kleinruppin Forever initially reinforces the differences between the two states, relying on the clash between cultures that had been a mainstay since the earliest post-unification films, albeit with a West German experiencing the East. Though the film's premise hinges on a case of mistaken identities, the eastern twin's progress in the west hardly features. As a 'Popper', Fiebeler's western protagonist appeals to both the contemporary fascination for one of the 1980s' most iconic styles (ostentatious, conceited, the 'Popper' embodied the decade's financial immodesty and its political conservatism, thereby distinguishing it from the radical politics associated with the previous decade). The film's early scenes establish Tim's 'Popper' credentials, focusing on his affluent social circle – moneyed teenagers dressed in the period's designer clothes, who play tennis and attend cocktail parties. Tennis, which in the 1980s enjoyed unprecedented and widespread popularity in the FRG following Boris Becker's success, is here associated with the affluent elite, a view that corresponds with the GDR authorities' view of the sport as a bourgeois pursuit that was undeserving of any significant financial support. The portrait of the FRG as a prosperous, materialistic society largely confirms east German suspicions, old and new.

The depiction of West German society is more than a parody of the 'greedy 1980s'. The image the young director presents echoes the post-unification stereotype of the west as a superficial society that values status and wealth. The East, by contrast, is a more authentic, if pitiably run-down society, though Fiebeler's film is not intended as a critique of the east's sclerotic economy. Denying that *Kleinruppin Forever* glorifies the east, the director did, however, confirm that the film is intended as a celebration of values considered to have been more manifest in the East (among them solidarity and friendship). Like *Sonnenallee*, Fiebeler's film seeks to redress the imbalanced accounts of life in the East but also to emphasize the similarities between the two societies:

> The 80s in East and West – that's the theme of my film. It symbolized two different worlds in Germany but its young people had the same problems and concerns – where is my life going, first love, and finding the next good party.[41]

Fiebeler naturally endeavours to acknowledge the state's repressive nature in his portrait of life in the GDR. The Stasi, the VoPo, and the *Nationale Volksarmee* (NVA – National People's Army) are all present. However their representatives are not the formidable and ruthless figures of popular memory, but dim-witted and corrupt individuals unable to get the better of the local population, a depiction that is perhaps less improbable than it might at first seem, given that the Stasi were, as Catherine Epstein has argued, often 'surprisingly inefficient, ineffective, and counterproductive'.[42] Despite the state's obvious material shortcomings and the comic-insidious figures who appear throughout the film, the East German society that Fiebeler recreates is largely defined by strong bonds between young people and a general, if passive, opposition to the state. While the state agents are immediately identifiable as such – uniformed policemen and army officers, Stasi officers in leather coats – their narrative function is ultimately little different to that of the authority figures found in most teen nostalgia films. In keeping with this generic paradigm, they are depoliticized, and represented as a nuisance to the local population rather than as a sinister threat or as representatives of a corrupted ideology.

More controversial than this tame depiction of those notorious figures is the reverse migration that takes place in *Kleinruppin Forever*.[43] Having succeeded in returning to his home in the FRG, Tim recognizes that it was in the GDR that he discovered true love, friendships based on common values and genuine affection. Surrendering his tennis career, his glittering social life and all his western possessions, he returns to the true Heimat of the east. Despite the restrictions of state socialism, the West German interloper is able to connect with an 'emotional community' in the East, one that the West lacks – then and now, according to the director.[44] In targeting the West German society of the 1980s in particular, Fiebeler's film effectively reverses the western criticism of Ostalgie. In the same way that Peterson's film invokes east German nostalgia only to undermine it, the nostalgic look at a period regarded by west Germans as their last decade of prosperity, which Fiebeler's film initially promises, soon gives way to a version that aligns the economic success of the 1980s with moral vacuity and exposes western society as one lacking in warmth or solidarity.

Fiebeler's film did not live up to expectations. It received some favourable press (winning a special prize at the little-known International Film Festival in Emden), but most critics took objection to the film and pronounced it clichéd and derivative. One reason might be the ill-advised decision to satirize a period that held nostalgic significance for audiences in the west, who, unlike their eastern cousins, are offered no positive reference points. One might also ascribe the film's failure to the absence of irony, which, as I have already indicated, was a key ingredient in each of the Ostalgie films. If the film demonstrated an 'excessive and heavily ironic use of stereotyping' as one scholar has claimed, it was an approach that no other reviewer was able to discern.[45] Andreas Hahn's review in the former FDJ organ, *Junge Welt*, was sceptical about the producer's claim that the film's theme – 'to find a home' – was universal, and objected to the reductive representations: 'Home is the slow paced and depoliticized ("chummy") GDR village community as opposed to the "alienated", urban pop-nonsense world of the west'.[46] The acerbity of Hahn's tone is revealing, given that much the same could have been said of those other films that envisage the east as a cosy community attempting to preserve some autonomy against the assimilationist tendencies of (globalized) western capital. This image, as we have seen, has been a mainstay of many post-unification films, particularly those released soon after the Wende. But where those films offered refuge in a depoliticized Heimat, Fiebeler's situates his narrative specifically in the GDR of the 1980s, a decade not generally considered to have been one of the GDR's happiest, though perhaps fondly remembered by the young east German director.[47]

It is interesting also to consider Fiebeler's film in light of the success enjoyed by the previous films. Despite the superficial similarity to the other Ostalgie comedies – the focus on teenagers, the pop soundtrack, retro-appeal, even a smart website that resembled those of *Sonnenallee* and *Good Bye, Lenin!* – the film attracted only 122,382 viewers.[48] A further explanation for the film's poor box-office performance may be a degree of Ostalgie fatigue. Fashions come and go and even the enthusiasm for this version of the East German past can only be sustained for so long. Yet there is no evidence at present that the market interest in the GDR has waned. Online Ossi shops continue to sell original East German goods and anyone visiting the eastern districts of Berlin will notice that GDR icons are still very much in evidence. Retro t-shirts bearing eastern brands and stirring political phrases resurrected for a generation too young to remember their original context, and the authentic and much prized home furnishings, are not hard to find.[49]

A more reasonable explanation of the film's failure lies in its portrayal of the two German states. Despite the director's claim that the film uses 'exaggeration and irony as stylistic device … in order to show the absurdity of many situations', it lacks the ironic, self-reflexive distance that informs some of the other films discussed in this chapter.[50] Only the lyrics to the film's title track (a song taken from Claude Pinoteau's 1980 coming-of-age film, *La Boum*) could be regarded as ironic: 'dreams are my reality/a wondrous world where I like to be/illusions are a common thing/I try to live in dreams although it's only fantasy'.[51] This ironic touch, if indeed it is intended as such, risks being missed completely since the film offers no other indicators or signals that prompt such inference – and, not least, because the lyrics are in English.[52] *Kleinruppin Forever* does not imply that its twisting of history is ironically intended; nor does it foreground its own artificiality as do the Brussig adaptations. Indeed, it can be said of each of the previous films that they emphasize the subjective construction of the past. In *Sonnenallee*, it is evident in both the film's appearance, which offers a conscious mock-up of the GDR, and in the narrative. When the hero sets about writing a volume of backdated diaries with which he hopes to convince a girl of his subversive credentials, Brussig joins other writers in satirizing those east Germans who manipulated their past, a theme that is also raised in *Helden wie Wir*.[53] Becker's film, too, acknowledges the manipulation involved in restaging the past: Christiane's world is nothing more than a reproduction GDR – stage-managed in much the same way that Schier's protagonist supervises his theme park in *Alles Lüge* and Lobek profits from the GDR made kitsch.

Fade to Grey: *NVA*

As *Sonnenallee* nears its conclusion, the camera retreats from the carniva-lesque scene of the teenagers dancing in step with parents and authority figures at the border crossing; the colour drains from the film and viewers are left with a more familiar black and white version of the GDR. That the film score, which has hitherto consisted mainly of western pop numbers from various eras, should end with Nina Hagen's cult East German tune 'Du hast den Farbfilm vergessen' (You've Forgotten the Colour Film') is significant. Stepdaughter of the expatriated dissident Wolf Biermann, Hagen counted as an unconventional and provocative figure in her own right not just in the GDR, where the authorities were uncharacteristically prompt in yielding to her demand to leave the state, but also in the FRG where she became one of the leading figures in the German punk scene. It was not the singer but the song that had a particular relevance for the film-makers. In it a girl expresses her disappointment that her boyfriend has forgotten the colour film for the camera and that the black and white images of their holiday will not accurately convey either the location's beauty or their happiness. The lyrics, which would be well known to many east Germans (and understood, as Thomas Lindenberger has pointed out, as a protest against monotony in the GDR), acquired a new and obvious relevance in the post-GDR context.[54] The GDR had come to be represented monochromatically, not just in terms of its visual representation, the black

Figure 6.4 *NVA*
Young guns and army goons in *NVA* (1999, Leander Haußmann) © Boje Buck
Produktion

and white images of the SED-state seen in documentaries and in historical accounts, but also in the black and white assessment of the GDR as a society of victims and villains, targets and spies. With its bold colour scheme, *Sonnenallee* broadened this spectrum. The colourful GDR artefacts that the film flaunts (against a regulation grey backdrop) may allow east Germans to reconnect with their youth but their inclusion is, in a sense, an attempt to colour in the GDR, an attempt to vivify the state. Haußmann's and Brussig's next east German narrative, the much criticized *NVA* (2005), even managed to envision the life of the East German conscript soldier as a life that was more colourful than conventional representations suggested. While the filmmakers had been admired for their simultaneously senti-mental and ironic look at the GDR, *NVA*, was widely regarded as a disap-pointing production, which, instead of providing a much-needed reckoning with an important agency of the state, an institution through which the majority of East German men passed, relied on lazy stereotypes and clichés. In fact, these were also features of Haußmann's and Brussig's earlier collaboration (the visitors from Dresden who marvel at the western television programmes that their Berlin hosts are able to tune into; Micha's family's wide-eyed encounter with unremarkable technology and gad-getry). That the film was not quite the box-office failure that the reviews might suggest (it was among the fifty highest grossing films in Germany that year) may be attributable to other characteristics that it shared with *Sonnenallee*. As well as the same scriptwriters, the film had the same pro-ducers, Claus Boje and Detlev Buck, with the latter playing a humourless NVA officer, which required only a slight adjustment to his role in Haußmann's earlier film. Marketing for the film certainly tried to capital-ize on the first film's popularity, with the strap line 'Out of the Sun Alley and into the National People's Army'. What, then, was so objectionable to critics about the later film? Partly it was the film's milieu. While barracks and military training films have a long history, falling generally into two categories, the tense drama and the broad comedy, few critics thought East Germany's national conscription a subject well suited for the makers of *Sonnenallee*. Where some critics had recognized that the earlier film fulfilled an important function, namely in providing some balance to the usual ac-counts of the GDR without becoming a hagiography of the state, the ra-tionale for making *NVA* was harder to understand. It may have been the film's ambiguity. Although it briefly acknowledges the army's brutality when the previously rebellious recruit Krüger (Oliver Bröcker) returns from the infamous military prison in Schwedt a broken man, other in-stances of mistreatment are comically configured and not used as an example of the army's determination to deindividualize the soldiers. Military training has been portrayed in a similar way in dozens of films. Often following the structure of the bildungsroman, barracks narratives typically trace an individual's development and maturation during their time in the army. Some concentrate on institutional abuse, others focus more on comical, albeit quasi-sadistic, episodes during training. In this regard, Haußmann's film is little different. It even features the kind of retro soundtrack associated with those Hollywood films, thereby erasing certain cultural differences between east and west, and offering further confirmation of the director's previous remark that the GDR was always stuck in the 1970s. The genre's stock figures are in place (the intellectual, the rebel, the romantic, the bully and so on), and Henrik Heidler's (Kim Frank) voice-over commentary is a device frequently employed.

It is doubtful that such adherence to generic convention would have raised any eyebrows had the film been set within the west German *Bundeswehr*. The NVA, however, was quite different. The absence of a critical engagement with the GDR was arguably permissible in *Sonnenallee*, but a film set within the GDR military could hardly avoid some of the state's opprobrious features, among them the attempt to indoctrinate recruits with a view to fostering a hatred of the west, the abuse, the harsh disciplinary measures that existed for even minor offences, and the poor living standards at the military bases.[55] If these feature in *NVA*, they do so in a comic arrangement intended to highlight the absurdity of the system and its representatives. This is particularly apparent in the depiction of the officers, a series of grotesques, whose presence did not endear the film to critics, partly because the film suggests that the feared military personnel were nothing more than laughable, though not entirely unsympathetic, *Spießer* (petty bourgeois), as exemplified by Colonel Kalt (Detlev Buck) tending his garden in his uniform and chequered slippers.

Such crude characterizations had been routine in the first decade after unification. By 2005, they seemed anachronistic. This was in part due to a general feeling that Germany had begun to move beyond Ostalgie (though no one had told the vendors or consumers of GDR kitsch this). A number of critics noted that the film lacked the ironic tone that had made *Sonnenallee* a critical success, with some suggesting that *NVA* was little better than the Ostalgie Shows.[56] This comparison would have doubtless piqued Haußmann and Brussig, who had each criticized those television programmes and their weekly parade of 'East Zombies'.[57] The allusion to the shows was also inaccurate. As a satire, the film falls flat, not least because it operates somewhere between genres – part drama, part romantic comedy, part grotesque satire; nevertheless, it does not celebrate or trivialize the GDR in the way the television programmes do. Absent are the post-modern sensibilities that made *Sonnenallee* such a success. Indeed, it is easy to forget how unconventional *Sonnenallee* was in its depiction of the GDR. There is a tendency to overlook its significance because of the trite productions that came in its wake, but its parodic quality was important in the sense outlined by Hutcheon when she describes parody as 'a value-problematizing, de-naturalizing form of acknowledging the history (and through irony, the politics) of representations', however recent these may have been.[58] Had *NVA* been released some years earlier, critics might well have considered it as counter-discursive, a satire which boldly ridiculed the East German army, something that would have been unthinkable during the GDR. Instead, Ostalgie's place in mainstream popular culture means that *NVA* is less likely to be regarded as subversive narrative than it is an example of the 'consensus cinema' as classified by Rentschler. The filmmakers are presumably conscious of this. Each has declared himself tired of discussing the GDR. This weariness with the subject may have to do with the cognitive dissonance previously mentioned. Over the years, they have made their views of the SED-state clear ('The GDR was a shitty system. Even today I can't find anything good about it') but have also sought to challenge the reductive accounts of the East German state, which pictured it as either a dictatorship or as a 'harmless fairytale land'.[59]

Stasiland GDR

If the closing credit in *NVA*, which reads 'In Memorium 1949–1989', was intended to signal the filmmakers' apparent conclusion with the GDR, it was a little premature. Both *Sonnenallee* and *Good Bye, Lenin!* were to become key reference points for the scores of reviewers and scholars contemplating German cinema's greatest international success, *Das Leben der Anderen*. Many regarded von Donnersmarck's Stasi drama as a welcome return to serious cinema, which was considered more appropriate for examining the GDR than the Ostalgie films. Certainly, von Donnersmarck, who spent over a year promoting the film, ostensibly a sombre study of a dedicated Stasi officer and the artists who are the subjects of his surveillance operation, intended that his film provide some balance to Ostalgie, a phenomenon that he describes as 'somewhat understandable, but definitely dangerous'.[60] Donnersmarck's misgivings about the east Germans' nostalgia are also evident in the film: in one of the final scenes set after the state's collapse, the film's most odious figure, former Politbüro member Bruno Hempf (Thomas Thieme), comments that, 'Life was good in our little Republic. Many people only realize that now'. According to the director, then, nostalgia for the East German past is not a matter of celebrating the ordinary, of separating personal experiences from the state's heinous activities. The implication is that only those who benefited from high ranking and corrupt office might look wistfully back to those days; one might infer, moreover, that these people seek to mobilize such nostalgia in an effort perhaps to defend their own (mis)conduct.[61]

What von Donnersmarck and the critics and commentators who viewed the film as an important and necessary corrective to the Ostalgie films failed to acknowledge was that those films had originally provided a corrective to the standard representation of the GDR. There was a tendency, too, to conflate all the later films set in the GDR as feel-good Ostalgie films. Journalists and reviewers may have talked of the tendency towards idealized versions of the GDR, but Ostalgie films and cheery portraits of the East German community were in fact few in number. Those films set in the GDR, meanwhile, invariably represented a state that was both moribund and unpopular. Reviewers generally limited their reference to *Sonnenallee* and *Good Bye, Lenin!*, which as I have suggested were not as uncritically nostalgic as some claimed; that their success was partly attributable to Ostalgie does not of course mean that they were intended as nostalgia narratives. Those few films that did indulge Ostalgie and which offered a far less sceptical view of the East German state were fewer still and did not fare well at the box-office.

Das Leben der Anderen enjoyed a plethora of favourable reviews, a fact that the director was keen to impress upon interviewers: 'any really serious newspaper – the kind of newspaper that would be read by educated people – gave me incredibly positive reviews'.[62] This was perhaps just as well given that the director was as sensitive to negative reviews as he was immodest about his film's achievement. Those who detracted, he suggested, either did so in order to buck the trend or because they were misinformed about the GDR. Surprisingly, Anna Funder, author of the critically acclaimed, prize-winning 'Stasiland', was one of those whose research von Donnersmarck questioned.[63] In fact, Funder is not dismissive of the film; it is the film's fundamental inaccuracies and the senior Stasi officer's sudden transformation that she finds problematic. What especially concerns Funder is the invention of a good Stasi officer (Captain Wiesler, played by Ulrich Mühe) where none existed, though others have noted that there was evidence of increasing scepticism towards the SED if not wide-scale insubordination during the GDR's final years.[64] Whilst the ex-Stasi employees whom Funder interviewed ranged from the fiercely impenitent to those who claimed only to be following orders, there was no evidence to suggest that any Stasi officer experienced a revelation that led them to betray their office. Wolf Biermann noted something similar in his review. But the errors and fictions of von Donnersmarck's film were ultimately unimportant according to Biermann. For him, the film's strengths lay in its ability to convey 'what it felt like to be subjugated by a Kafkaesque dictatorship' and, on a more personal level, for personifying his erstwhile and long unimaginable tormentors.[65]

In a sense, this was one of von Donnersmarck's objectives. The director hoped to delve deeper into the psyche of the Stasi officers, to go beyond the hackneyed characterizations of the state's security officers as brutish officials or inept careerists in an effort to understand their motivation, behaviour and actions and so arrive at a more realistic account of GDR life. In many Stasi dramas, Stasi employees are coded as one-dimensional figures, obsequious to their superiors, abusive of ordinary East Germans. For them, ideology sanctions repression; seldom is there any sense of the Stasi employees retaining some genuine belief in socialism. Wiesler is an exemplary officer. To be thus, he needs to engage in the usual Stasi abuses, which he does, albeit in scenarios that avoid any sensationalism – something that was important to the director if his film was to be understood as an authentic portrait and not simply a Stasi drama. Indeed, the director stressed the film's authenticity by repeatedly emphasizing the considerable research he had undertaken in preparation for the film and pointing to the endorsements offered by prominent figures (from politicians to Stasi victims). Not all critics were persuaded by these claims, but few were in doubt as to the director's filmmaking talents or the cast's performance, particularly Ulrich Mühe. Yet a significant number found Wiesler's transformation unconvincing. Previously the consummate and dedicated Stasi man, Wiesler's faith in the system and in his office is gradually undermined by a number of insights. One is the realization that his colleagues and peers do not serve the socialist cause as deeply and selflessly as he, a point that Donnersmarck presumably intends as a reflection on the fraudulent nature of GDR socialism. His immediate superior, Grubitz (Ulrich Tukur) is a careerist whose actions are both practical and tactical. Minister Hempf (Thomas Thieme), meanwhile, exploits his ministerial status to pursue and force into a sexual relationship the actress Christa-Maria Sieland (Martina Gedeck), and his motives for having her partner, the playwright Georg Dreyman (Sebastian Koch), placed under surveillance are personal and not political. Wiesler's other insight reveals the redemptive power of art, specifically Brecht's poetry

Figure 6.5 *Das Leben der Anderen*
Ulrich Mühe as the dedicated but troubled Stasi officer in *Das Leben der Anderen* (Florian Henckel von Donnersmarck, 2006) © Wiedemann & Berg Film GmbH & Co KG

and classical music ('The Sonata of the Good Man', the piece by Gabriel Yared specially commissioned for the film) that he (over)hears at the suspects' apartment, and which compounds his crisis of ideology. No longer certain of his own beliefs and, for the first time, indecisive in some of his conduct, he finally attempts to manipulate the surveillance operation in order to protect the couple for whom he feels responsible.

Mühe's subtle reading of the character was widely admired; the rigidity of his gestures and the blank expressions emphasize both Wiesler's self-discipline, his lack of interiority, and his unyielding devotion to his occupation. But von Donnersmarck does not extend such subtlety to his representation of the GDR. While the attention to minimally rendered period detail, the interest in procedure and even the film's naturalistic palette evoke a GDR that for many reviewers rang true (whether or not they had direct experience of the state), the East German people are remarkable by their absence. The GDR that von Donnersmarck restages is one populated almost exclusively by Stasi agents and dissidents. Such narrow focus is not a new thing for films set in the GDR: the victims-and-villains narrative marks a return to earlier representations of the Workers' and Peasants' State. Representing the East through such a binary was always a safe option, and the steady media exposure of new victims and new villains ensured a useful and seemingly accurate organizing principle. Wiesler's transformation may be unprecedented (in both film and GDR history), but von Donnersmarck's film is predicated on a similarly conventional representation. An assortment of civil servants, ranging from odious politicians to menacing subordinates, represents the state, and these are set up in opposition to the bohemians gathered around Dreyman. The distinctions between the two are most obvious in the portrayal of Wiesler, the state automaton to Dreyman's passionate artist. Where one is profiled as an unemotional servant of the state (whose sterile apartment, unremarkable clothing and lifestyle depersonalize him still further), the other is coded as a vital being, a writer who lives in a suitably bohemian apartment full of books and music and art, and who enjoys an intense relationship with Christa-Maria, the actress who will eventually be compromised into betraying him. For fellow director Andreas Dresen, much appreciated for his subtle studies of everyday life in post-unification Germany, the East Germany that von Donnersmarck portrays is a 'fantasy GDR', not just because of the rarified world that is here presented but because of von Donnersmarck's lone Stasi protagonist. 'I'd like to see a different film', Dresen explained. 'One that depicts everyday betrayal, one whose hero is not a lone wolf but a Stasi man with wife and kids, who drives a Trabi or a Wartburg and has a barbeque with friends at the weekend – and then goes to the office at nine on Monday morning to destroy people's lives.'[66]

Despite the enduring interest in the Stasi, finding people willing to invest in his portrait of the GDR was, as the director frequently noted, far from simple.[67] This is ironic, given the problems that the producer Katrin

Schlösser had experienced in sourcing money for *Sonnenallee*, whose description of the GDR when first pitched had also aroused consternation, albeit for different reasons. A less generous assessment would be that in a business that is as risk averse as the film industry, investors were apprehensive about financing a novice (feature) filmmaker such as von Donnersmarck. The director's project did eventually appeal to two of his fellow alumni of the Munich Academy of Television and Film, producers Quirin Berg and Dieter Wiedemann (of Wiedemann and Berg Filmproduktion), who were able to secure enviable distribution through Walt Disney Studio's distribution arm, Buena Vista International. The producers may have been aware of the waning interest in Ostalgie. Though the viewing figures for the retro shows of 2003 marked Ostalgie's zenith, the critical response suggested its nadir and a subsequent 'Ostalgie fatigue' was perceptible. In addition to the controversial portrayal of a redeemed Stasi officer, the producers presumably recognized in von Donnersmarck's script a list of generic conventions that would cater to audiences: the film combines aspects of both the surveillance thriller (it is particularly reminiscent of Francis Ford Coppola's understated *The Conversation* (1974), a film whose focus is even more on those surveying than those surveyed) and mainstream melodrama.[68] Furthermore, while the film engages specifically with the communist dictatorship, international reviewers especially were prone to referencing the Hitler dictatorship, which has long been a lucrative topic for film. No less important to the film's domestic success is the nostalgia that it apparently gainsays. While the film was widely seen as a counterpoint to Ostalgie, it too indulges in retrospection, only the fascination here is with the GDR as a repressive dictatorship and especially the state's infamous security operations. The exhibits may differ to those on display in *Sonnenallee* and *Good Bye, Lenin!* but the attention given to period artefacts is hardly different. The title of both Becker's and von Donnersmarck's films are programmatic but not unambiguous: *Good Bye, Lenin!* implies valediction, a farewell to the past; in truth it facilitates a view of a GDR that is uncoupled from its corrupted ideology, a view of what the GDR might have been. Though the title of von Donnersmarck's film was originally intended as a reference to those under Stasi surveillance, *Das Leben der Anderen* may for future generations come to signify how Germany's others, the former GDR citizens, once lived.

Notes

1. D. Lowenthal, *The Past is a Foreign Country*, 3rd ed., Cambridge: Cambridge University Press, 1990, p. 384.
2. J.R. Gillis, 'Memory and Identity: The History of a Relationship', in J.R. Gillis (ed.). *Commemorations: The Politics of National Identity*, Princeton: Princeton University Press, 1996, 3–24, p. 17.
3. Lowenthal (1990), p. xxiii.

4. E. Hobsbawm, 'Introduction: Inventing Tradition', in Hobsbawm and Ranger (eds) (2003), 1–15, p. 6.
5. C Dieckmann, *Das wahre Leben im Falschen. Geschichten von ostdeutscher Identität*, Berlin: C. Links, 2000, 15.
6. T. Roethe, *Arbeiten wie bei Honecker, verdienen wie bei Kohl. Ein Plädoyer für das Ende der Schonfrist*, Frankfurt am Main: Eichborn Verlag, 1999.
7. 'Blindes Gekaufe', *Der Spiegel* 19, 1991: 121.
8. S.T. Ostovitch, 'Epilogue: Dangerous Memories', in A. Confino and P. Fritzsche (eds), *The Work of Memory. New Directions in the Study of German Society and Culture*, Urbana: University of Illinois Press, 2002. Retrieved 25 September 2008 from http://www.press.uillinois.edu/ epub/books/confino/
9. I am distinguishing between those socialized in the GDR rather than those simply born there. The latter often profess to miss the East German state even though their experience of life under socialism was negligible.
10. The unification comedies' reliance on members of established cabaret groups was often seen as a weakness. One reviewer of *Go Trabi Go* also grumbles about the film's debt to cabaret. *Film Dienst* 44, 1991: 26 (no author).
11. The original line is 'Entwicklung des volkseigenen Humors'. The Volkseigener Betrieb (people-owned enterprise) was the GDR's legal form of publicly owned industrial enterprises.
12. Thompson summarizes this disappointment when he suggests, 'they imagined they would get the West Germany of the 1950s, but got that of the 1990s. They wished for the *Wirtschaftswunder* [economic miracle] but got the *Standortskrise* [economic crisis] instead'. See P. Thompson, '"CSU des Ostens"? – *Heimat* and the Left', in Taberner and Finlay (eds) (2002), 123–41, p. 126.
13. Interview with M. Worthmann, 'Die leicht verderbliche Vereinigung', *Berliner Zeitung*, 10 April 1992.
14. T. Brussig, *Am kürzeren Ende der Sonnenallee*, Berlin: Verlag Volk und Welt, 1999.
15. Though nowhere near as successful as *Sonnenallee*, Peterson's film did tempt almost 200,000 viewers to the screen, a respectable figure for a German film in a market typically dominated by Hollywood.
16. K. Sontheimer, 'United Germany: Political System Under Challenge', *SAIS Review* (Special Issue) 15, 1995: 39–54, 48. For a hostile review see for example G. Decker, 'Freiheit zu lachen', *Neues Deutschland*, 6 October 1999.
17. Brussig offered a more rational response in an open letter. See T. Brussig, 'Opfer politischer Gewalt haben ein Recht auf Wiedergutmachung', *Der Tagesspiegel*, 29 January 2000.
18. Brussig was less disingenuous, and suggested that the director thought the decade more fashionable. See S. Maischberger, 'Sonnenallee. Interview mit Thomas Brussig und Leander Haußmann'. Retrieved 12 September 2008 from http://www.thomasbrussig.de/interviews/sonnenallee.htm
19. C. Löser, 'Sonnenallee', *Film-Dienst*, 1999, 52. Among the film's many faults, according to the reviewer, were the idioms and descriptions that post-date the Wende.
20. In Maischberger, 'Sonnenallee. Interview mit Thomas Brussig und Leander Haußmann'.
21. Cooke (2005), p. 116.
22. See Hodgin (2004), p. 40.
23. V. Gunske and S.S. Poser, 'Nachdenken Über Thomas B', *Tip-Magazin* 21, 1999. The book to which Brussig refers is his own: T. Brussig, *Am kürzeren Ende des Sonnenallees*, Berlin: Volk und Welt, 1999.
24. It is worth noting that the script underwent numerous changes before final approval. Among the suggested changes was the inclusion of a Stasi element proposed by the film's west German co-producer, Detlev Buck, a suggestion that was not welcomed by Brussig.
25. T. Brussig, *Helden wie Wir*, Berlin: Volk und Welt, 1995, p. 300.
26. At a press conference in November 1989, SED Politbüro member Schabowki mistakenly announced that restrictions on border crossings to the west had been lifted with

immediate effect, which statement led to thousands of east Germans descending on the East/West Berlin border.

27. P. Ensikat, 'Filmtipp der Woche', *Der Tagesspiegel*, 9 December 1999.
28. S. Boym, *The Future of Nostalgia*, New York: Basic Books, 2001, 50.
29. See T. Brussig,'Der Brechreiz ist ein aktueller', *Der Tagesspiegel*, 31 August 2003, and 'Wir sind nostalgisch weil wir Menschen sind' (originally published 2001). Retrieved 12 August 2008 from http://www.thomasbrussig.de/publizistik/sehnsucht.htm
30. J. Sparschuh, *Der Zimmerspringbrunnen. Ein Heimatroman*, Köln: Kiepenhauer & Witsch, 1995.
31. See Cooke (2005), p. 17.
32. H. Bhabha, *The Location of Culture*, London and New York: Routledge, 1994, p. 86.
33. Among the titles published around the same time of Becker's release were C. Rausch, *Meine freie deutsche Jugend*, Frankfurt am Main: Fischer Verlag, 2003, and Michael Tetzlaff, *Ostblöckchen*, Frankfurt am Main: Schöffling, 2004. As with the film's producers, the publishers were often keen to distance their titles from an unreconstructed Ostalgie (whilst exploiting exactly the kind of imagery associated with the trend for the books' sleeves).
34. A similar emigration had been envisaged in one mock historical account. See R. Andert, *Rote Wende. Wie die Ossis die Wessis besiegten*, Berlin: Elefanten Press, 1994.
35. A number of reviewers ironically noted that the most successful Ostalgie/unification film was a western production (the cast includes some actors from the east but the scriptwriter, director and lead actor are all from the west).
36. See Cooke (2005), p. 141.
37. See H. Witzel, 'Das Märchen von der Ostalgie. Die DDR-Welle im Fernsehen', *Der Stern* 37, 2003: 190–4. The series had its detractors. A particularly arch review is to be found in C. Dieckmann, 'Honis heitere Welt', *Die Zeit* 36, 28 August 2003. Retrieved 1 January 2006 from http://zeus.zeit.de/text/2003/36/Ostalgie_
38. H.-J. Maaz, 'Ich fürchte, wir kommen wieder nicht vor', *MDR-Online*, 1 January 2003. Retrieved 13 September 2008 from http://www.mdr.de/kultur/896480.html
39. F. Illies, *Generation Golf*, Frankfurt am Main: Fischer Verlag, 2000. Writers' nostalgia for the FRG is discussed in A. Plowman,'"Westalgie"? Nostalgia for the "Old" Federal Republic in Recent German Prose', *Seminar* 40(3), 2004: 249–61.
40. The fact that one of the better films documenting the old West Germany was made by an east German director did not draw nearly as much attention as had the western provenance of *Good Bye, Lenin!*'s director.
41. *Kleinruppin Forever* Press Pack, p. 26.
42. C. Epstein, 'The Stasi: New Research on the East German Ministry of State Security', *Kritika: Explorations in Russian and Eurasian History* 5(2), 2004, 321–48, p. 323.
43. Emigration was overwhelmingly a one-way affair – and a fraught one at that. The GDR authorities arrested as many as 2,000 people a year for attempting to flee the state. See http://www.bpb.de/themen/P2F402,2,0,Glossar.html#art2 (retrieved 12 September 2008). There are other narratives in which those who have escaped the GDR finally choose to return – *Der Boss aus dem Westen*, or Delius's protagonist (F.C. Delius, *Der Spaziergang von Rostock nach Syrakus*, Reinbek: Rowohlt-Verlag, 1995) – but the important difference is that the protagonists in each case are east German.
44. M. Maffesoli, cited in G. Delanty, *Community*, London: Routledge, 2003, p. 139.
45. G. Mueller, 'Going East, Looking West: Border Crossings in Recent German Cinema', *Seminar* 44(4), 2008: 453–69, p. 466.
46. A. Hahn, 'Ins Gehege', *Junge Welt*, 9 September 2004. Retrieved 23 June 2008 from http://www.jungewelt.de/2004/09-09/021.php. See also M. Stöhr, *Schnitt*, 2004. Retrieved 23 June 2008 from http://www.schnitt.de/filme/artikel/kleinruppin_forever.shtml
47. Lest one should think Fiebeler an east German revisionist, it is important to note that east Germans who are unable to separate themselves from their past come in for some

criticism in *Die Datsche* (2003), his previous (graduation) film, a 'psychothriller', in which a couple are held hostage in their simple holiday home.

48. Statistics from *Filmförderungsanstalt. FFA-info*, 2, 26 August 2005. Retrieved 23 June 2008 from http://www.filmfoerderungsanstalt.de/downloads/publikationen/ffa_intern/FFA_info_2_2005.pdf , p. 10.

49. Of course, these t-shirts are not, strictly speaking, retro, since no such t-shirts existed in the GDR. They are evidence of a postmodern design principle that jumbles the new with the authentic – original East German mottos and symbols are re-contextualized, divorced from their political and historical origins and given a new life as design statements. Authentic or not, we might agree with Lowenthal's point that 'imitations, fakes, and new works inspired by earlier prototypes extend and further alter the aura of antiquity. The scarcity of originals spurs the making of replicas that at least echo the old'. He may be discussing older civilizations but the idea is the same. See Lowenthal (1990), p. xxiii.

50. *Kleinruppin Forever* Press Pack, p. 28.

51. 'Reality' performed by Eskobar (written by Jeff Jordan/Vladimir Cosma and originally performed by Richard Sanderson).

52. Admittedly, irony operates at different levels and requires different degrees of decoding. Other post-unification films have used far more elaborate structures with which to address a point. In *Tolle Lage*, Sören Voigt introduces a character called Michi Fanselow, a former GDR *Schlagersänger* (crooner) whose career has hit rock bottom, forcing him to tour east German campsites. Many reviewers (and presumably audience members) failed to recognize that the character was invented but factualized by the director, who acknowledged 'Michi Fanselow' in the credits. *Tolle Lage* thus makes a satirical point about the unreliability of memory (and the quality of reviewers' research). The joke went so far as to record Michi's 'original' hit, 'Mauerblümchen' ('Little Wall Flower'), and an accompanying video.

53. See Cooke (2005), p. 118. Also Taberner (2005), p. 37.

54. T. Lindenberger, 'Zeitgeschichte am Schneidetisch', in G. Paul (ed.), *Visual History. Ein Studinebuch*, Göttingen: Vandenhoeck & Ruprecht, 2006, 353–73, p. 359.

55. See F. Zilian, *From Confrontation to Cooperation. The Takeover of the National People's (East German) Army by the Bundeswehr*, London: Praeger, 1999, pp. 31–59.

56. See C. Dieckmann, 'Zonenkindereien', *Die Zeit 40, 29 September 2005*.

57. L. Haußmann, 'Es Kam dicke genug', *Der Spiegel*, 8 September 2003: 220–2, p. 220.

58. L. Hutcheon, *The Politics of Postmodernism*, London: Routledge, 1989, p. 93.

59. Dieckmann (2005).

60. *Lives of Others* Press Booklet, p. 12. http://www.sonyclassics.com/thelivesofothers/externalLoads/TheLivesofOthers.pdf

61. In the audio commentary, the director stresses that Thieme, who had been persecuted by the East German authorities, 'hates the GDR with a vengeance'. It is interesting to note that Donnersmarck was also conscious that he might alienate some of the east German audience and thus decided to remove from the same scene dialogue that revealed the former politician's post-unification success and connection to the PDS. According to the audio commentary, that party's existence as a successor party to the SED is as inconceivable to the director as would have been the continuation of Hitler's NSDAP after 1945.

62. M. Guillénn, 'The Lives of Others – Interview With Florian Henckel Von Donnersmarck', 2007. Retrieved 12 July 2009 from http://twitchfilm.net/archives/008825.html

63. A. Funder, *Stasiland*. London: Granta, 2003.

64. See G. Dale, 'Heimat, "Ostalgie" and the Stasi: The GDR in German Cinema, 1999-2006', *Debatte. Journal of Contemporary Central and Eastern Europe*, 15 (2), 2007: 158.

65. W. Biermann, 'Warum Wolf Biermann über den Stasi-Film *Das Leben der anderen* staunt', *Die Welt*, 22 March 2006. Retrieved 20 October 2009 from http://www.welt.de/printwelt/article205586/Warum_Wolf_Biermann_ueber_den_Stasi-Film_Das_Leben_der_Anderen_staunt.html

66. A. Borcholte and W. Höbel, '"Ich hasse dieses Gestöhne"', *Der Spiegel*, 3 September 2008. Retrieved 12 December 2009 from http://www.spiegel.de/kultur/kino/0,1518,575840,00.html

67. For more on Stasi films see See N. Hodgin 2011 (forthcoming). 'Screening the Stasi: The Politics of Representation in Postunification Film', in N. Hodgin and C. Pearce (eds), *The GDR Remembered. Representations of the East German State Since 1989*, Rochester, NY, and Woodbridge, Suffolk: Camden House, 2011 (forthcoming).

68. For an interesting analysis of the film's reliance on melodrama see O. Evans, 'Redeeming the Demon? The Legacy of the Stasi in *Das Leben der Anderen*', *Memory Studies* 3(2), 2010: 164–77.

CONCLUSION

A Community Apart?

Although the films considered in this book address a broad range of issues and represent dissimilar approaches to screening the east, the majority coincide in their representation of the east Germans as a separate community. From *Go Trabi Go* to *Good Bye, Lenin!* the majority of post-unification narratives emphasize the continued differences between east and west. Even those films that allow for a degree of reconciliation or mutual understanding do so while underlining the cultural distinctiveness of the two communities (though, in truth, the west barely features in any meaningful way). While this was to be expected in the films that immediately followed unification, it is perhaps surprising that, two decades later, the east Germans continue to be portrayed as a community apart.

Before 1989, invoking the other Germany had been crucial to each state's image of itself and reflected an adversarial process of self-definition (of the self against the other) that was anchored in the politics of the Cold War. While a common national culture survived the opposing ideologies, the disintegration of the East German state did not collapse all differences between the Germans. Forty years of education, of economic and political separation, of cultural and ideological influence that stemmed from opposing ends of the political spectrum could not be undone with the simple dismantling of the wall. The differences that remained were no longer rooted in ideology, and seemed sometimes only trivial. Yet seemingly insignificant differences between ostensibly similar cultures can, as Freud noted, be magnified out of all proportion and problematize relationships between neighbours.[1] It had been expected that unification would re-establish a German cultural dialogue that had survived the states' opposing ideologies; instead, new distinguishing features have emerged, of which the economic disparity between east and west is perhaps the most significant. Similarly, divergent political and cultural values, which appear to confirm that a separate consciousness had developed in the GDR, even if the final product was not true to the original SED design, means that the adjectival designation 'east' or 'west' is not simply a reference to geographical origin but carries with it certain assumptions about political and cultural orientation that have not been fully resolved in the period since unification. Surveys conducted in 2009 certainly bear out marked differences in the east and west Germans' attitudes to the GDR and unification: east Germans are far more sceptical of the market economy than are their western neighbours and a significant number still see consider themselves second class citizens; and while few of the west Germans who were polled see much merit in the GDR, half of the east German interviewees believe that there were more positives than negatives in the GDR.[2]

Heimat, once vilified by the GDR authorities because of its conservative associations, returned as a foundation for building new post-communist communities. In the films of the early 1990s, the Heimat community offers a place of refuge, a shelter where friendship and common values bind the east Germans. The return of community to political discourse was by no means unique to the former GDR. Gerard Delanty has suggested that 'community was the ideology of the 1990s', and that it assumed a new potency in the political campaigns of that decade.[3] Its proponents (Delanty mentions Bill Clinton and Tony Blair) found it useful as a means of countering the individualism favoured by their predecessors – the hallmark of the selfish 1980s – and the social policies of New Labour's 'Third Way' and Gerhard Schröder's 'neue Mitte' were clearly embedded in community discourse. The new commitment to community championed by Blair, Schröder, and others was not an appeal to an older way of living, a return to tradition, even if the new discourse of community – 'a response to the failure of society to provide a basis for the three core components of community: solidarity, trust and autonomy' – implicitly acknowledged the loss of certain values associated with the past.[4] Community seen in these terms obviously has some resonance for the east Germans. Certainly, a parochial vision of community, which is central to the films' depiction of post-GDR Heimat, has been recognized by, among others, the PDS/Die Linke.[5] In re-connecting with the idea of community, east Germans are attempting to safeguard factors that are fundamental to their group identity. In many of the films, the appeal to community *does* herald a return to old traditions, since community living is repeatedly linked to a particularly bucolic vision of life, one that resists modernity entirely.

Paradoxically, this post-GDR Heimat, which is as anachronistic as it is invented, is seen to provide an authentic alternative to the impersonal, superficial society beyond, a distinction between community (intimate, congenial) and society (impersonal, artificial) first theorized over a century ago by the sociologist Ferdinand Tönnies and which has been a mainstay of Heimat discourse.[6] As previously mentioned, the restored Heimat had no real equivalent in East German filmmaking, but is the result of grafting a specifically west German film aesthetic onto an east German theme. This allows different viewers different means of identifying with the films. Those in the west may respond positively to a visual style that facilitates some connection to their own past and visual culture; at the same time, it allows east Germans a return to a depoliticized Heimat of the kind that had been anathema to the East German authorities.

Though a sentimental conception of community is not intrinsically east German, it is presented as such in some of the period's films. East Germans may therefore imagine themselves as a more wholesome counterpart to their western neighbours. It also allows west German audiences the possibility to see the east as a quaint, unsophisticated region which, freed from the tyranny of state socialism, has reverted to a romantic vision of Germany rooted in the traditional view of Heimat, albeit one from which they are excluded. Where these films make use of the east German countryside as a symbolic site of imagined harmony, a romanticized vision of the rural east in which community offers a refuge from western materialism and its attendant dangers, the films discussed in the third and fourth chapters offer a corrective to this idealized vision. With the focus on geographic, cultural, and social alienation, these critical narratives reject the fantasy communities of nostalgia that are revived in the post-unification Heimatfilm. The community that is represented in these films no longer provides any such shelter and the 'vocabulary of values' that traditionally binds communities has ceased to provide any meaning.[7] There are, nonetheless, traces of the original Heimat genre, particularly in the arrival of strangers in remote environments and the perceived threat to the local community. The contact between those inside the community and those from without does not lead to any resolution as it does in the simple east/west encounters, but frequently provides the catalyst for extreme (and extremist) reactions. These films seek to dissociate the eastern locality from any post-unification idea of a natural idyll; they refuse to facilitate a return to the mythical territories imagined in the Heimatfilme. The occasional documentary tone found in these films distinguishes them from the contrived and sentimental Heimat that features in other narratives. Focusing on the region's despoiled surroundings, its ruins, and the disintegration of community, the films invariably communicate a sense of loss. This loss is not nostalgia for an irretrievable past but for the utopian aspirations associated with the GDR rather than the empty promises of the SED-state. Just as the idyllic surroundings captured in *Der Brocken* and *Das war der wilde Osten* are encoded and offered as a physical representation of its inhabitants' psychological and social well-being, the neglected eastern geography in other films reflects the communities' social and psychological decline.

In contrast to the Heimat iconography, which transcends regional borders and ignores the geopolitical details of the recent past, the films that focus on the east as a landscape of loss acknowledge the local environment as a critical space of inquiry. Concentrating on the region's myriad difficulties, they underline the east as a territory that will not easily be incorporated within the newly expanded national imaginary. Equally, the films deny any official historicized memory of the GDR, rejecting both the west's post-unification account and the SED-state's self-depiction. In choosing images constitutive of the east's economic collapse and characters whose politics and behaviour contradict the east's apparently core socialist values (internationalist, anti-fascist, progressive), they underline the failure of the GDR national project. The films also remain sceptical as to an undifferentiated, unified German society. The protagonists remain 'extracommunitari', to borrow Morley's and Robins' term, not just from the Berlin Republic but also from their local community.[8] With the GDR Heimat gone, and their position within the wider German community not (yet) established, they remain disconnected from both the past and from the present. Placing particular emphasis on the eastern geography, these films represent the east less as a lost Heimat than as a ruined Heimat.

Few of these films are able to offer a positive resolution. Unlike the celebratory mood that characterizes the endings in the Wende comedies, the east is given no glimmer of hope for a better future. In many of the films the final image is one of flames. Fire provides a common metaphor, for as various buildings burn, so, too, do the hopes for a better future. In *Herzsprung*, the local yobs set fire to the roadside café in which the Stranger has been working. Fire is the result of incendiary hostilities in several other films, including *Endstation: Tanke* in which the protagonists are forced to escape their roadside sanctuary when it is set alight by a drunken mob. The drunken righteousness and inebriated courage of the mob figures again in *Tolle Lage*, where angry east German campers finally round on the site's west German owner, setting fire to the camp shop – an impotent act as it turns out, since he has just sold the premises. In other films, characters are consumed by fire in road accidents (*Landschaft mit Dornen* and *Vergiss Amerika*), while Simon's film concludes with its protagonists dancing around the flames of his blazing shelter. The death of the protagonist is, in fact, not an unusual ending. *Herzsprung*, *Die Vergebung*, *Bis zum Horizont und weiter*, *Wege in die Nacht* and *Schultze gets the Blues* are among those that end in a tragic, usually violent fashion. Those films that do not close with an image of fire or death are no more upbeat. Final scenes typically emphasize the uncertain future that the east Germans face: in films such as *Ostkreuz*, *Asphaltflimmern*, *Stilles Land*, and *Neben der Zeit*, characters are left wondering, or waiting for something, or they are seen heading off into the distance, having succeeded only in escaping their Heimat. The motivation behind this desire to escape varies slightly and the characters react differently to their circumstances, but boredom, unemployment and the deterioration of the community typically account for the chronic provincial pessimism for which escape appears to be the only cure.

Pessimism is not, of course, a condition that affects only those habitués of the eastern provinces. City residents are, according to several urban narratives set in and around east Berlin, likewise lacking in confidence and isolated from those around them. Disorientated by the changes in their physical and social environment, the figures in these Berlin films struggle to adjust to life after the GDR, and inevitably seek refuge in their memories of the past, memories that focus not on old-fashioned and ahistorical notions of community as in the Heimatfilme, but on the security and social order associated specifically with the GDR. The protagonists' attempts to impose the order that they associate with the life before 1989 only worsens their situation, and the films count as a warning against such recourse to the past, while acknowledging the reasons for the characters' retrospection. Conversely, retrospection of a rather different kind has been central to the most significant trend in the development of a post-communist identity. Faced with the possible erasure of their past, some east Germans took to reconstructing the past that they preferred to remember, a process that Foucault, in a discussion about post-war French films, called a 're-programming of popular memory'.[9] This version of the GDR is a backwards projection of the past the east Germans wish they had experienced rather than a realistic re-enactment of those times, as the narrator of *Good Bye, Lenin!* makes clear. Ostalgie blocks complete cultural assimilation as a means of guarding the east Germans' memory and identity. It strives to promote a collective memory that necessarily denies what is typically regarded as a master narrative imposed by outsiders (i.e. the west) and subdues or ignores any competing or alternative voices within – the non-native Germans who lived in the GDR, for example, are not generally involved or invited to participate in the retrogressive celebration of the East German yesteryear. The importance of Ostalgie lies in its potential to celebrate and therefore reinforce an east German distinctiveness. Ostalgie is significant for what it does not celebrate as much as what it does. It is not the GDR's unpalatable features that are the focus, but the unremarkable, everyday items and lives. Possessing some totemic values for the east Germans, the GDR products that were on view in the Ostalgie films seem to gratify the east Germans' nostalgic tastes, even if the films were satirizing such retrogressive yearning. Sometimes they were doing both – legitimizing the east Germans' right to reminisce whilst also satirizing the related commodification of memory, and targeting both proponents and consumers. That Christiane Kerner in *Good Bye, Lenin!* is ultimately unable to identify the ersatz gherkins that Alex has transferred to an original Spreewald jar is just one example in which the films gently highlight Ostalgie's hollowness. Of the (so-called) Ostalgie films discussed, two were among the most successful German productions of the post-unification period. While *Sonnenallee* was considered (even accused) by several critics to advance an east German identity that was rooted in a falsely conceptualized past – erroneous though this assessment was – the other, *Good Bye, Lenin!*, appeared to bury both the GDR and the hatchet between east and west. Only *Kleinruppin Forever* can be said to promulgate an account of the GDR according to which life in the East was not only better than post-unification discourse often allows but actually preferable to life in the West, a claim that is anchored in a celebration of apparently innate eastern values.

In his exhaustive survey of post-unification literature, Frank Thomas Grub wonders whether Ostalgie texts rely so heavily on contemporary readers' recognition of the products of the east's former consumer culture that the narratives will become meaningless to future generations. 'Who', he asks, 'will remember the products referenced in 20 years, let alone connect them to positive childhood and adolescent memories?'[10] The question is apposite; yet Ostalgie (and by implication its referents) may not fade as quickly as some have suggested. If the inequitable situation in east Germany continues –social policy reforms such as 'Harz IV' led to sizeable demonstrations in the east, where these belt-tightening measures are most keenly felt – the impulse behind Ostalgie might not die out with the generation socialized in the SED-state but, as Patricia Hogwood has observed, 'pass on to the post-unification generation of east Germans, and form the basis of a lasting cultural myth'.[11] This notion of a post-memory, which was first theorized by Marianne Hirsch in relation to the children of Holocaust survivors, is gaining ground in post-GDR studies. While successive generations with no direct experience of the GDR will certainly be influenced by their parents' and local communities' (variously mediated and often contradictory) experiences, future views of the past will also be shaped by those accounts offered by, among other media, film.

Towards Normalization?

Given that the eastern states remain Germany's poor region, and that the Federal Republic's faltering economy, seen by some as a consequence of financing the east, has put an end to many west Germans' sympathy for their eastern neighbours and further exacerbated the latter's frustration and disappointment with their post-unification lives, some points of division between the two communities are likely to persist. But the interest in the GDR shows no immediate signs of abating and the fascination for the state's uglier aspects are liable to prolong suspicions about the east Germans. Filmmakers will doubtless continue to probe issues related to the former state. Film and television productions such as *Hundsköpfe* (Karsten Laske, 2001), *Die Mauer – Berlin 61* (*The Wall – Berlin 61*, Hartmut Schoens, 2006), *Der Tunnel* (*The Tunnel*, Roland Suso Richter, 2001, *Drei Stern Rot* (*Three Star Red*, Olaf Kaiser, 2002), *Der rote Kakadu* (*The Red Cockatoo*, Domink Gräf, 2006), *Die Frau vom Checkpoint Charlie* (*The Girl from Checkpoint Charlie*, Miguel Alexandre, 2007), *An die Grenze* (*To the Border*, Urs Egger, 2007), *Das Wunder von Berlin* (*The Miracle of Berlin*, Roland Suso Richter, 2008), *Das Leben der Anderen*, and *Liebe Mauer* (Peter Timm, 2009), attest to a continued curiosity about certain subjects – the Stasi, the border patrols, the East German military – from which many east Germans have tried to distance themselves. By contrast, but no less significant, is the abiding comic depiction of the east, an approach that is evident and exploited in genre films, from buddy movies to black comedies to crime capers. These narratives do little to challenge the homogenous view of the east and rely instead on the usual eastern topoi. The representation of the east in *Ossi's Eleven* (2007), Oliver Mielke's provincial pastiche of Steven Soderbergh's Hollywood hit *Ocean's Eleven* (2001), for example, still relies on the kind of stereotypes that were common currency in the immediate post-unification period. Socialist era apartment blocks provide the back-drop, where a crew of eastern losers (comprising victims of the SED's no-torious athlete-doping programme, a former Stasi employee, etc.) are gathered together in order to rob a bank by the eponymous Ossi. Despite the east Germans' usual improvisation, the plan fails to make the gang richer, but succeeds in binding together disparate individuals made des-perate by circumstances. Such formulaic fare is perhaps to be expected from a director best known for television work (mostly sitcoms and comedy shows), but other, better known and more respected directors have engaged in similar portraits. The Berlin and Dresden based Filmkombinat must have hoped that Michael Schorr's *Schröders Wunderbare Welt* (2007) would prove as successful as his earlier surprise hit, *Schultze gets the Blues*. The director and the cast, which included a number of well-regarded east and west German actors (Eva-Maria Hagen and Hollywood favourite Jürgen Prochnow) must have seemed a safe bet, as must its location at Germany's eastern borders (with Poland and the Czech Republic). *Schröders Wunderbare Welt* does not quite abandon the documentary tone of its predecessor, but the film suffers from an inconsistency of style, seeking simultaneously to combine satire, realism and comedy as well as an accu-rate account of the lives of ordinary people in this seemingly remote part of Germany. In the accompanying press notes, the director claims that his film 'defies genre, switching between and fusing satire and reality'.[12] Perhaps it was this bold, genre-defying approach that Filmkombinat, self-declared producers of 'unusual and ambitious documentaries and feature films', felt suited their portfolio. But neither critics nor audiences were much impressed by Schorr's second feature, which was criticized for its clichés, its messy plot and a general lack of focus. Contemporary though the themes of Schorr's film were, especially in terms of the cross-border dialogue between the Germans and their eastern neighbours, his portrayal of the region aligned it with the crude farces rather than the subtle satires of earlier post-unification films.

Representations of east Germany are not limited to GDR dramas or post-unification farces, however. A tendency towards normalized portraits of the east, a trend that has also been recognized in contemporary literature, is increasingly apparent.[13] A few of the films made during the first decade after unification had consciously avoided the standard references to the GDR and the well-worn post-unification issues which underpinned so many other eastern narratives. This was not driven by a desire to have done with the GDR, to overlook or negate the crimes of the SED-state, but rather a means of addressing issues in contemporary Germany without needing to invoke the overused and exaggerated features – an 'attempt to get away from the extremes', as Boym says.[14] *Heidi M.* (2001), Michael Klier's much-admired follow up to *Ostkreuz*, for example, offers an intimate city portrait of a woman in her forties in a touching drama that avoids contextualizing the east German experience in terms of the GDR or unification. By far the most interesting (and critically acclaimed) representations of contemporary eastern Germany are those critical realist films made by Andreas Dresen, who has proved to be one of the country's most versatile directors, working successfully in a number of formats, from documentaries to television and feature films. More than any other director, Dresen has applied himself to the task of narrating life in the east in films that do not have recourse to the past and which deliberately avoid the topoi of post-unification film. The stock characterizations (provincial simpletons, brooding loners) and trite unification issues (the east/west conflict, confrontation with the past) are all noticeably absent in his films.[15] Instead, they offer realistic, often affecting, sometimes bittersweet portraits of everyday east Germans, young and old, though Dresen is keen to point out that his films are not intended as chronicles specific to east Germany and that the challenges facing his characters, their preoccupations and concerns, are universal, not regional.[16] Since unification, his films have explored life in both the provinces and in Berlin, from *Halbe Treppe*, which follows the lives of a group of thirty-something friends living in a dismal Frankfurt an der Oder and whose marital infidelities threaten their relationships but also finally motivate them to reassess their lives, and the raw portrait of life in Rostock as seen through the eyes of a woman police officer in *Die Polizistin* (*The Policewoman*, 2000), to the Berlin films, *Willenbrock*, *Sommer vorm Balkon* and *Wolke 9* (*Cloud Nine*, 2008). Dresen's normalizing approach is evident, too, in other recent representations of life in the east. Critics welcomed Bernd Böhlich's *Du bist nicht allein* as a realistic portrait of the east, which foregrounds the east German post-unification experience but also avoids the usual references. The same is true of films such as Valeska Grisebach's *Sehnsucht* (*Desire*, 2006) and *Yella* (2007), Christian Petzold's haunting drama, which ostensibly follows a woman's escape from her eastern *Heimat* to a brave new world of private equity in the west, where the eponymous protagonist (Nina Hoss) hopes to prosper. *Yella* may be one of the few post-wall films to trace an east German's journey into the west but the filmmaker is ultimately less interested in examining any east/west cultural clash or contextualizing Yella's journey in terms of unification politics than he is than he is in exposing the strangeness of modern capitalism, a world made peculiar and alienating by Peztold's characteristically dispassionate direction. Petzold's subsequent film, the prize-wining *Jerichow* (2008), a loose adaptation of James M. Cain's 'The Postman Always Rings Twice', is set in Germany's north east, an area whose coast and desolate landscape has become a preferred setting for German filmmakers. As with *Yella*, the realities of east German life – unemployment, deindustrialization, the search for Heimat – are thematized without recourse to the usual figures and visual markers. Indeed, most reviewers commented on the film's eastern location in terms primarily of geography and not of socio-political context.

While the attention paid to the SED-state has not yet declined, the obvious markers of 'easternness' are thus no longer a pre-requisite for east German stories. Nor do these filmmakers seek to include the 'typical' east German, whether the underdog and everyman figures embodied by Wolfgang Stumph, or the agitated characters consummately played by Michael Gwisdek. Since most of these normalized narratives centre on young east Germans, it follows that former DEFA actors are increasingly absent from such portraits. Berlin continues to feature in many of these films, offering a location for a series of edgy city portraits as in Sören Voigt's *Identity Kills* (2003), Vanessa Jopp's *Komm näher* (*Happy as One*, 2005) and Detlev Buck's *Knallhart* (*Tough Enough*, 2006). Most of these narratives – one might also include Martin Gypkens's *Wir* (*Us*, 2003) and Robert Thalheim's *Netto* (2004) – follow the experiences of (east) Berlin's youth, the first post-GDR generation, and seldom reference the East German past or place the lives depicted in the context of unification, but opt instead for universal stories rendered through a new critical realist aesthetic.[17]

The focus on young people in contemporary east Germany extends also to those films set in the provinces. For the first time in post-unification film, some of these narratives comment on Germany's eastern borders, usually with Poland, and have begun to consider the experiences of non-Germans at the eastern border. It was surprising, given the substantial migration that took place after the borders between east and west were opened and the large numbers of new arrivals from the former Eastern Bloc and beyond, that their stories had so rarely featured. In the first decade after unification, the appearance of non-Germans generally fulfilled a narrative function, in which their otherness set off a chain of calamitous events that exposed the east German community as one hostile to outsiders, however innocent they might be (as in *Endstation: Tanke* and *Herzsprung*, for example). Outsiders, typically eastern Europeans, briefly figured in other films where they were problematically linked to criminal activities (car thieves in *Vergiss Amerika* and *Asphaltflimmern*, pornography in *Berlin is in Germany*, the mafia in *Neben der Zeit*), an example of 'othering the immigrant' that was increasingly common in the decade after unification.[18] But films such as *Klassenfahrt* (*School Trip*, Henner Winkler, 2002), *Lichter* (*Distant Lights*, Hans-Christian Schmid, 2003), *Das Lächeln der Tiefseefische* (*The Smile of the Monsterfish*, Till Endemann, 2004) and *Am Ende Kommen Touristen* (*And Along Came Tourists*, Robert Thalheim, 2007) provide less skewed representations of Germany's eastern neighbours, who have come to assume a more central role.[19] The new interest in and awareness of these neighbouring states and of the Germans' relationship to them has led Randall Halle to observe that 'What was once a strict geopolitical border, becomes a new and under-theorized transnational boundary.'[20]

It is too early to say whether interest in Germany's newer arrivals will continue, though the acclaim that some of these films have received will give directors and producers cause to exploit what seems like a good thing. Films that reflect the experiences of non-native Germans could enhance Germany's multicultural profile and support the notion of a culturally heterogeneous society, which recognizes and celebrates pluralism. But it might also be that the emergence of a new 'other' arriving from the east once again (whether Balkan refugees, Polish smugglers, or Russian criminals) will challenge the east Germans' eastern identity in terms of their supposed geographical and cultural distinctiveness and indirectly confirm their 'Germanness', as the Germans recognize their similarities against different eastern communities.

Notes

1. Freud terms this the 'narcissism of small differences' and discusses it with regard to 'closely related' communities and to anti-Semitism. S. Freud, *Civilization and Its Discontents*, trans. D. McLintock, London: Penguin Books, 2002, pp. 50–1.
2. See 'Ergebnisse der Emnid-Umfrage: Wie bewerten die Deutschen die Ereignisse von 1989'. Retrieved 20 October 2009 from http://www.bmvbs.de/jsp/fotoreihe/ fotoreihe_einzelbild.jsp?doc-id=1083277&curr_img_nr=1&sprache=de and R. Köcher, '42 Prozent der Ostdeutschen fühlen sich als Bürger zweiter Klasse', 26 September 2009. Retrieved 20 October 2009 from http://www.wiwo.de/politik-weltwirtschaft/42- prozent-der-ostdeutschen-fuehlen-sich-als-buerger-zweiter-klasse-409340/
3. G. Delanty, *Modernity and Postmodernity. Knowledge, Power and the Self*, London: Sage, 2000, p. 120.
4. Ibid., p. 128.
5. See, for example, B. Harper, 'Why does the PDS reach the parts that Bündnis 90/Die Grünen Cannot?' in P. Barker (ed.), *The Party of Democratic Socialism in Germany. Modern Post-Communism or Nostalgic Populism? German Monitor*, Amsterdam; Atlanta: Editions Rodopi, 1994, p. 84.
6. See F. Tönnies, *Gemeinschaft und Gesellschaft. Grundbegriffe der reinen Soziologie*, Darmstadt: Wissenschaftliche Buchgesellschaft, 1991. It is worth noting that the west's encroachment into the traditional homeland, the symbolic site of the nation, was also a theme in post-communist Russian films. See S. Larsen, 'In Search of an Audience: The New Russian Cinema of Reconciliation', in Barker (1994), p. 207.
7. Weeks, 'Rediscovering Values', in Squires (ed.) (1993), p. 182.
8. Morley and Robins, 'No Place Like *Heimat*: Images of Home(land) in European Culture', in Carter, Donald and Squires (eds) (1993), p. 76.
9. M. Foucault, 'Film and Memory. An Interview with Michael Foucault ', *Radical Philosophy* 11, 1975: 25.
10. Grub (2003), p. 569.
11. P. Hogwood, 'Identity in the Former GDR: Expressions of "Ostalgia" and "Ossi" Pride in United Germany', in P. Kennedy and C.J. Danks (eds), *Globalization and National Identities. Crisis or Opportunity?* Basingstoke: Palgrave, 2001, 64–79, p. 78.
12. *Schroeder's Wonderful World* (press notes). Retrieved 13 June 2009 from: www.filmkombinat.de/download/.../PresseheftSchroederTextEng.doc
13. See Taberner (2005), p. 54.
14. Boym (2001). Boym is referring to post-war discourse but her point is applicable to post-communist dialogue.
15. To date, the director has only made one film about the GDR. His television film, *Raus aus der Haut* (1997), offered a view of growing up in the East that neither glorified nor vilified the GDR but managed to be both sentimental and critical.

16. Author's interview with Dresen.
17. Films featuring central characters old enough to have had some experience of the GDR are much less common, though the characters in *Sehnsucht*, *Jena Paradies* (*Jena Paradise*, Marco Mittelstaedt, 2004) and Mittelstaedt's other films *Elbe* and *Im Nächsten Leben* (*In the Next Life*, 2005, 2008 respectively) are old enough to remember life in the East.
18. A. Triandafyllidou, *Immigrants and National Identity in Europe*, London: Routledge, 2001, p. 76.
19. Edgar Reitz, meanwhile, has considered the ambivalent reception offered to east Germans and renaturalized Germans from eastern Europe arriving in the provincial west in the final series of his television epic, *Heimat 3* (2004).
20. R. Halle, 'Views from the German-Polish Border: The Exploration of Inter-national Space in *Halbe Treppe* and *Lichter*', *German Quarterly* (80)1, 2007: 77–96, p. 90.

FILMOGRAPHY

Abschied von Agnes (Michael Gwisdek, 1994)
alaska.de (Esther Gronenborn, 2001)
Alle der Kosmonauten (Susann Reck, 1998)
Allemagne Neuf Zero (Jean-Luc Godard, 1991) Doc.
Alles Lüge (Heiko Schier, 1992)
Alte Lied, Das (Ula Stöckl, 1991)
Am Ende Kommen Touristen (Robert Thalheim, 2007)
American Graffiti (George Lucas, 1974)
An die Grenze (Urs Egger, 2007)
Apfelbäume (Helma Sanders-Brahms, 1992)
Asphaltflimmern (Johannes Hebendanz, 1994)
Der Baader Meinhof Komplex (Uli Edel, 2008)
Badlands (Terence Malick, 1974)
Befreite Zone (Norbert Baumgarten, 2002)
Berlin Babylon (Hubertus Siegert, 2001)
Berlin is in Germany (Hannes Stöhr, 2001)
Berlin. Die Sinfonie der Grossstadt (Walter Ruttmann, 1927)
Berlin: Sinfonie einer Großstadt (Thomas Schadt, 2002)
Bicycle Thieves, The (Vitorrio De Sica, 1948)
Bis daß der Tod euch scheidet (Heiner Carow, 1978)
Bis zum Horizont und weiter (Peter Kahane, 1999)
Blaue, Der (Lienhard Wawrzyn, 1993)
Blaue Wunder, Das (Peter Kahane, 2004) TVM
Boum, La (Claude Pinoteau, 1980)
Brocken, Der (Vadim Glowna, 1992)
Buntkarierten, Die (Kurt Maetzig, 1949)
Bürgschaft für ein Jahr (Hermann Zschosche, 1982)
Burning Life (Peter Welz, 1994)
Camper, Die (Peter Lichtfeld, 1996–2005) TVS
Cosima's Lexikon (Peter Kahane, 1991)
Conversation, The (Francis Ford Coppola, 1974)
Countdown (Ulrike Ottinger, 1991) Doc.
Daheim sterben die Leut' (Klaus Gietinger, 1985)
Datsche, Die (Carsten Fiebeler, 2003)
Denk ich an Deutschland – Herr Wichmann von der CDU (Andreas Dresen, 2003) Doc.

Deutsche Kettensägenmassaker, Das (Christoph Schlingensief, 1990)
Deutschfieber (Niklaus Schilling, 1992)
Drei Stern Rot (Olaf Kaiser, 2002)
Elbe (Marco Mittelstaedt, 2005)
Endstation: Tanke (Nathalie Steinbart, 2001)
Engelchen (Helke Misselwitz, 1996)
Erinnerung an eine Landschaft – Für Manuela (Kurt Tetzlaff, 1983) Doc.
Erst die Arbeit und dann? (Detlev Buck, 1985)
Die Fälscher (Stefan Ruzowitzky, 2007)
Fernes Land Pa-isch (Rainer Simon, 1993; released 2000)
Flieger, Der (Erwin Keusch, 1986)
Frau vom Checkpoint Charlie, Die (Miguel Alexandre, 2007)
Germany Year Zero (Roberto Rossellini, 1946)
Go Trabi Go (Peter Timm, 1990)
Go Trabi Go II. Das war der wilde Osten (Wolfgang Büld, Reinhard Klooss, 1992)
Good Bye, Lenin! (Wolfgang Becker, 2003)
Grüß Gott, Genosse! (Manfred Stelzer, 1993) TVM
Grüß Gott, ich komm' von drüben (Tom Toelle, 1978)
Halbe Treppe (Andreas Dresen, 2002)
Heidi M. (Michael Klier, 2001)
Helden wie Wir (Sebastian Peterson, 1999)
Heimat 3 (Edgar Reitz, 2004) TVS
Heinrich der Säger (Klaus Gietinger, 2001)
Herr Lehmann (Leander Haußmann, 2003)
Herzsprung (Helke Misselwitz, 1992)
Hundsköpfe (Karsten Laske, 2001)
Identity Kills (Sören Voigt, 2003)
Im Lauf der Zeit (Wim Wenders, 1976)
Im Nächsten Leben (Marco Mittelstaedt, 2008)
Im Namen der Unschuld (Andreas Kleinert, 1997) TVM
Jadup und Boel (Rainer Simon, 1980–81)
Jagdszenen aus Niederbayern (Peter Fleischmann, 1969)
Jaider, der einsame Jäger (Volker Vogeler and Ulf Miehe, 1970/71)
Jana und Jan (Helmut Dziuba, 1992)
Jena Paradies (Marco Mittelstaedt, 2004)
Jerichow (Christian Petzold, 2008)
Karbid und Sauerampfer (Frank Beyer, 1963)
Karniggels (Detlev Buck, 1991)
Kaspar Hauser, Jeder für sich allein und Gott gegen alle (Werner Herzog, 1974)
Klassenfahrt (Henner Winkler, 2002)
Kleinruppin Forever (Carsten Fiebeler, 2004)
Knallhart (Detlev Buck, 2006)
Knockin' on Heaven's Door (Thomas Jahn, 1997)
Kombat Sechzehn (Mirko Borscht, 2005)
Komm näher (Vanessa Jopp, 2005)

Kontrolleur, Der (Stefan Trampe, 1994)
Kroko (Sylke Enders, 2004)
Lächeln der Tiefseefische, Das (Till Endemann, 2004)
Land hinter dem Regenbogen, Das (Herwig Kipping, 1992)
Landschaft mit Dornen (Bernd Böhlich, 1992) TVM
Leben der Anderen, Das (Florian Henckel von Donnersmarck, 2006)
Leben ist eine Baustelle, Das (Wolfgang Becker, 1997)
Leere Mitte, Die (Hito Steyerl, 1998) Doc.
Legende von Paul und Paula, Die (Heiner Carow, 1973)
Letztes aus der DaDaeR (Jörg Foth, 1990)
Lichter (Hans-Christian Schmid, 2003)
Lichter aus dem Hintergrund (Heide Reidemeister, 1998) Doc.
Liebe Mauer (Peter Timm, 2009)
Liebesau – die andere Heimat (Wolfgang Panzer, 2001) TVS
Local Hero (Bill Forsyth, 1982)
Lola Rennt (Tom Tykwer, 1998)
Mauer, Die (Jürgen Böttcher, 1991) Doc.
Mauer – Berlin 61, Die (Hartmut Schoens, 2006)
Mediocren, Die (Matthias Glasner, 1995)
Miraculi (Ulrich Weiß, 1992)
Mr. Bluesman (Sönke Wortmann, 1993)
Nachtgestalten (Andreas Dresen, 1998)
Naked (Mike Leigh, 1993)
Neben der Zeit (Andreas Kleinert, 1995)
Netto (Robert Thalheim, 2004)
Nikolaikirche (Frank Beyer, 1993) TVS
Not a Love Song (Jan Ralske, 1997)
Novemberkatzen (Sigrun Koeppe, 1985)
NVA (Leander Haußmann, 2005)
Ocean's Eleven (Steven Soderbergh, 2001)
Ossi's Eleven (Oliver Mielke, 2007)
Ostkreuz (Michael Klier, 1991)
Plötzliche Reichtum der armen Leute von Kombach, Der (Volker Schlöndorff, 1971)
Plus-minus-null (Eoin Moore, 1998)
Polizistin, Die (Andreas Dresen, 2000) TVM
Rodina heisst Heimat (Helga Reidemeister, 1992) Doc.
Rote Kakadu, Der (Domink Gräf, 2006)
Salto Kommunale (Ralph Gregan and others, 1998–2001) TV Series
Salto Postale (Bernhard Stephan and others, 1993–1996) TV Series
Schröders Wunderbare Welt (Michael Schorr, 2007)
Schuh des Manitu, Der (Michael Herbig, 2001)
Schultze gets the Blues (Michael Schorr, 2004)
Sehnsucht (Valeska Grisebach, 2006)
Siedler am Arsch der Welt, Die (Claus Strigel, 2004)
So schnell geht es nach Istanbul (Andreas Dresen, 1991)

Solo Sunny (Konrad Wolf, 1980)
Sommer vorm Balkon (Andreas Dresen, 2005)
Sonnenallee (Leander Haußmann, 1999)
Sophie Scholl – die letzten Tage (Marc Rothemund, 2005)
Status Yo! (Till Hastreiter, 2004)
Stilles Land (Andreas Dresen, 1992)
Stroszeck (Werner Herzog, 1977)
Sumo Bruno (Lenard Fritz Krawinkel, 1999)
Superstau (Manfred Stelzer, 1990)
Tal der Ahnungslosen (Branwen Okpako, 2003) TVM
Texas Chainsaw Massacre (Tobe Hooper, 1974)
Thelma and Louise (Ridley Scott, 1991)
Tolle Lage (Sören Voigt, 1999)
(T)Raumschiff Surprise – Periode 1 (Michael Herbig, 2004)
Tunnel, Der (Roland Suso Richter, 2001)
Überall ist es besser wo wir nicht sind (Michael Klier, 1988)
Untergang, Der (Oliver Hirschbiegel, 2004)
Verfehlung (Heiner Carow, 1991)
Vergangen, Vergessen, Vorüber (Jan Ralske, 1994) Doc.
Vergebung, Die (Andreas Höntsch, 1994)
Vergiss Amerika (Vanessa Jopp, 2000)
Verlorene Landschaft (Andreas Kleinert, 1992)
Versprechen, Das (Margarethe von Trotta, 1994)
Wedding (Heiko Schier, 1990)
Wege in die Nacht (Andreas Kleinert, 1999)
Weltstadt (Christian Klandt, 2008)
Wer anhält Stirbt (Olaf Kaiser, Alexander Ris, 1995) TVM
Willi-Busch-Report, Der (Niklaus Schilling, 1977)
Willenbrock (Andreas Dresen, 2005)
Winter adé (Helke Misselwitz, 1985) Doc.
Wir (Martin Gypkens, 2003)
Wir können auch anders (Detlev Buck, 1993)
Wunder von Berlin, Das (Roland Suso Richter, 2008)
Yella (Christian Petzold, 2007)
Zeit zu leben (Horst Seemann, 1969)
Zimmerspringbrunnen, Der (Peter Timm, 2001)
Zutaten für Träume (Gordian Maugg, 2001)
TVS denotes television series
TVM denotes television film.
Doc. Denotes documentary film.

BIBLIOGRAPHY

Adorno, T.W. and M. Horkheimer. 1979. *Dialectic of Enlightenment*. London, New York: Verso.

Ahbe, T. 2000. '"Hammer, Zirkel, Kaffeekranz." Ostalgie als Methode. Wie sich die Ostdeutschen stabilisieren und integrieren', *Berliner Zeitung* (Ressort Magazin), 5 February. Retrieved 8 June 2002 from http://www.kulturinitiative-89.de/Texte/Ahbe_Thomas.html

Aitken, I. 2002. *European Film Theory and Cinema. A Critical Introduction*. Bloomington: Indiana University Press.

Allan, S. and J. Sandford (eds). 1999. *DEFA. East German Cinema, 1946–1992*. New York and Oxford: Berghahn.

Alter, R. and P. Monteath (eds). 1997. *Rewriting the German Past. History and Identity in the New Germany*. Atlantic Highlands, New Jersey: Humanities Press.

Amis, M. 2003. *Koba the Dread. Laughter and the Twenty Million*. London: Vintage.

Anderson, B. 1991. *Imagined Communities. Reflections on the Origin and Spread of Nationalism*, 2nd ed. London: Verso.

Anderson, C., K. Kaltenthaler and W. Luthardt (eds). 1993. *The Domestic Politics of German Unification*. London and Boulder: Lynne Rienner Publishers.

Andert, R. 1994. *Rote Wende. Wie die Ossis die Wessis besiegten*. Berlin: Elefanten Press.

Andrew, G. 1998. *Stranger than Paradise. Maverick Film-makers in Recent American Cinema*. London: Prion.

Arnold, F. 1993. 'Wir können auch anders', *epd Film* 4: 40.

'Aufbruch Ost'. 2005. *Der Spiegel*, 47.

Augé, M. 1995. *Non-Places. Introduction to an Anthropology of Supermodernity*. London: Verso.

Baer, V. 1998. 'Das andere Gesicht der DEFA', *Film Dienst* 8: 12–14.

Barker, P. (ed.). 1994. *The Party of Democratic Socialism in Germany. Modern Post-Communism or Nostalgic Populism? German Monitor*. Amsterdam; Atlanta: Editions Rodopi.

Bauman, Z. 2000. *Liquid Modernity*, Cambridge: Polity Press.

_____. 2001. *Community. Seeking Safety in an Insecure World*, Cambridge: Polity Press.

Bausinger, H. 2002. *Typisch Deutsch. Wie deutsch sind die Deutschen?* 3rd ed. Munich: C.H. Beck.

Becher, J.R. 1956. *Schöne Deutsche Heimat*. Berlin: Aufbau-Verlag.

Behrends, J.C., T. Lindenberger and P.G. Poutrice (eds). 2003. *Fremde und Fremd-Sein in der DDR. Zu historischen Ursachen der Fremdenfeindlichkeit in Ostdeutschland*. Berlin: Metropol Verlag.

Benjamin, W. 1992. *Illuminations*. London: Fontana.

_____. 1969. *Charles Baudelaire: Zwei Fragmente: ein Lyriker im Zeitalter des Hochkapitalismus*. Frankfurt am Main: Suhrkamp.

Berger, S., L. Eriksonas and A. Mycock (eds). 2008. *Narrating the Nation. Representations in History, Media, and the Arts*. New York and Oxford: Berghahn.

Bergfelder, T. 2005. *International Adventures. German Popular Cinema and European Co-Productions in the 1960s*. New York and Oxford: Berghahn.

Berghahn, D. 2005. *Hollywood Behind the Wall. The Cinema of East Germany*. Manchester and New York: Manchester University Press.

Betts, P. 2000. 'The Twilight of the Idols: East German Memory and Material Culture', *The Journal of Modern History* 72: 731–65.

Bhabha, H. 1994. *The Location of Culture*. London and New York: Routledge.

Biermann, W. 2006. 'Warum Wolf Biermann über den Stasi-Film *Das Leben der anderen* staunt', *Die Welt*, 22 March. Retrieved 20 October 2009 from http://www.welt.de/printwelt/article205586/Warum_Wolf_Biermann_ueber_den_Stasi-Film_Das_Leben_der_Anderen_staunt.html

Billig, M. 1995. *Banal Nationalism*. London and New Delhi: Sage.

Blacksell, M. 1997. 'State and Nation: Germany Since Reunification', *Europa* 3. Retrieved 23 August 2008 from http://www.intellectbooks.com/europa/number3/blacksel.htm

Blickle, P. 2002. *Heimat. A Critical Theory of the German Idea of Homeland*. Rochester and Woodbridge: Camden House.

'Blindes Gekaufe.' 1991. *Der Spiegel* 19: 121.

Bloch, E. 1995. *The Principle of Hope*, trans. N. Plaice, S. Plaice and P. Knight. Cambridge, MA: MIT Press.

Blunk, H. 1988. 'Heimat und Vaterland in DEFA-Spielfilm', *Deutsche Studien* 26(103): 226–38.

Boa, E. and R. Palfreyman. 2000. *Heimat. A German Dream. Regional Loyalties and National Identity in German Culture 1890–1990*. Oxford: Oxford University Press.

Borcholte, A. and W. Höbel. 2008. '"Ich hasse dieses Gestöhne"', *Der Spiegel*, 3 September. Retrieved 12 December 2009 from http://www.spiegel.de/kultur/kino/0,1518,575840,00.html

Boym, S. 2001. *The Future of Nostalgia*. New York: Basic Books.

Brussig, T. 2003.'Der Brechreiz ist ein aktueller.' Retrieved 12 August 2008 from http://www.thomasbrussig.de/publizistik/ostalgie.htm

_____. 2001. 'Wir sind nostalgisch weil wir Menschen sind.' Retrieved 12 August 2008 from http://www.thomasbrussig.de/publizistik/sehnsucht.htm

_____. 2000. 'Opfer politischer Gewalt haben ein Recht auf Wiedergutmachung', *Der Tagesspiegel*, 29 January.

_____. 1999. *Am kürzeren Ende der Sonnenallee*. Berlin: Volk und Welt.

_____. 1995. *Helden wie Wir*. Berlin: Volk und Welt.

de Bruyn, G. 1998. *Vierzig Jahre*. Frankfurt am Main: Fischer Verlag

Bullivant, K. (ed.). 1997. *Beyond 1989. Re-reading German Literary History since 1945*. Providence: Berghahn Books.

Bulmahn, T. 2000. 'Modernity and Happiness – The Case of Germany', *Journal of Happiness Studies* 1(3): 375–400.

Calhoun, D. 2004. 'Afghan Aftermath', *Sight and Sound*, February: 20–22.

Cameron, K. (ed.). 1999. *National Identity*. Exeter: Intellect Books.

Carter, E., J. Donald and J. Squires (eds). 1993. *Space and Place. Theories of Identity and Location*. London: Lawrence & Wishart.

Clark, D.E. and M. Wildner. 2000. 'Violence and Fear of Violence in East and West Germany', *Social Science & Medicine* 51: 373–9.

Clarke, D. 2004. 'Representations of East German Masculinity in Hannes Stöhr's *Berlin is in Germany* and Andreas Kleinert's *Wege in die Nacht'*, *German Life and Letters* 55(4): 434–49.

Cohan, S. and I. Rae Hark (eds). 1997. *The Road Movie Book*. London; New York: Routledge.

Confino, A. and P. Fritzsche (eds). 2002. *The Work of Memory. New Directions in the Study of German Society and Culture*. Urbana: University of Illinois Press. Retrieved 25 September 2008 from http://www.press.uillinois.edu/epub/books/confino/

Conboy, M. 1999. 'The Discourse of Location. Realigning the Popular in German Cinema', *European Journal of Communication* 14(3): 366.

Cooke, P. 2005. *Representing East Germany since Unification. From Colonization to Nostalgia*. Oxford: Berg Publishers.

Cooke, P. and C. Homewood (eds). 2011 (forthcoming). *New Directions in German Cinema*. London: I.B. Tauris.

Costabile-Heming, C.A., R.J. Halverson and K.A. Foell (eds). 2004. *Berlin. The Symphony Continues. Orchestrating Architectural Change in Germany's New Capital*. Berlin and New York: Walter de Gruyter.

Dahn, D. 1994. *Wir bleiben hier oder, wem gehört der Osten. Vom Kampf um Häuser und Wohnungen in den neuen Bundesländern*. Reinbeck bei Hamburg: Rowohlt.

Dale, G. 2007. 'Heimat, "Ostalgie" and the Stasi: The GDR in German Cinema, 1999-2006', *Debatte. Journal of Contemporary Central and Eastern Europe*, 15 (2), 155–175

Daly, P.M. et al. (eds). 2000. *Images of Germany. Perceptions and Conceptions*. New York: Peter Lang.

Davidson-Schmich, L.K., K. Hartmann and U. Mummert. 2002. 'You Can Lead a Horse to Water, But You Can't (Always) Make It Drink: Positive Freedom in the Aftermath of German Unification', *Communist and Post-communist Studies* 35: 325–52.

Decker, G. 1999. 'Freiheit zu lachen', *Neues Deutschland*, 6 October.

Decker, K. and G. Decker. 2000. *Gefühlsausbrüche, oder ewig pubertiet der Ostdeutsche. Reportagen, Polemike, Porträts*. Berlin: Das Neue Berlin.

Defa Nova-nach wie vor? Versuch einer Spurensicherung. 1993. Berlin: Freunde der Deutschen Kinemathek eV., No. 82.

Delanty, G. 2003. *Community*. London: Routledge.

_____. 2000. *Modernity and Postmodernity. Knowledge, Power and the Self*. London: Sage.

Delius, F.C. 1995. *Der Spaziergang von Rostock nach Syrakus*. Reinbek: Rowohlt-Verlag.

Dieckmann, C. 2005. 'Zonenkindereien', *Die Zeit* 40, 29 September.

_____. 2003. 'Honis heitere Welt', *Die Zeit* 36, 28 August. Retrieved 1 January 2006 from http://zeus.zeit.de/text/2003/36/Ostalgie_

_____. 2000. *Das wahre Leben im Falschen. Geschichten von ostdeutscher Identität*. Berlin: Ch. Links.

Dresen, A., T. Schulz and A. Leusink. 1999. *Nachtgestalten*. Berlin: Aufbau Taschenbuch Verlag.

Dümcke, W. and F. Vilmar (eds). 1995. *Kolonisierung der DDR. Kritische Analyse und Alternativen des Einigungsprozesses*. Münster: Agenda.

Durrani, O., C. Good and J. Hillard (eds). 1995. *The New Germany. Literature and Society After Unification*. Sheffield: Sheffield Academic Press.

Dyer, R. and G. Vincendeau (eds). 1992. *Popular European Cinema*. London and New York: Routledge.

Eagleton, T. 2002. *Literary Theory. An Introduction*. London: Blackwell.

Eberstadt, N. 1994. 'Demographic Shocks in Eastern Germany, 1989–93', *Europe-Asia Studies* 46(3): 519–33.

Elsaesser, T. 2003. *European Cinema: Face to Face with Hollywood*. Amsterdam: Amsterdam University Press.

_____. 1989. *New German Cinema. A History*. London: BFI Publishing.

Eniskat, P. 1999. 'Filmtipp der Woche' (*Helden wie Wir* review), *Der Tagesspiegel*, 9 December.

Epstein, C. 2004.'The Stasi: New Research on the East German Ministry of State Security', *Kritika. Explorations in Russian and Eurasian History* 5(2): 321–48.

_____. 2003. 'East Germany and Its History since 1989', *Journal of Modern History* 75(3): 634–61.

Evans, O. 2010. 'Redeeming the Demon? The Legacy of the Stasi in *Das Leben der Anderen*', *Memory Studies* 3(2): 164–77.

Facius, G. 1990. 'Integration of the East German Media into an All-German Structure', *Aussenpolitik* 41(4): 388–399.

Fehrenbach, H. 1995. *Cinema in Democratizing Germany. Reconstructing National Identity after Hitler*. Chapel Hill and London: University of North Carolina Press.

Finger, E. 2005. 'Der Ossi als Wessi', *Die Zeit*, 25 August: 35.

Fleischhauer, J. 1990. '"Ick will meine Ruhe wieder"', *Der Spiegel* 19: 117–24.

Flockton, C. and E. Kolinsky (eds). 1999. *Recasting East Germany. Social Transformation after the GDR*. London: Frank Cass and Company.

Foucault, M. 1975. 'Film and Memory. An Interview with Michael Foucault', *Radical Philosophy* 11: 24–9.

Freud, S. 2002. *Civilization and Its Discontents*, trans. D. McLintock. London: Penguin Books.

Freyermuth, G.S. 1993. *Der Übernehmer. Volker Schlöndorff in Babelsberg*. Berlin: Ch. Links.

Fulbrook, M. and M. Swales (eds). 2000. *Representing the German Nation. History and Identity in Twentieth Century Germany*. Manchester: Manchester University Press.

Funder, A. 2003. *Stasiland*. London: Granta.

Galle, B. 1999. 'Das mit uns geht so tief rein', *Berliner Zeitung*, 28 January.

Gillis, J.R. (ed.). 1996. *Commemorations: The Politics of National Identity*. Princeton: Princeton University Press.

Gilloch, G. 1996. *Myth and Metropolis. Walter Benjamin and the City*. Cambridge: Polity Press.

Gless, F. and H. Witzel. 2002. 'Interview with Thierse', *Stern* 18: 58.

Golombeck, D. and D. Ratzke (eds). 1991. *Facetten der Wende. Reportagen über eine deutsche Revolution.* Frankfurt am Main: Institut für Medienentwicklung und Kommunikation GmbH.

Goodbody, A. 2005. 'Veränderte Landschaft: East German Nature Poetry Since Reunification', *GFL-Journal*, 2.

'Go Trabi Go' (review; no author). 1991. *Film Dienst* 3: 26.

Gransow, K.H. and V. Gransow (eds). 1994. *Uniting Germany Documents and Debates, 1944–1993.* Oxford: Berghahn Books.

Grub, F.T. 2003. *'Wende' und 'Einheit' im Spiegel der deutschsprachigen Literatur. Band 1: Untersuchungen.* Berlin; New York: Walter de Gruyter.

Guillénn, M. 2007. 'The Lives of Others – Interview With Florian Henckel Von Donnersmarck'. Retrieved 12 July 2009 from http://twitchfilm.net/archives/008825.html

Gunske, V. and S.S. Poser. 1999. 'Nachdenken Über Thomas B', *Tip-Magazin* 21.

Habermas, J. 1990a. *Die nachholende Revolution.* Frankfurt am Main: Suhrkamp.

_____. 1990b. *Vergangenheit als Zukunft.* Zürich: Pendo-Verlag.

Hahn, A. 2004. 'Ins Gehege', *Junge Welt*, 9 September. Retrieved 23 June 2008 from http://www.jungewelt.de/2004/09-09/021.php

Hahn, H.-J. 1993.'Ossis, Wessis and the Germans: An Inner-German Perception of National Characteristics', *Journal of Area Studies* (Perspectives on German Unification) 2: 114–28.

Hake, S. 2002. *German National Cinema*, 2nd ed. London and New York: Routledge.

Halbwachs, M. 1992. *On Collective Memory*, trans. L.A. Coser. London and Chicago: University of Chicago Press.

Halle, R. 2007. 'Views from the German-Polish Border: The Exploration of International Space in *Halbe Treppe* and *Lichter*', *German Quarterly* (80)1: 77–96.

Halle, R. and M. McCarthy (eds). 2003. *Light Motives German Popular Film in Perspective.* Detroit: Wayne State University Press.

Hancock, M.D. and H.A. Welsh (eds). 1994. *German Unification. Process and Outcomes.* Oxford: Westview Press.

Hanisch, M. 1993. 'Eine lustige Reise zum stillen Don', *Neue Zeit*, 1 April.

Haußmann, L. 2003. 'Es Kam dicke genug', *Der Spiegel*, 8 September: 220–2.

Hein, J. 2001. *Mein erstes T-Shirt.* München: Piper Verlag.

Henning, F. 1999. *Alles nur geklaut.* München: btb Verlag.

Herold, K. and J. Scherer. 1998. *Wegzeichen. Fragen von Filmstudenten an Regisseure. Beiträge zur Film-und Fernsehwissenschaft.* Berlin: Vistas.

Heym, S. 1990. *Auf Sand Gebaut. Sieben Geschichten aus der unmittelbaren Vergangenheit.* Munich: Bertelsmann.

Hill, J. and P. Church Gibson (eds). 2000. *World Cinema. Critical Approaches.* Oxford: Oxford University Press.

Hjort, M. and S. Mackenzie (eds). 2002. *Cinema & Nation.* New York, London: Routledge.

Höbel, W. 2000. 'Mach nur einen Plan', *Der Spiegel* 45: 360–2.

Hobsbawm, E. and T. Ranger (eds). 2003. *The Invention of Tradition*, 10th ed. Cambridge: Cambridge University Press.

Hochhuth, R. 1993. *Wessis in Weimar. Szenen aus einem besetzten Land*. Berlin: Verlag Volk und Welt.

Hochmuth, D. 1993. *Defa Nova-nach wie vor? Versuch einer Spurensicherung*. Berlin: Freunde der Deutschen Kinemathek eV.

Hockenos, P. 1993. *Free to Hate. The Rise of the Right in Post-Communist Eastern Europe*. London: Routledge.

Hodgin, N. and C. Pearce (eds), 2011 (forthcoming). *Remembering the GDR: Representations of the East German State since 1989*, Rochester, NY, and Woodbridge, Suffolk: Camden House.

Hodgin, N. 2011 (forthcoming). 'Eastern Blues, Southern Comforts: Searching for *Heimat* on the Bayous', *Mississippi Quarterly*.

_____. 2007. 'Marginalized Subjects, Mainstream Objectives. Insights on Outsiders in Recent German Film', *New Readings* 8. Retrieved 3 December 2009 from http://www.cf.ac.uk/euros/subsites/newreadings/volume8/articles/hodgin article.pdf

_____. 2004. '*Berlin is in Germany* and *Good Bye, Lenin!* Taking Leave of the GDR?', *Debatte: Review of Contemporary German Affairs* 12(1): 25–46.

Holloway, R. 1999. 'Wege in die Nacht' (review). Retrieved 22 August 2008 from http://www.filmfestivals.com/cannes99/html/quinzaine2.htm

Horton, A. (ed.). 1991. *Comedy/Cinema/Theory*. Berkeley: University of California Press.

Hosking, G. and G. Schöpflin (eds). 1997. *Myth and Nationhood*. London: Hurst & Co.

van Hoven, B. 2001. 'Women at work – experiences and identity in rural East Germany', *Area* 33(1): 38–46.

Howard, M. 1995. 'An East German Ethnicity? Understanding the New Division of Unified Germany', *German Politics and Society* 13(4), 49–70. Retrieved 8 May 2002 from http://www.kulturinitiative-89.de/Texte/Ahbe_Thomas.html

Hutcheon, L. 1989. *The Politics of Postmodernism*. London: Routledge.

Huyssen, A. 2003. *Present Pasts. Urban Palimpsests and the Politics of Memory*. Stanford: Stanford University Press.

_____. 1995. *Twilight Memories. Marking Time in a Culture of Amnesia*. London: Routledge.

Illies, F. 2000. *Generation Golf*. Frankfurt am Main: Fischer Verlag.

'Interview mit Peter Timm', *Dirk-Jasper Filmlexikon* [no author]. Retrieved 12 January 2007 from http://www.djfl.de/entertainment/stars/p/peter_timm_i_01.html

Ireland, P.R. 1997. 'Socialism, Unification Policy and the Rise of Racism in Eastern Germany', *International Migration Review* 31(3): 541–68.

James, H. and M. Stone. 1992. *When the Wall Came Down. Reactions to German Unification*. New York: Routledge.

James, N. 2006. 'German Cinema. All Together Now', *Sight and Sound*, December: 26–31.

Jameson, F. 1984. 'Postmodernism, or the Cultural Logic of Late Capitalism', *New Left Review*, July/August: 53–92.

'Jammertal Ost.' 2004. *Der Spiegel* 39.

Jarausch, K.H. (ed.). 1999. *Dictatorship as Experience. Towards a Socio-Cultural History of the GDR*. New York and Oxford: Berghahn Books.

_____. (ed.). 1997. *After Unity. Reconfiguring German Identities*. Oxford: Berghahn.

Kaes, A. 1992. *From Hitler to Heimat. The Return of History as Film*. Cambridge, MA and London: Harvard University Press.

Kaminer, W. 2001. *Schönhauser Allee*. Munich: Goldmann.

Kannapin, D. 2005. '"GDR identity" in DEFA Feature Films', *Debatte* 13(2): 185–200.

Kaschuba, W. (ed.). 1989. *Der deutsche Heimatfilm*. Tübingen: Tübingen Vereinigung für Volkskunde e.V.

Kaupp, C.M. 2003. *Good Bye, Lenin! Film-Heft*. Bonn: Bundeszentrale für politische Bildung.

Kellner, D. and H. O'Hara. 1976. 'Utopia and Marxism in Ernst Bloch', *New German Critique* 9: 11–34.

Kennedy, P. and C.J. Danks (eds). 2001. *Globalization and National Identities. Crisis or Opportunity?* Basingstoke: Palgrave.

Kleßmann, C. (ed.). 2001. *The Divided Past. Rewriting Post-War German History. German Historical Perspectives XV*. Oxford and New York: Berg.

Klug, T. 1992. '"Go, Trabi, Go 2." Stumpi jetzt im wilden Osten', *Volksstimme* (Magdeburg), 13 August.

Kocka, J. 1995. *Vereinigungskrise. Zur Geschichte der Gegenwart*. Göttingen: Vandenhoeck und Ruprecht.

Kolker, R.P. and P. Beicken. 1993. *The Films of Wim Wenders. Cinema as Vision and Desire*. Cambridge: Cambridge University Press.

Körte, P. 1992. 'DDR adé', *Frankfurter Rundschau*, 20 November.

Kroker, E.J.M. and B. Deschamps (eds). 1993. *Die Deutschen auf der Suche nach ihrer neuen Identität?* Frankfurt am Main: Frankfurter Allgemeine Zeitung.

Krueger, A.B. and J.-S. Pischke. 1997. 'A Statistical Analysis of Crime against Foreigners in Unified Germany', *The Journal of Human Resources* 32(1): 192–209.

Kühn, D. 1992. 'Der Brocken', *epd Film* 5: 40.

Ladd, B. 1997. *The Ghosts of Berlin. Confronting the German History in the Urban Landscape*. Chicago and London: University of Chicago Press.

Lange, G. 1973. *Heimat. Realität und Aufgabe. Zur Marxistischen Auffassung des Heimatgefühls*. Berlin: Akademie Verlag.

Lasch, C. 1991. *The True and Only Heaven. Progress and Its Critics*. New York and London: E.E. Norton.

Leeder, K. 1996. *Breaking Boundaries. A New Generation of Poets in the GDR*. Oxford: Clarendon Press.

Levitin, J., J. Plessis and V. Raoul (eds). 2003. *Women Filmmakers. Refocusing*. New York: Routledge.

'Liebesgeschichte ertrinkt in DDR-Klischees.' 1992. *Sächsische Zeitung*, 16 July.

Löser, C. 1999. 'Sonnenallee', *Film Dienst* 52.

Lowenthal, D. 1998. *The Heritage Crusade and the Spoils of History*. Cambridge: Cambridge University Press.

_____. 1990. *The Past is a Foreign Country*, 3rd ed. Cambridge: Cambridge University Press.

Lubowski, B. 1992. 'Vom Herzsprung in Herzsprung', *Berliner Moregenpost*, 19 November.

Ludewig, A. 2001. 'Heimat, City and Frontier in German National Cinema', *Debatte* 9(2): 181.

Lux, S. 1993. 'Wir können auch anders', *Film Dienst* 6.

Maaz, H.-J. 2003. 'Ich fürchte, wir kommen wieder nicht vor', *MDR-Online*, 1 September. Retrieved 13 September 2008 from http://www.mdr.de/kultur/896480.html

———. 1991. *Das gestürtzte Volk, oder, die unglückliche Einheit*. Berlin: Argon.

Magdoff, H. and J.B. Foster. 2003. 'Notes from the Editor', *Monthly Review*, October. Retrieved 5 May 2008 from http://www.monthlyreview.org/nfte1003.htm

Maier, C.S. 1999. *Dissolution. The Crisis of Communism and the End of East Germany*, 4th ed. Princeton, NJ: Princeton University Press.

Maischberger, S. 'Sonnenallee. Interview mit Thomas Brussig und Leander Haußmann.' Retrieved 12 September 2008 from http://www.thomasbrussig.de/interviews/sonnenallee.htm

Mast, G. 1979. *The Comic Mind. Comedy and the Movies*, 2nd ed. Chicago and London: University of Chicago Press.

Matussek, M. 1990. 'Rodeo im Wilden Osten', *Der Spiegel* 22: 194–206.

Mazierska, E. and L. Rascaroli. 2006. *Crossing New Europe. Postmodern Travel and the European Road Movie*. London: Wildflower.

McGowan, M. 2002. 'Waiting for Waiting for Godot: Echoes of Beckett's Play in Brecht's Chosen Land', *Brecht-Jahrbuch* 27: 133.

Mehr, M.Y. and R. Sylvester. 1992. 'The Stone Thrower From Eisenhuttenstadt' [sic], *Granta* (Krauts!) 42: 133–43.

Meißner, I. 2000. 'Die neunziger Jahre'. Retrieved 25 August 2008 from http://www.deutsches-filminstitut.de/sozialgeschichte/dt105a.htm

'Mercedes statt Wolga'. 1990. *Der Spiegel* 3: 124.

Meyer, B. 2003. 'Much Ado about Nothing? Political Representation Policies and the Influence of Women Parliamentarians in Germany', *The Review of Policy Research* 20(3): 401–21.

Milful, J. 1997. 'Who Owns GDR Culture? Against Analogy', *Debatte* 5(2): 194–201.

Moeller, R.G. 2001. *War Stories. The Search for a Usable Past in the Federal Republic of Germany*. London and Berkeley: University of California Press.

von Moltke, J. 2005. *No Place Like Home. Locations of Heimat in German Cinema*. Berkeley: University of California.

Moran, J. 2004. 'November in Berlin. The End of the Everyday', *History Workshop Journal* 57: 220.

Morley, D. 2000. *Home Territories. Media, Mobility and Identity*. London: Routledge.

Mueller, G. 2008. 'Going East, Looking West: Border Crossings in Recent German Cinema', *Seminar* 44(4): 453–69.

Muir, R. 2000. 'Conceptualising Landscape', *Landscapes* 1: 4–21.

Müller, J.-W. (ed.). 2000. *Another Country. German Intellectuals, Unification and National Identity*. New Haven and London: Yale University Press.

Münter, M. and R. Sturm. 2002. 'Economic Consequences of German Unification', *German Politics* 11(3): 179–94.

Naughton, L. 2002. *That was the Wild East. Film Culture, Unification and the 'New' Germany*. Ann Arbor: University of Michigan Press.

Nora, P. 1989. 'Between Memory and History: Les Lieux de Mémoire', *Representations* 26: 7–24.

Nothnagle, A.L. 1999. *Building the East German Myth. Historical Mythology and Youth Propaganda in the German Democratic Republic, 1945–1989*. Michigan: University of Michigan Press.

Ostow, R. 1993. 'Restructuring Our Lives: National Unification and German Biographies', *The Oral History Review. Journal of the Oral History Association* 21(2): 1–8.

Palmowski, J. 2009. *Inventing a Socialist Nation: Heimat and the Politics of Everyday Life in the GDR, 1945–1990*. Cambridge: Cambridge University Press.

Papadakis, A.C. (ed.). 1991. *Berlin Tomorrow. International Architectural Visions*. London: Architectural Design.

Parmalee, P.L. 1993. 'Movies Document a Turn', *German Politics and Society* 29: 112–33.

Paul, G. (ed). 2006. *Visual History. Ein Studienbuch*. Göttingen: Vandenhoeck & Ruprecht.

Peifer, D. 2001. 'Commemoration of Mutiny, Rebellion, and Resistance in Postwar Germany: Public Memory, History, and the Formation of "Memory Beacons"', *Journal of Military History* 65: 1013–52.

Pickering, M. 2001. *Stereotyping. The Politics of Representation*. Basingstoke and New York: Palgrave.

Plowman, A. 2004. '"Westalgie"? Nostalgia for the "Old" Federal Republic in Recent German Prose', *Seminar* 40(3): 249–61.

Poggioli, R. 1968. *The Theory of the Avant-Garde*. Cambridge, MA: Belknap Press/Harvard University Press.

Prase, T. and J. Kretzschmar. 2003. *Propagandist und Heimatfilmer. Die Dokumentarfilme des Karl-Eduard von Schnitzler*. Leipzig: Leipzig Universitäts Verlag.

Püschel, A. 1991. 'Grenzenloses Grenzgebiet Der "Zonenrand" außer Rand und Band', in *Facetten der Wende. Reportagen über eine deutsche Revolution Band II*. Frankfurt am Main: Institut für Medienentwicklung und Kommunikation GmbH in der Verlassungsgruppe Frankfurter Allgemeine Zeitung GmbH.

Ranze, M. 2004. 'Schultze gets the Blues' (review), *epd Film* 5: 22.

Rausch, C. 2003. *Meine freie deutsche Jugend*. Frankfurt am Main: Fischer Verlag.

Regener, S. 2001. *Herr Lehmann*. Frankfurt am Main: Eichborn Verlag.

Reif, C. 1993. 'Die Provinz schlägt zurück. Über die Tugenden des Ländlers und Detlev Bucks neuen Heimatfilm "Wir können auch anders"', *Film und Fernsehen* 2: 28–9.

Reißig, R. 1999. 'Die Ostdeutschen – zehn Jahre nach der Wende. Einstellungen, Wertemuster, Identitätsbildungen.' Retrieved 21 February 2003 from http://www.biss-Online.de/download/Die_Ostdeutschen_zehn_Jahre_nach_der_Wende.PDF

Reißig, R. and G.J. Glaeßner (eds). 1991. *Das Ende eines Experiments. Umbruch in der DDR und deutsche Einheit*. Berlin: Dietz Verlag.

Rentschler, E. 2002. 'Post-Wall Prospects: An Introduction', *New German Critique* 87 (Special Issue on Post-Wall Cinema): 3–5.

Richter, E. 1996. 'Anarchie und Menschlichkeit', *Film und Fernsehen* 5+6: 52–5.

Roethe, T. 1999. *Arbeiten wie bei Honecker, leben wie bei Kohl. Ein Plädoyer für das Ende der Schonfrist*. Frankfurt am Main: Eichborn Verlag

Rogier, F. 1996. 'Growing Pains: From the Opening of the Wall to the Wrapping of the Reichstag', *Assemblage* 29: 45.

Römer, R. 1992. 'Dein Lebens-Budget voll ausschöpfen', *Junge Welt*, 21 February.

Rossi. A. 1982. *The Architecture of the City*. Cambridge, MA and London: MIT Press.

Rother, H.-J. 1994. 'Die Provinz als Reservoir der Utopie', *Film und Fernsehen* 4+5: 68–9.

Sannwald, D. 2000. '"Ich heiße Alex, wie der Platz." Berlin-Film der anderen Art: "Plus minus null" von Eoin Moore', *Der Tagesspiegel*, 30 March.

Schenk, R. 1996. 'Zerissene Seelen und gefundene Fressen', *Berliner Zeitung*, 20 May. Retrieved 4 March 2002 from http://www.berlinOnline.de/wissen/berlin-erzeitung/archiv/1996/0520/kultur/0004/index.html

———. (ed.). 1994. *Das Zweite Leben der Filmstadt Babelsberg DEFA-Spielfilme 1946–1992*. Berlin: Henschelverlag.

———. 1993. 'Schattenboxer und Kinderspiele. Über einige neue deutsche Spielfilme während und im Umfeld der Berlinale', *Film und Fernsehen* 2: 23–7.

Schmiechen-Ackermann, D. 2002. *Diktaturen im Vergleich*. Darmstadt: Wissenschaftliche Buchgesellschaft.

Schnödel, H. 1990. 'Würstel aus Krauts', *Die Zeit*, 14 December.

Schoenbaum, D. and E. Pound. 1996. *The German Question and Other German Questions*. New York: St. Martin's Press.

Schöpflin, G. 2000. *Nations, Identity, Power. The New Politics of Europe*. London: Hurst.

Schulze, I. 1999. *Simple Storys. Ein Roman aus der ostdeutschen Provinz*. Munich: Deutscher Taschenbuch Verlag.

Seesslen, G. 1996. 'Deutschland, Niemandsland', *Potsdamer Neueste Nachrichten*, 26 September.

Segert, A. 1998. 'Problematic Normalisation – Eastern German Workers Eight Years After Unification', *German Politics and Society* 16(3): 105–24.

Seidel, C. 1990. 'Von Metzgern und Menschen', *Der Spiegel* 49.

Short, J.R. 1991. *Imagined Country. Society, Culture and Environment*. London: Routledge.

Simonoviecz, A. 1992. 'Gartenlaube', *TIP* 12.

Simons, D. 1991. 'Ein flacher Film über den doofen Ex-DDR-Bürger', *Volksstimme* (Magdeburg), 30 January.

Smith, A.D. 1999. *Myths and Memories of the Nation*. Oxford: Oxford University Press.

———. 1991. *National Identity*, London: Penguin Books.

———. 1986. *The Ethnic Origins of Nations*. Oxford: Blackwell.

Smith, G. et al. (eds). 1992. *Developments in German Politics*. Durham: Duke University Press.

Sobe, G. 1992. 'Heimkehr und Aufbruch des Udos', *Berliner Zeitung*, 21 August.

Sontheimer, K. 1995. 'United Germany: Political System Under Challenge', *SAIS Review* (Special Issue) 15: 39–54.

Sparschuh, J. 1995. *Der Zimmerspringbrunnen. Ein Heimatroman*. Köln: Kiepenhauer & Witsch.

Squires, J. (ed.). 1993. *Principled Positions. Postmodernism and the Rediscovery of Value*. London: Lawrence and Wishart.

Staab, A. 1998. *National Identity in Eastern Germany. Inner Unification or Continued Separation?* Westport and London: Praeger.

Steußloff, H. 2000. 'Zur Identität der Ostdeutschen. Merkmale und Tendenzen eines Phänomens', *Hefte zur ddr-geschichte* 66, Berlin: Forscher- und Diskussionskreis DDR Geschichte.

Stevenson, P. and J. Theobald (eds). 2000. *Relocating Germanness. Discursive Unity in Unified Germany.* London: Macmillan.Stöhr, M. 2005. 'Kleinruppin Forever' (review), *Schnitt.* Retrieved 23 June 2008 from http://www.schnitt.de/filme/artikel/kleinruppin_forever.shtml

Straub, S. 2000. 'Der Suizid und "die Wende" in der DDR. Zur Tragfähigkeit von Durkheims Konzeption des (anomischen) Selbstmords am Beispiel Thüringens', *System Familie* 13: 68.

Taberner, S. 2005. *German Literature of the 1990s and Beyond. Normalization and the Berlin Republic.* Rochester, NY: Camden House.

Taberner, S. and F. Finlay (eds). 2002. *Recasting German Identity. Culture, Politics and Literature in the Berlin Republik.* Rochester, NY, Camden House.

Tapper, R. (ed.). 2002. *The New Iranian Cinema. Politics, Representation and Identity.* London: I.B. Tauris.

Tetzlaff, M. 2004. *Ostblöckchen.* Frankfurt am Main: Schöffling.

Teusch, W. (ed.). 1998. *Heimat in der DDR-Medien. Arbeitsheft zum Medienpaket 8.* Bonn: Bundeszentrale für politische Bildung.

Thompson, P. 2005. *The Crisis of the German Left. The PDS, Stalinism and the Global Economy.* New York and Oxford: Berghahn Books.

Tilman, J. 1990. 'Grüsse aus der neuen Heimat', *Geo-Spezial DDR* 2, 11 April: 39–49.

Tok, H.-D. 1991. 'Wir sind doch ganz schön naiv. Auskünfte des Hauptdarstellers Wolfgang Stumph zu "Go Trabi Go"', *Thüringer Allgemeine*, 20 March.

Tönnies, F. 1991. *Gemeinschaft und Gesellschaft. Grundbegriffe der reinen Soziologie.* Darmstadt: Wissenschaftliche Buchgesellschaft.

Töteberg, M. (ed.). 1999. *Szenenwechsel. Momentaufnahmen des jungen deutschen Films.* Reinbek: Rowohlt Verlag.

Triana-Toribio, N. 2003. *Spanish National Cinema.* London and New York: Routledge.

Triandafyllidou, A. 2001. *Immigrants and National Identity in Europe.* London: Routledge.

Umard, R. 1992. 'Im Kleinen Ganz Gross', *TIP* 17: 26–8.

van der Vat, D. 1991. *Freedom Was Never Like This. A Winter's Journey in East Germany.* London: Hodder and Stoughton.

Vidler, A. 2000. *Warped Space. Art, Architecture and Anxiety in Modern Culture.* Cambridge, MA: MIT Press.

Walser, M. 1968. *Heimatkunde. Ausfätze und Reden.* Frankfurt am Main: Suhrkamp.

Weidenfeld, W. and K.-R. Korte (eds). 1999. *Handbuch zur deutschen Einheit 1949–1989–1999.* Frankfurt am Main: Bundeszentrale für politische Bildung.

Wiegand, W. 1991. 'Anpassung als Katastrophe. Ein ungewöhnliches "Kleines Fernsehspiel": "Ostkreuz"', *Frankfurter Allgemeine Zeitung*, 25 July.

Wilson, E. 1992. 'The Invisible Flaneur', *New Left Review* 191: 90–110.

Winter, S. 2005. 'Wölfe am Wasser', *Der Spiegel* 26: 56–8.

Witte, J.C. and G.G. Wagner. 1995. 'Declining Fertility in East Germany after Unification: A Demographic Response to Socioeconomic Change', *Population and Development Review* 21(2): 387–97.

Witzel, H. 2003. 'Das Märchen von der Ostalgie. Die DDR-Welle im Fernsehen', *Der Stern* 37: 190–4.

_____. 2002. 'So sind wir, wir Ossis', *Stern* 18: 40–52.

Woderich, R. 1999. 'Ostdeutsche Identität zwischen symbolischer Konstruktion und lebensweltlichem Eigensinn', Schriftfassung des Referats auf der Konferenz 'The German Road from Socialism to Capitalism', Harvard University, Centre for European Studies, 18–20 June. Retrieved 21 March 2003 from http://www.biss-Online.de/download/ostdeutsche_identitaeten.pdf

Wolf, C. 1994. *Auf dem Weg nach Tabou. Texte 1990–1994*. Köln: Kiepenheuer & Witsch.

Wolle, S. 1998. *Die Heile Welt der Diktatur. Alltag und Herrschaft in der DDR, 1971–1989*. Bonn: Bundeszentrale für politische Bildung.

Worthmann, M. 1993. 'Dann setzen wir eben eine Kalaschnikow ein', *Berliner Zeitung*, 1.April.

_____. 1992. 'Die leicht verderbliche Vereinigung', *Berliner Zeitung*, 10 April.

Zhang, Y. 2004. *Chinese National Cinema*. New York and London: Routledge.

Zilian, F. 1999. *From Confrontation to Cooperation. The Takeover of the National People's (East German) Army by the Bundeswehr*. London: Praeger.

Schroeder's Wonderful World (press notes). Retrieved 13 June 2009 from: www.filmkombinat.de/download/…/PresseheftSchroederTextEng.doc

http://www.bpb.de/themen/P2F402,2,0,Glossar.html#art2

INDEX